D0717641

library

WITHDRAWN

C016799991

ALSO BY

*The Thatcher Government* (1983)

*The Thatcher Decade* (1989)
Republished in a substantially revised version as
*The Thatcher Era, and its Legacy* (1991)

*Honest Opportunism: The Rise of the Career Politician* (1993)

*Parliament Under Pressure* (1998)
Republished in a substantially revised version as
*Parliament Under Blair* (2000)

*Hug Them Close: Blair, Clinton, Bush and the
Special Relationship* (2003)

*The Unfulfilled Prime Minister:
Tony Blair's Quest for a Legacy* (2005)

*In Defence of Politicians (in spite of themselves)* (2011)

# 15 MINUTES OF POWER

## THE UNCERTAIN LIFE OF BRITISH MINISTERS

## PETER RIDDELL

PROFILE BOOKS

First published in Great Britain in 2019 by
PROFILE BOOKS LTD
3 Holford Yard
Bevin Way
London
WC1X 9HD

www.profilebooks.com

Copyright © Peter Riddell, 2019

10 9 8 7 6 5 4 3 2 1

Typeset in Fournier by MacGuru Ltd
Printed and bound in Great Britain by Clays Ltd, Elcograf S.p.A.

The moral right of the author has been asserted.

All rights reserved. Without limiting the rights under copyright reserved
above, no part of this publication may be reproduced, stored or introduced
into a retrieval system, or transmitted, in any form or by any means
(electronic, mechanical, photocopying, recording or otherwise), without the
prior written permission of both the copyright owner and the publisher of
this book.

A CIP catalogue record for this book is available from the British Library.

ISBN 978 1 78816 218 0
eISBN 978 1 78283 533 2

FSC
www.fsc.org
MIX
Paper from
responsible sources
FSC® C018072

To David Sainsbury and to all my former colleagues at the
Institute for Government for making this book possible

# Contents

# Foreword

This book is about power and those who seek to exercise power as ministers – and the flaws in the political system which encourage the appointment of too many ministers serving for too brief a time, creating an excessively short-term outlook. The following chapters reflect a professional lifetime of conversations with politicians, civil servants and advisers – more than forty years that I have been observing British politics and government as a journalist, author of half a dozen books, commentator and, particularly, as chief executive/director of a think tank, the Institute for Government, which has interviewed a large number of former ministers. I start from a position of sympathy with the position of ministers: their powers and influence are balanced by the uncertainties of their existence. In every role I have occupied my longevity has, for better or worse, exceeded that of ministers with whom I have worked.

Much has been written about ministerial life in a multitude of memoirs and diaries. Many perceptions have been, and are still being, shaped by two products of the early 1980s: the late Gerald Kaufman's entertaining and astute *How to be a Minister* of 1980; and, even more, the thirty-eight episodes of the television series *Yes Minister* (shown from 1980 to 1984) and its sequel *Yes, Prime Minister* (1986–8) with the memorable exchanges between Jim Hacker (played by the late Paul Eddington) and Sir Humphrey Appleby (played by the late Nigel Hawthorne). Both, though appearing during the Thatcher years, were inspired by the Wilson and Callaghan governments of the late 1970s and, indeed, Bernard Donoughue, head of the Policy Unit in this period, was one of the advisers to the late Sir Antony Jay and Jonathan Lynn, the writers of the series. The overlapping, and popular, *Spitting Image* satirical puppet series from 1984 to 1996 portrayed Cabinet ministers as weak and argumentative school children with Margaret Thatcher as a dominant teacher.

More recently, Armando Iannucci's *The Thick of It*, appearing intermittently between 2005 and 2012, portrayed the Blairite and Brownite world in which politically appointed special advisers cowed and bullied ineffective ministers struggling for a role and influence, before finally depicting the manoeuvrings of the coalition. The diaries of Chris Mullin, who was twice a minister in the Blair years, though much longer a Labour backbencher, portrayed a junior minister often vainly seeking to be more than a dogsbody of the Whitehall machine and of more senior ministers in making unreported speeches, signing letters and meeting obscure delegations, while achieving little, and attracting little notice compared with when he chaired a Select Committee.

These accounts all contain insights into how ministers operate, and about their relationships with civil servants and, more recently, with special advisers. This is why they are still widely cited and have influence, even though both Kaufman's book and the *Yes Minister* series can now appear dated in the era of twenty-four-hour news, social media and constant tweeting. Moreover, the truths can easily be turned into caricatures which present a misleading overall impression of ministers and their lives. *Yes Minister* depicts ministers as being manipulated by wily civil servants who have their own agendas and policy preferences. In the case of *The Thick of It*, the running is made by special advisers supplying policies and soundbites to hapless ministers with few ideas of their own. Of course, there are examples of both. There is no single accurate version. The picture I have observed is different. Only relatively few ministers may be strong, dominant figures successfully driving forward their plans, but most have views and policy priorities which they seek to advance in the face of constraints of time and a short-termist political and media outlook. Few are the passive ciphers satirised on television in recent decades.

I am also indebted to the work of my friend of fifty years, Professor Peter Hennessy, now ennobled, who has caught the essence of the attitudes of the post-war Permanent Secretary cadre in many books and lectures. No writer on Whitehall can neglect the pathbreaking work on the world and influence of the Treasury by Hugh Heclo and Aaron Wildavsky in their 1974 work *The Private Government of Public Money* – combined with the largely neglected *Ministers and Mandarins*, produced in 1986 by Jock Bruce-Gardyne, a Conservative politician, briefly a minister, and perceptive observer of power. A nuanced historical analysis of the role of ministers has come in the wide-ranging work of Professor Kevin Theakston of Leeds University. Former Cabinet minister John (now Lord) Hutton and former Permanent Secretary Sir Leigh Lewis have offered discreet insights in their *How To be a Minister* (over thirty years after Gerald Kaufman wrote his book with the same title). I would also highlight a series of reports over the past two decades by various House of Commons Select Committees on public administration and the constitution chaired by Tony Wright, Graham Allen and Sir Bernard Jenkin. All three have a commitment to good government and it is a pity that many of their recommendations were not accepted, and implemented, by the governments of the day.

There is a tendency to focus largely, if not exclusively, on those at the top – the Secretaries of State and heads of department, and, of course, Prime Ministers – and, with the exception of Chris Mullin and a few like him, largely to ignore the much more numerous ranks of Ministers of State and under-secretaries. But they also matter and feature in the following chapters.

The general portrayal of ministers on television is of the fully formed man or woman (as Rebecca Front showed in *The Thick of It*) with little discussion of how they arrived there, what preparation or training they had (usually very little in the formal sense), or what they were trying to achieve. It is the world of spin and crises, not the undramatic world of Commons adjournment debates, ministerial visits and meeting interest groups.

The direct inspiration for this book is a programme in which I was involved as, first, Senior Fellow, and then, for nearly five years as Director of the Institute for Government. The Institute was founded in 2008 by David Sainsbury, Lord Sainsbury of Turville, because, from his own experience as a long-serving minister for science and research, he did not think that government worked well. He believed that the way that government operated could be improved. One important strand of that work was preparing politicians for serving as ministers and then assisting them while in office.

This programme had a number of different innovative features, but the linking theme was that it is possible to make ministers more effective. The precise definition of 'effective' is a question that runs through this book. The Institute has not just been an observer but has actively sought to help potential and actual ministers, through working with the Conservative shadow implementation team in 2009–10 in arranging sessions about how Whitehall worked, and then in intensive sessions with a number of Labour shadow teams ahead of the 2015 general election, as discussed in a report by Nehal Davison. A number of induction sessions were developed with new ministers after the 2010, 2015 and 2017 general elections, and following numerous mid-term reshuffles. Zoe Gruhn pioneered private appraisals to help develop ministers, which were innovative for them, though common in many other large organisations. She organised revealing 360-degree assessments of some Conservative and Liberal Democrat ministers, which to the credit of her and those directly involved never leaked, to the surprise and scepticism of many in the gossipy political world.

A linked and longer-lasting initiative, the core of this book, was a series of exit interviews with former ministers which I launched as Director in the aftermath of the 2015 general election. This built up on an earlier report, *The Challenge of Being a Minister*, which I jointly wrote with Zoe Gruhn and Liz Carolan, and which was published in 2011. The roughly hour-long interviews are entitled Ministers Reflect, and concentrate on what it is like to work as a minister, more than on particular policies. The transcripts of all the interviews have been put on the Institute's website, along with commentary and some audio interviews. Ministers Reflect was run in its formative years with good humour, patience and persistence by Nicola Hughes, with the support of Jen Gold and myself. Two of the three of us did most of the early interviews: Nicola and Jen putting up with my tendency to reminisce with interviewees, most of whom I had known for several years, if not decades. The programme was then developed by Daniel Thornton and Catherine Haddon, with the help of other members of the Institute staff. I also worked closely with Catherine on the two reports on Transitions in 2009 and 2011, to which I refer in Chapter Three. The use of the title's 'Reflect' by chance and coincidence overlaps with the *Reflections* series of radio interviews which Peter Hennessy and Rob Shepherd have conducted with household name figures about their lives in politics. But there is very little overlap of substance, since the aim of the Institute series has been to look at how ministers of all kinds, not just the big names, have developed their careers, have worked with the Civil Service, and their achievements and frustrations.

The initial intention of Ministers Reflect was to collect the views of Conservative and Liberal Democrat former members of the 2010–15 coalition – and the interviews are an invaluable source about how that fascinating experiment in government operated in practice. Seen by some of my colleagues as a one-off initiative, I am glad to say the programme expanded both backwards to include several Labour ministers from before 2010, and then forwards, during the hectic politics from 2015 onwards, to include a succession of former Conservative ministers as they lost office. Several of the interviewees have returned to ministerial office again after being interviewed, in some cases twice; such has been the churn in appointments and resignations since 2015. There is so far only one case of someone being interviewed for a second time: David Jones, the former Secretary of State for Wales and then Brexit minister, after his second departure from office. The increased pace of ministerial changes and mainly Brexit-related resignations since the June 2017 general election is hard to keep up with, but is broadly accurate as of completion of the manuscript in January 2019, since when several more ministers have resigned. This hectic activity does not, however, affect the thrust of the conclusions about the uncertain life of ministers and their struggle to make an impact.

A key feature of the interviews is that they have not just been with well-known former Cabinet ministers (though most of the leading figures of recent governments feature); rather they include junior ministers, 'Goats' (ministers appointed to the Lords from outside politics) and law officers. That provides a depth of understanding about how ministers operate not found elsewhere, as well as a richness, and generally candour, of reflection. We found it best to leave it a few weeks, if not months, after someone had been sacked, resigned or been defeated at a general election before interviewing them.

At the time of writing, the eighty-six interviewees consist of fifty-one former Conservative ministers, twenty-one former Labour ones and fourteen Liberal Democrats – of whom thirty-eight served as full Cabinet members at one stage, sixteen are female, who are more open about the personal and the time pressures they faced. Seventeen served in the Lords for most of their ministerial careers. Their experiences and views have little to do with their party affiliation, and the differences have much more to do with their positions, as a junior or senior minister, or being in the Commons or Lords. The transcripts of the interviews can be directly called up on the Institute website, but the following chapters draw on them along with many other sources, both from my personal experience and written to fulfill my aim to illuminate the work of ministers, the constraints they face and the ways they can have influence. The main focus is on the last twenty years, but where ministers, such as Kenneth Clarke, Sir George Young, Francis Maude, Andrew Mitchell, Alistair Burt and others, served in the Thatcher and Major administrations, that earlier experience has been drawn upon, and I have also provided some historical background in the first two chapters.

Whenever a Ministers Reflect interview is mentioned, it appears as (MR, with dates of ministerial office). A full list is provided after the bibliography. Another stylistic point: I have identified people as they were known at the time they were in office, except at times to clarify any confusion about identity. So I hope currently retired distinguished knights, dames and peers will forgive the use of the names they were known by during their ministerial careers. The main exceptions are politicians who have taken on a title different from their previous name.

I must emphasise one important disclaimer. I am currently Commissioner for Public Appointments, the regulator of appointments made to public bodies by ministers. I am a public office holder independent of government, but I work closely with ministers and civil servants. Nothing in this book reflects my experience as Commissioner since April 2016. There is nothing in the following chapters about the public appointments process or ministers and civil servants with whom I have worked.

This book represents a welcome reunion with Andrew Franklin, twenty-six years after he published *Honest Opportunism*, an account of the rise of the career politician, which was intended as a warning but was seen by some subsequent MPs as a training manual. There is a clear link between the two books in their accounts of political life, though with the focus here much more on what politicians as ministers can, and cannot, achieve in office.

It has been a pleasure working with Andrew again after so long, though our conversations have been as much about the tumultuous political scene as the book itself. I am grateful to him and his team at Profile Books for their support. I would also like to thank David Sainsbury for suggesting that I should write this book back when I was still running the Institute, and to Bronwen Maddox, my successor as Director, for her strong support in ensuring that the book has materialised. We always agreed that it would be my book, and not an Institute report, but, of course, it would not have been possible without the enthusiasm and commitment of Institute staff, past and present, several of whom I have consulted during the course of writing, notably Catherine Haddon and Gavin Freeguard, while Jill Rutter's work on policymaking and policy successes has been influential on my thinking. My thanks to the IfG is reflected in the dedication.

I am, as ever, grateful for the love and encouragement of Avril, who was not yet my wife when the first edition of *Honest Opportunism* appeared, and our now adult daughter Emily.

Over the decades, they have supported and encouraged my fascination with government and politics, and Avril has revived her proofreading skills from long ago at *The Economist* in spotting, and preventing, misspellings and misuse of words, for which I am very grateful.

Finally, a word on the title. I wanted to indicate the temporary, always uncertain and provisional, nature of ministerial office. John Nott has already taken *Here Today, Gone Tomorrow* as the title of his memoirs, derived from his famous vituperative interview with Robin Day in October 1982, from which he memorably walked out – before he left the government barely three months later. I quite liked 'Temporary Kings', one of the titles in Anthony Powell's great *Dance to the Music of Time* series. But this book is not about Prime Ministers or party leaders as such, and is primarily about other ministers who form 99 per cent of governments. So after considerable debate over wording, and rejecting 'Temporary Princes' as too narrow, not least on gender, we settled on *Fifteen Minutes of Power: The Uncertain Life of British Ministers*, which captures the central contradiction of ministerial life, its provisional nature, unpredictable term, yet the exalted status temporarily given to ministers.

Peter Riddell
*April 2019*

# Preface

'When you first arrive, you are overwhelmed. All this stuff,
people talk to you about all kinds of things – and if you are not
careful, you will get a moment of panic. The next stage, after six
months is you have got an agenda. You know exactly what you
are going to do. The next stage, after two years, you are really on
top of it – you are really comfortable, you are doing things. And
then the phone rings and the Prime Minister is having a reshuffle
and you move on to the next department and you are back at the
beginning; there you are, panicking again.'

– Kenneth Clarke, holder of eight Cabinet posts between 1985 and
2014, Ministers Reflect interview, 2016

'If Prime Ministers had their way, they would appoint all the
MPs on their benches to ministerial office. The payroll vote is an
essential parliamentary tool, and the bigger it is the better.'

– Jonathan Powell, *The New Machiavelli*, 2011, p142

The British breed ministers more than any other country, but
they tend to have a much shorter active life in office than our
favourite pets. Most ministers survive longer than the twelve
months of a chameleon but few make it past the four years of
the golden hamster and only the most successful remain in the

same position as long as the five years of a queen bee. So the life of a minister is generally precarious, and many politicians are unsure whether they will last beyond the annual cull, or 'reshuffle', as it is known in the political world. The only consolation is that most last longer than UK football managers, whose average tenure is around fifteen months.

This book is about uncertainty and achievement – the uncertain life of ministers and their attempt to make an impact. One of the conclusions is that, despite all the frustrations, some ministers can make a difference and can point to policy changes of greater or lesser scale.

There are eight main themes affecting the life of ministers.

First, there are a lot of ministers, and Prime Ministers are always trying to increase the number of MPs receiving jobs from them (the 'payroll vote', as it is known), even if quite a few do not receive additional pay for their work. Unusually in Western democracies, most ministers are drawn from the limited talent pool of the House of Commons and, to a much less significant extent nowadays, from the House of Lords.

Second, the length of ministers' time in office is not only uncertain and unpredictable but is shorter than in virtually any other leadership position in Britain. This situation has got worse in recent years, with an accelerating rate of change thanks to mainly Brexit-related resignations and replacements. By the beginning of 2019, barely a quarter of ministers in the House of Commons had been in the same posts only eighteen months earlier after Theresa May reshuffled her administration following the 2017 general election. Only half as many MPs, fourteen, had been in the same ministerial post since before the general election campaign. (There has been much greater continuity amongst Lords ministers.) Two ministers, Amber Rudd and Chris Skidmore, had left the government and rejoined within the same calendar year of 2018, as did James Brokenshire after major surgery.

The result of these two long-standing trends, a rising number of ministers and their short tenures, is to create, what John (Lord) Birt, the former head of the BBC and adviser to Number 10 in the Labour years, has called 'the something must be done' approach. 'I need to attract attention because I am keen to have promotion.' So, as he told the Commons Public Administration Committee (2009, p9), 'a lot of junior ministers are extremely keen when they get into office to find the six sound bites that can get them noticed by the higher ups in their party over the twelve months that they are likely to be in position'. From the Civil Service perspective, Jonathan Baume, former General Secretary of the senior officials' union, the First Division Association, argued (2009, p10):

> The more junior ministers you have – and we have more than ever – the more work you have to find for them. One of the biggest single frustrations about the political process within the Civil Service is just the number of junior ministers you have and the work projects that then have to be designed and engineered to satisfy their particular interests.

Third, few new ministers have much idea of what doing the job involves – or have received sufficient, if any, preparation – apart from the still small, though prominent and influential, group of former special/political advisers. Future

Labour Cabinet minister Patricia Hewitt, who helped organise briefing sessions at Templeton College, Oxford, before the 1997 election, remembers (MR, in office 1998–2007) 'what was really depressing was that the Shadow Cabinet really didn't feel they needed any training or development'. They thought that as ministers they would be making decisions and implementation would be somebody else's problem. Parliamentary, and political, skills are important but are not sufficient to make for an effective minister.

Fourth, the initial experience of office has often been a shock for new ministers: from the circumstances of appointment by the Prime Minister by phone at Kempton racecourse or in the loo of a First Great Western train, to trying to work out what they can, and want to, do. Few ministers, at any rate junior ones, are given specific objectives, and many end up doing something in which they have no interest. Conservative Patrick McLoughlin was made responsible for shipping and aviation in 1989. When he said he had the most landlocked constituency in the UK and hated flying, his Secretary of State, the late Cecil Parkinson, said, 'Excellent, you'll bring an open mind to the subject'. What junior ministers do is heavily influenced by their relations with their Secretary of State. New ministers frequently complain of the stresses and strains of office, of how tired they are when faced with red boxes, decisions, constant meetings and travel, particularly when taking account of constituency and family commitments. At least now maternity leave for ministers who become mothers is established practice.

Fifth, how long will they serve in a post? Even if ministers master the intricate relationship with the Civil Service – 'we're the roadies, you're the talent', as Liberal Democrat

Steve Webb was told – they still have the problem of working out what they can do over the relatively short period they are likely to be in office. Damian Green, who served under Theresa May in the Home Office from 2010 until 2014, and then in two Cabinet posts after she became Prime Minister, notes (MR, in office, 2010–14 and 2016–17) that 'the amount of time it took from even everyone agreeing with a decision to actually seeing anything change on the ground is a number of years. And inherent in the way of politics is that you're very unlikely to see your successes through'. Many ministers therefore pick small-scale objectives which they may hope to achieve, or influence, in their couple of years in post.

Sixth, attempts to pull in talent from outside Parliament to become ministers via, for example, Gordon Brown's over-hyped experiment of the Government of All the Talents (Goats) had a mixed, and generally limited, impact. Former businessman Paul (Lord) Myners recalls (MR, in office 2008–10) how he and former banker Mervyn (Lord) Davies used to meet occasionally for coffee to reflect, and laugh, at how government makes decisions – and their rather naive belief that all ministers work to the same agenda with a common purpose instead of, in fact, being rivals and competitors. Perhaps unsurprisingly, few outsiders last more than a year or two in office, unless they have a clearly defined specialist role.

Seventh, in many ways it is surprising how much ministers can, and do, achieve. They are seldom pawns in the hands of the Civil Service or of special advisers, as *Yes Minister* and *The Thick of It* suggest. Ministers can, and do, alter policy. Nor is the story all one of failure, as in *The Blunders of our Governments*, the 2013 book by the late Anthony King and Ivor Crewe. The reasons for the disasters they describe

– from the poll tax to all too many wasteful IT projects – are complicated, and can only partly be attributed to the excessive turnover and short life of ministers. There have been plenty of successes too, from the Olympics to the introduction of the national minimum wage, via behavioural changes such as the reduction in drink driving and the banning of smoking in public places, to improvements in school performance and the NHS. The Chris Mullin version of the junior minister largely wasting their time is contradicted by many more stories of junior ministers playing a key role in implementing changes in policy.

Eighth, the key to success is longevity in office – giving a minister time to prepare, discuss and take through new policies and to implement them. Time is not always the answer to policy innovation, as Andrew Lansley's six years shadowing Health in opposition, and twenty-eight months in office, and Iain Duncan Smith's near six-year tenure bringing in Universal Credit showed. But in other cases a long spell in one post can help a minister make an impact – reinforced by a clear focus on a limited number of priorities and an outward-looking collaborative attitude towards working with civil servants and key outside groups. Alistair Darling, who served at Cabinet level in a variety of posts in the Blair and Brown governments (MR, in office 1997–2010), does not think that a minister can make much of an impact inside three years. 'I think six years is probably too long. I thought four years was as long as you need to stay because you need fresh impetus. You're not a career specialist – it's not like being managing director of a company or something – so you can become departmentalised. But in a year you can do very, very little more than hold the fort frankly.' If you are involved in a major infrastructure project, you are highly unlikely to be involved from beginning to end.

We have too many ministers and they are moved around too often. That produces a bias in favour of activity rather than reflection and preparation. Most of what ministers decide is what any minister, of whatever party, would probably do, so there is a narrow margin for any minister, however senior, to make a personal difference. George Osborne reckoned that just 10 per cent of decisions were his own, in which he could hope to leave his mark. Many ministers do leave office with positive achievements. There have been a number of clear policy successes as well as failures reflecting the positive impact of ministers. But in order to make an impact, ministers have to master uncertain, and often unfavourable, circumstances, as well as being lucky.

**CHAPTER ONE**

# The Strange World of Ministers

'If we think of the civil servants as marine animals and the politicians as fishermen operating on the surface, we will have some idea of the relations between the two. The Civil Service takes a long view. It knows that the boatloads of politicians now anchored above them are certain to be changed within five years.'

– Richard Crossman, Godkin lectures, Harvard University, 1970, published as *Inside View*

The transience of ministers has a profound effect on what has been called the governing marriage between them and civil servants. They have very distinct cultures, which overlap but are not the same, as I explore later in this book. That uncertainty about how long they will be in office affects both how ministers see themselves and how they work with others, notably with the Civil Service.

Nearly half a century ago two American political scientists, Hugh Heclo and Aaron Wildavsky, developed the concept of the 'Whitehall Village', in their study of how the Treasury operated (which appeared in 1974 as *The Private Government of Public Money*). While the particular personalities and events they discussed have long gone, many of the features of the 'village' remain – the sense of a close-knit community of rivals who combine an allegiance to the entity of the Civil Service against the outside world but also a fierce loyalty to the departments which they run. The late Jock Bruce-Gardyne, briefly a Treasury minister, and a shrewd commentator on the Whitehall scene, took up the concept of the village in his 1986 book *Ministers and Mandarins*. He says

> the politicians are the tourists in the village. They come, and go. Their habits are not always to the taste of the villagers, who do their best to educate them in village ways. Since the village lives on tourism, it has no choice other than to accommodate the visitors. Fortunately they are guaranteed eventually to depart. Some contrive to shift the villagers around. Some successfully impose new religions. Some are so uncouth that the villages manage to evict them, or at least to lock them up in the village tollbooth. But the villagers know they will outstay them all.

These expectations and constraints have a powerful influence on what ministers think they can do, and then do.

The rise in the number of middle-ranking and junior ministers in recent decades, reinforced by the appointment of additional 'unpaid' ministers – and their frequently brief tenure, of much less than a full Parliament – are damaging to good government. New ministers both take time to master their new responsibilities and are then aware they may not have much time to make an impact and to impress party leaders. The two parallel trends of increased numbers and frequency of change both have negative effects, reinforced by the inherently adversarial nature of British politics and the pressures of social media and twenty-four-hour news. As the number of ministers has grown, they have sought to demonstrate activity, and be noticed, in order to impress party leaders and whips, ahead of their rivals for survival and promotion. The focus is on the short-term, and on immediate results, when the solutions to Britain's problems generally take a longer time to appear. As the Public Administration Select Committee pointed out in a report in June 2009 (Good Government, p11): 'the system for making ministerial appointments can work to undermine good government by encouraging behaviour that is focused on short-term political advantage rather than the long-term interests of stable, effective government'.

In the Brown and Blair years, the average tenure for individual ministerial posts was 1.7 years, rising to just 2.2 years for members of the Cabinet. Of those appointed by Tony Blair in May 1997, just nineteen (including four in the Lords) were in the same post at the time of the 2001 general election, and a mere four overall following his post-election reshuffle, with none at below Cabinet level. This sense of 'do the most while you can' reflects widespread, and justified, uncertainty, since ministers never know when they are either going to lose office or be shifted somewhere else.

The existence of the Conservative/Liberal Democrat coalition meant more stability than before or since, but that is now long gone. David Cameron began with a deliberate policy of trying to reduce the frequency of ministerial changes and largely succeeded for the first three to four years of the 2010–15 Parliament. He was helped, as in, say, Germany and the Netherlands, by the existence of the coalition, which made it more cumbersome to switch around portfolios between parties. But that was a brief interlude. By the time of the 2015 general election, just eighteen ministers out of 121 MPs and peers remained in the same post as when the coalition was formed five years earlier. Fewer than 10 per cent of junior ministers appointed in May 2010 held on to the same position until the end of the Parliament. Six departments retained no ministers in the same post throughout the five years, and three (DFID, Defra and DCMS) had three different Secretaries of State.

The upheavals of 2015–19, with the Brexit referendum, the change of Prime Minister, the 2017 general election and the subsequent voluntary and involuntary departures from government, mainly associated with Brexit, have produced an unprecedented level of ministerial turnover. As the Whitehall Monitor from the Institute for Government records, just over half of all ministers were appointed to their current posts in early 2019. This includes half of those who attend Cabinet meetings. Since 2010, there have been seven DCMS Secretaries, and six Justice and DWP Secretaries (in the latter case five in less than three years). All ministers in the Ministry of Justice and the Cabinet Office were new to their roles in 2018. This extraordinary rate of change is inevitably disruptive, as new ministers adjust to their new responsibilities.

A contrarian view – at least until a year or two ago – was that the short tenure of ministers has not been that unusual, and is similar to that of corporate chairs or chief executives. But that is only partially true because, while the tenure of the chief executives of the top 300 British companies has been falling, it is still a median of nearly five years in the top post. This is down from more than eight years in 2010, according to a study by PwC. Yet that is in itself worrying, and is anyway much longer than senior ministers. It represents a more rapid turnover than any country apart from Brazil, Russia or India. The firm commented (in a *Financial Times* report in 2017) that 'less than five years is a very short time to make real and tangible changes to a business. Stakeholders are demanding ever faster results, but should consider the long term too, to ensure stability.'

The problem of ministerial turnover has also been aggravated by an excessive rate of change in the Civil Service (see Sasse and Norris, 2019), with senior civil servants changing jobs much faster than their opposite numbers in other countries or those in the private sector. In some London-based departments, turnover rates have hit 20 to 25 per cent, while according to the study, a new minister in six departments is likely to find that four out of ten of his senior officials have been in post for less than a year. This rate is both expensive in itself but also undermines institutional memory and the ability to offer policy advice.

Ministers themselves believe that their turnover is too rapid. Ben Bradshaw, who served in five different departments (MR, in office 2001–10), acknowledges the rationale for moving ministers around to broaden their experience, but

for junior ministers four years is probably enough, while anything less than two years is not long enough because it's only really after two years, particularly as a junior minister, that you know enough to be fully effective and to challenge the civil servants and ask the questions that need to be asked. I think you are at your most effective when you are at least a year and a half or two years into a job.

That rate of turnover of ministers shortens political horizons over decisions which will take many years to implement and work through. New ministers do not have much time to understand their briefs and decide priorities. This encourages a short-term approach to policymaking, as well as affecting the balance between often inexperienced ministers and experienced civil servants. It makes it harder for Parliament to hold a minister to account if the person responsible for a decision has been moved on, or dropped. This is in marked contrast with many other countries. Germany, including the former West Germany, had fifteen business ministers between 1949 and 2010, as opposed to thirty-five in a comparable position in the UK. A particularly damaging result of frequent changes in the British government is in international relations, since ministers in other countries are likely to remain in office for much longer. A new British minister is likely to have less influence at international meetings than a more experienced European or other overseas opposite number. British interests were unlikely to have been advanced by having nine Africa ministers in the thirteen Blair and Brown years, or thirteen Europe ministers over that period. Revealingly, where ministers stay in post for longer, they have the chance to show greater strengths in policymaking, and possibly, improved results. Chancellors of the Exchequer have tended to remain in post for longer than many of their colleagues, and this has produced greater consistency and impact.

The time cycle of any major infrastructure decision often covers more than one parliamentary cycle, and is therefore presided over by several ministers. David Freud, who served for six years as welfare reform minister, notes (MR, in office

2010–16) that he worked with five different ministers at the then Communities and Local Government Department. He complains not only about high turnover amongst civil servants but also amongst ministers:

> Basically people who haven't been in the job a long time find it difficult to make decisions with confidence. If you move people around, you don't get big decisions, you get little decisions. You don't get that energy and determination of someone who understands it: 'Yes, we should do that, we must do that,' and then drives it. Moving people around is the bane of one's life as a minister.

Nick Raynsford, a long-serving middle-ranking member of the Blair and Brown governments, told an inquiry on 'Skills in Government' by the Commons Public Administration Committee, in 2006–7, that

> Inevitably, a new minister coming in is going to look at 'What new can we do to make an impact?' because they have their reputation. If there is a culture where they are assumed to have to make their mark within a year or two in order to move on and up, they are going to want to do something quickly. The last thing they are going to want to do is to focus on maintaining a programme that is going to take ten years to produce results when they will not be there to get the benefit and the praise. That, I think, is an insidious culture.

An interesting, and revealing, exception was the late Tessa Jowell, who not only devised and coordinated the London

bid for the 2012 Olympics, awarded in 2005, but who continued to oversee the project under various ministerial titles
until 2010, even when she was replaced as Culture Secretary
in June 2007. She also worked on a cross-party basis with Sir
Hugh Robertson, the Conservative shadow spokesman on
the Olympics, and then Olympics minister after the 2010
election, thus ensuring much-needed continuity on an obviously time-sensitive project. That was, however, a notable
exception; more generally, ministers are preoccupied with
what they can do if they are only in office for a couple of
years.

The uncertainty, and generally short tenure in office, is
combined with low public standing. As I have argued elsewhere (2011, Chapter One, pp11–12), there is nothing novel
in criticism of politicians, and of ministers in particular: just
look at all the eighteenth- and early-nineteenth-century
satires of ministers and the coruscating cartoons of Gillray
and Rowlandson. But the trends are still startling. IPSOS
Mori has a Veracity Index which lists various professions and
occupations and asks interviewees whether or not they would
generally trust them to tell the truth. Nurses came top at 96
per cent in October 2018, followed by other groups with
whom voters have direct contact: doctors on 92 per cent,
teachers on 89 per cent, then professors, scientists, judges,
weather forecasters. Right down the bottom are politicians,
generally on 19 per cent, with government ministers on 22
per cent, lower than estate agents on 30 per cent and journalists on 26 per cent. If you measure net trust (the percentage
generally trusting a group to tell the truth minus those not
trusting them to tell the truth), the figure was minus 51 per
cent – and that was a slight improvement compared with

twelve months earlier. These figures show the mountain that ministers have to climb to persuade voters that they are trying their best in the public interest. The only minimal consolation is that the figures have always been bad. Ministers have seldom been popular, or trusted.

That exposes a recurring dilemma throughout this book that those who are often best prepared to handle the challenges of being ministers from their time as special advisers or political researchers are the most mistrusted, being regarded as part of a metropolitan elite and insufficiently aware of ordinary people's problems – the essence of the populist appeal.

Ministers are also operating in a much more hostile and difficult public environment than in the past. A blame culture has been fostered by a more partisan media and by the frenetic pressures of twenty-four-hour news and the Internet. Virtually nothing is believed or taken on trust. There is no room for the greys, the relative/on balance judgements which governing involves. This applies not just to policy but also to ministers' personal lives. The spread of social media has led to more resignations by Cabinet ministers because of such personal problems/scandals. Such personal accountability may in one sense be desirable, though even at the time, let alone in retrospect, some resignations reflect more a media/political frenzy than a balanced assessment of responsibility. This is not the place for a lengthy discussion of the impact of the populist revolt, apart from saying that it has obviously made the life of a minister much harder.

Nonetheless, there is no lack of desire by politicians to be ministers. Some MPs do turn down the opportunity to join the government, but not many. The list includes three later

Labour leaders, Michael Foot, Neil Kinnock and John Smith, though the first and third did later become ministers. The opportunity to be a minister tempts most: even MPs who have had a successful time as backbenchers – chairs of Select Committees such as Chris Mullin, for example, who spent two periods as a junior minister, despite talking down the role in his later published diaries. John Whittingdale went in 2015 from chairing the then Culture, Media and Sport Select Committee to being, for fourteen months, the DCMS Secretary of State, which, as he admitted (MR, office 2015–16) meant that he was up to speed on the issues even if he knew little about the workings of government. After barely a year chairing the Defence Select Committee, Rory Stewart accepted office as a junior Environment minister after the 2015 election.

In many cases, whether or not someone becomes a minister primarily reflects the swing of the political pendulum and timing. Labour's Giles Radice spent over two-thirds of his twenty-eight years in the Commons in opposition. After a brief spell in the Shadow Cabinet, he made the most mark chairing the Public Services Committee and then the Treasury Committee. If Labour had been in power earlier in his parliamentary career, he would almost certainly have become a minister. Oliver Heald (MR, in office 1995–97, 2012–14 and 2016–17) reflects on the fates of politics:

> I was very lucky to get a chance at office. My generation missed out a bit, because I was a bit of a rising star under John Major, minister after two or three years and then we had thirteen years in opposition. Of course I was in the Shadow Cabinet for five years, did all these great jobs, but they're not as rewarding in opposition as they are in

government. Because you're talking about and don't actually get anything done. So the great lesson is if you get a chance of office make sure you do some things.

Above all, there is no shortage of posts. Demand and supply are, of course, linked. England, more accurately the United Kingdom for the past three centuries, has been known as the Mother of Parliaments, but it is more clearly and unambiguously the Mother of Ministers. The UK has far more ministers than similar parliamentary democracies. Definitions vary – and many countries have more politically appointed civil servants and advisers – but the UK current total is around ninety to ninety-four members of the Commons, including whips. Comparisons are not straightforward because of varying definitions and different constitutional arrangements, such as in federal or quasi-federal systems, where there are powerful ministers at regional and provincial levels, as in Germany, Australia and Canada. But whatever caveats are applied, it is clear that the UK has more ministers in government than most other countries. India has a constitutional limitation on the number of ministers at 15 per cent of the total number of members of the House of the People, or just under eighty. According to a comparison undertaken earlier in the decade (quoted in the Public Administration Committee report, 'Too Many Ministers?', 2009–10, pp3–4), among other Westminster systems, South Africa had sixty-six ministers, while Canada had sixty-three ministers and parliamentary secretaries (a total which has fluctuated from premier to premier). The UK has more ministers per head of population than these countries, though fewer than smaller countries like Australia and New Zealand.

Kevin Theakston (1987) has traced the growth in the number of ministers and the origins of junior ministers to the mid-nineteenth century. Before 1832 there was no real difference between permanent/bureaucratic and parliamentary roles. That distinction gradually became clearer, as a result of two parallel trends. First, increasing parliamentary demands required ministers to help heads of department in the Lords and the Commons. Second, a permanent Civil Service appointed on merit rather than by partisan patronage emerged during the second half of the century after the Northcote/ Trevelyan report of 1854. Nonetheless, the number of junior ministers remained small, at eleven to fifteen, from 1830 until 1914, and their skills were seen as primarily parliamentary, with no specialist or administrative knowledge expected or required. Moreover, over this eighty-four-year period, twenty-two of the 294 junior ministers were neither MPs nor peers at the time of appointment. But there was an increasing pattern from then on of ministers gaining experience in a junior role before entering the Cabinet – particularly for those in the Commons, who had an increasing burden of work, especially when the head of department was in the Lords, as was often the case then.

As the state expanded during the twentieth century, so did the number of ministers overall, as new departments were created to handle the range of welfare and other responsibilities being taken on by government. In 1900, there were sixty paid ministers, of whom only just over a half (thirty-three) were MPs. That total rose sharply during the First World War to ninety-five paid ministers, of whom sixty were MPs, before falling back to fifty-eight in the Labour minority government in 1930, then rising sharply again during the Second

World War, and afterwards. The total of paid ministers was eighty-one in 1950, including sixty-eight MPs, and 102, including eighty-six MPs, in 1970. There was broad stability during the Thatcher years before a steady rise in the Blair and Brown period. The formation of the coalition led to a further increase, as members of both parties had to be given posts, some unpaid, as discussed below. The total number of MPs in government posts has been in the ninety to ninety-four range since 2010, including fifteen to seventeen whips. So the number of MPs in government posts has risen by just under three times since Lord Salisbury's days as Prime Minister at the time of the Boer War and the peak of Empire.

In addition, there has been a sharp increase in the number of parliamentary private secretaries, who assist ministers but are not officially part of the government, and are not paid anything above their MP's salary – though they are required to vote with the government. Their number rose from nine in 1900 to twenty-seven by 1950, peaked at fifty-eight in 2001 but has generally been around forty-five in the last couple of decades. The total number of parliamentary private secretaries tends to be higher earlier in a party's period in power, and higher when it has a large majority, hence the figure for 2001.

The growth in the number of ministers has proved to be a one-way ratchet regardless of the scope of government. The end of Empire made virtually no difference. The India Office and then the Colonial Office disappeared, and the Commonwealth Relations Office was merged into the Foreign Office in 1968. The separate armed service ministries disappeared in 1964. In time, the growth of overseas aid, and the formation of a separate Department for International Development, was a partial offset, in creating new ministers, as did the formation in 1992 of a Department for the National Heritage, which developed into what is now the Department of Digital, Culture, Media and Sport. Two big developments towards the end of the twentieth century – privatisation and devolution – did not result in a net reduction in the number of ministers overall. The previously separate roles of dealing with utilities could be merged, and often downgraded in seniority, while substantial devolution to Edinburgh, Cardiff and Belfast resulted in machinery of government changes and a reduction in the number of members of the UK government dealing with Scottish, Welsh and Northern Irish affairs, from fourteen (including three in the Lords) before the 1997 election to six in total by the time Gordon Brown became Prime Minister a decade later, and two of the territorial secretaries also then headed UK-wide departments, Defence and Work and Pensions. Yet the total of Commons ministers rose as the Cabinet Office acquired new ministers, and new under-secretaries were appointed where none had existed before – for example, to the Leader of the Commons.

While Prime Ministerial patronage is extensive, there are statutory limits on the number of ministers, or, rather on the number of paid ministerial posts. Under a 1975 act, this is set at 109, consisting of no more than twenty-one Cabinet ministers and eighty-three ministers of all kinds, including parliamentary secretaries, as well as three law officers and up to twenty-two whips. Under another 1975 act, no more than ninety-five holders of ministerial office, including whips, may sit in the House of Commons at any one time. Recent Prime Ministers, starting with Tony Blair, have sought ways round this limit by inviting up to five or six other ministers to attend Cabinet without being full Cabinet ministers. This has partly been to allow Prime Ministers to claim that more women sit round the Cabinet table, as well as to ensure that, for instance, the Chief Secretary to the Treasury and the Attorney General attend.

In addition, over the past fifteen years, Prime Ministers have appointed ministers without giving them additional pay as ministers (as opposed to their salaries as MPs or allowances as members of the House of Lords). It has also helped having the odd millionaire around who can do without a ministerial salary. Theresa May's post-election administration in June 2017 had nine such unpaid ministers, who ranged between wealthy 'Goats' in the Lords to junior whips on the lowest rungs of the ministerial ladder. Some people simultaneously hold junior ministerial roles as under-secretaries and are whips, though only paid as the latter. The use of the term 'unpaid' is misleading, since ministers have private offices, staff and usually drivers, which even a decade ago was estimated to amount to around £500,000 – according to Sir Andrew (now Lord) Turnbull, the former Cabinet Secretary, in evidence to the 2009–10 committee enquiry. A further stream of patronage, separate from ministerial life but which expands the size of the payroll vote required to support the government, has been the introduction of paid party roles (with a dozen paid Conservative Party vice-chairs following the January 2018 reshuffle), as well as trade envoys and regional or subject representatives.

These figures on ministerial numbers apply to the UK government. If you add in the number of ministers in the Scottish, Welsh and Northern Ireland administrations, the total increases by around a further seventy-five, with, as mentioned earlier, no compensating fall in the overall UK total when devolution came in during the late 1990s.

The other distinguishing feature of British ministers is that they are largely drawn from a limited pool of politicians in the House of Commons. Even excluding parliamentary private secretaries, not far short of one in three MPs on the government side of the Commons are members of the administration – the exact number depending on the size of its majority in the Commons. That is apart from a small, but largely distinct, group of ministers in the Lords (as I will discuss in Chapter Nine). The number of peers in government, either as ministers or whips, has changed little, at around twenty to twenty-five compared with the total at the end of the nineteenth century. The total number of Lords ministers dipped during the mid-twentieth-century Labour governments, which had few, then solely hereditary, peers taking their whip to call upon to appoint as ministers. Labour's ability to have more ministers in the Lords was transformed by the creation of life peerages in 1958, including women. The big change is that there are now just one or two peers in the Cabinet, as against up to nine around 1900.

In many other countries even with parliamentary as opposed to presidential systems, ministers are drawn from outside the legislature – from leadership roles in regional or local government or from the private sector. In the USA, France, Sweden, Norway, the Netherlands, Belgium and Portugal, serving government ministers may not at the same time be members of the national legislatures. In Germany, Austria, Italy, Finland, Denmark and Japan, members of the Cabinet are permitted to be members of the legislature but do not have to be. That allows a much greater degree of choice in picking ministers. In the UK, direct switches from outside the ranks of national politicians or from the world of business have been rare, usually short-lived and not always successful. Some former local authority leaders, notably David Blunkett from Sheffield in the 1980s, have become MPs and worked their way up, but they have not moved directly from local leadership to the Cabinet. The relatively narrow parliamentary base for selecting ministers in itself raises questions about whether, and how, politicians elected primarily as representatives of their constituents are prepared for leading large executive organisations.

More significant over the past two decades have been moves in the opposite direction, with prominent members of the Commons seeking leadership of the devolved administrations (in the first wave in the 1990s and early 2000s, with Donald Dewar and Rhodri Morgan amongst several others, though that shift from the centre out to the capitals of the nations has now ended), and in recent years has been much more to become directly elected mayors in English cities and regions. All three London mayors since 2000 (Ken Livingstone, Boris Johnson and Sadiq Khan) and a number of the new cross-local authority mayors, such as Andy Burnham and Dan Jarvis, have come from the Commons. A number of former MPs have also been elected as Police and Crime Commissioners in England, a Conservative-inspired reform which has so far mainly benefitted former Labour MPs such as Jane Kennedy, Vera Baird and Paddy Tipping.

The link with the Commons – and to a lesser extent the Lords – is the key to ministerial appointments. Prime Ministers do not have a free hand either when forming governments or in undertaking later reshuffles (see Chapters Three and

Ten). They are not appointing after a competitive exam. Yes, they are looking for a high-quality Cabinet team, but above all it must be a team which works together reasonably harmoniously and can command not just the confidence of the House of Commons in key votes, but also broader support, even at times grudging, from MPs on the government side in the Commons.

It is striking how two very different Prime Ministers, Margaret Thatcher and Gordon Brown, expressed the pressures in very similar terms in their memoirs. First, Thatcher (1993, p25):

> It is not always understood how real are the constraints under which the choices take place. By convention, all ministers are members of either the Commons or the Lords, and there must not generally be more than three Cabinet members in the Lords, thus limiting the range of potential candidates for office. In addition, one has to achieve distribution across the country – every region is easily convinced it has been left out. You must also consider the spectrum of party opinion.

She noted the expectation that the list of ministers would be published within about twenty-four hours, 'otherwise it is taken as a sure sign of some sort of political crisis'. Her opposite numbers overseas 'are often astonished at the speed with which British governments are formed and announced'.

Similarly, Brown (2017, p202) noted that

> Picking a Cabinet is even more complicated than it might seem. You have to focus on the jobs in hand, choosing the

best person to deal with, say, education or health, and you also have to be aware of the overall balance – of ages, backgrounds, personalities and factions within the party – that needs to be struck. And, of course, there are the inexorable pressures of ambition: in the UK, unlike in America, if you are not a member of the government, you can hardly introduce a piece of legislation, and so for most MPs the test of success is not achievement as a backbencher but whether they make it into ministerial ranks.

That team is bound to be a mixture. Some ministers will know their departments from their careers and experience outside politics; others may have shadowed the area when in opposition, from serving on a Select Committee or, more generally, as backbenchers; others may have served in junior roles in the same department. But given the limited recruitment pool, not all, or even perhaps most, will have been appointed to match the specific needs of the department.

This limited pool of ministerial recruits, and the parliamentary link, are the reasons they are of such mixed quality. All but a tiny percentage of the population are excluded from the potential pool. But what are ministers for? What do they do? The next chapter explores the nature of ministerial life.

# CHAPTER TWO

# The Minister Will See You Now

'All the world's a stage,
And all the men and women merely players;
They have their exits and their entrances;
And one man in his time plays many parts.'

— Jaques, in Shakespeare's *As You Like It*

'My existence is now (after four months in post) almost entirely
pointless ... with hand on heart. I can say that I have less
influence now over government policy than at any time in the last
eight years. The only possible excuse for doing this is the hope
that it will lead to something better.'

— Chris Mullin, *A View from the Foothills*, 2009, pp43–4

Ministers still exist in an aura of at least formal respect and
deference – despite their impermanence and low public standing. A visit to a minister's office is a bit like waiting to see a
hospital consultant except the chair is likely to be more comfortable than in a hospital and you will be offered water, tea
or coffee. But there is a similar sense of being ushered into
the presence of a very busy person who has little time, who is
vaguely familiar with your case after a hurried look at the

papers, but is about to go on to a more important meeting. A partial exaggeration perhaps but indicative of the way ministers exist. They are in charge, for the moment at least, and are given the expected status, not least from their attendant civil servants.

The contrast between the minister with no certainty of tenure but public status and the civil servant with permanence (less so recently) but a constitutionally subservient role is brought when there is a change of minister. There is an immediate transfer of attention, and loyalty, from the former minister, who might almost no longer exist, to the new one. The virtues of the predecessor are forgotten as Whitehall works out how to deal with the successor. The observance of the constitutional principles can appear brutal. Yet that can lead to the *Yes Minister* trap of underrating the role of ministers.

David Freud, a journalist turned banker turned welfare expert/minister at Work and Pensions, summed up the dilemma well (MR, in office 2010–16):

> Picking up the satires on politics that there have been, when you analyse them, the *Yes Minister* satire is about the civil servants effectively having an agenda and running it through ministers who don't know what they're doing. The satire of *The Thick of It* is a political class desperate to claim they're doing important, dramatic things and not having anything to do. I can imagine that has been happening in different departments at any time in government, but that is absolutely not what was happening when we came in – with a very big agenda.

Norman Fowler was widely, and somewhat unfairly, derided for calling his memoirs *Ministers Decide*. Not only was he a long-serving, and effective, minister, particularly at Health and Social Services, but the title captures the constitutional essence of a minister's role. He or she will be the recipient of often persuasive, overwhelming advice from civil servants pointing towards decisions, but it is ministers who have to authorise a policy or statement.

A Secretary of State is both politically and legally the head of a department – the person who is accountable and responsible for what their officials do. It suits the Civil Service to have a politician as the public face of a department who takes the credit, and the criticism. The standing of Ministers of State and under-secretaries is less clear-cut – they operate in the name of the Secretary of State, and their powers are derived from their superior, but they are treated as a group apart from civil servants and other advisers. All ministers are bound by the doctrine of collective responsibility. They have to accept the policy of the government as a whole even when they have only taken a formal role in approving it, as is true most of the time for Cabinet ministers, or they have had no formal say in decisions, as is true for all non-Cabinet ministers.

Defining what a minister does is complicated, since their job really involves several roles (as we described in *The Challenge of Being a Minister*, 2011, p11).

Executive and policy – although ministers are more like executive chairs than chief executives, they have to lead their departments, approving all key decisions and public statements. They have to develop and set out policy objectives and personally take the lead when pushing through reform programmes, while monitoring progress. They also have to handle correspondence and case work, such as planning decisions and immigration appeals.

Parliamentary – ministers are creatures of Parliament, in the sense both that all nowadays are members of one or other House, and it is where they have to explain and justify their policies and performance. Appearing convincing in Parliament is vital for a minister's reputation and effectiveness. This includes the ability to answer questions; to make statements, particularly on urgent issues and new policies; to appear in front of Select Committees; and to take legislation through, either on the floor of the House of Commons or in a public bill committee. As is made clear in Chapter Eight, understanding the importance of Parliament, and the need to spend time there to maintain relationships with colleagues, is one of the dividing lines between politicians and civil servants.

Departmental advocate – ministers need strong advocacy and negotiating skills to argue their department's case, whether for resources with the Treasury, or on a policy and legislative priority in Cabinet, or more likely in a Cabinet committee and in inter-departmental exchanges within Whitehall, as well as directly with 10 Downing Street. Since 1973, there have also been responsibilities in Brussels and other EU institutions, although Brexit implies that this role will shift from negotiating as an insider to being an outsider.

Collective government and party role – ministers, especially Secretaries of State, participate in, and take responsibility for, collective decision-making by the government.

Public advocate – ministers have to give much of their time to presenting and defending what they and their departments have done and are proposing to the media and to their own parties, with the increased challenge now of the proliferation of social media. It is not just President Trump who is addicted to tweeting.

This list of roles is far from comprehensive. To adapt the quotation from *As You Like It* at the opening of this chapter, every minister is likely to play many parts during the course of their career, depending not only on their seniority and their department but also on their personality and preferences, as well as circumstances. But ministers have to master each of these roles if they are to make an impact.

Effectiveness does not, of course, just consist of a list of roles to perform. It is about how they are performed. There is a danger of confusing activity for achievement. Ministers can comfort themselves with busy diaries when it is harder to identify where they have made an impact. There is a very wide range of agreement about how ministers can be effective, though this differs substantially between Secretaries of State and more junior ministers. The former can hope to hold the same office for longer, enough time to introduce, and implement, policies which will really make a difference. The ambitions of the latter are bound to be more limited in both time and scope. But there are common factors.

For the Institute for Government report referred to above, we asked what made an effective minister. This question was put to both ministers and civil servants on an unprompted basis. Both agreed almost equally on the importance of having a clear vision, goals and objectives. Second was building constructive relationships, and then getting the best out of people. Every business school or leadership guru would agree. But there is a big gap between analysis and performance, not least because ministers have very different experiences and careers from business executives before taking office. Indeed, it is the very political nature of their roles – such as taking Parliament seriously – where ministers' assessments of effectiveness not only differ from business executives but also from civil servants. For ministers, a good performance in the Commons is a mark of success, even if nobody outside Westminster notices.

Michael Heseltine was, by a large margin, the most frequently mentioned example of an effective minister in the 2011 report (p23). One, far from starry-eyed, senior official described Heseltine as a 'dream minister' with clear vision, who was not distracted by day-to-day trivia, and able to translate a set of priorities into plans and to punch his weight in Cabinet. Another who worked with him closely says he was a 'magic combination – managed to do the job without being very high maintenance and having a sense of where he wanted to go. He had a magic wand.' He was seen by civil servants who worked with him as an exceptional motivator with an unusual ability to inspire and enthuse – and also, very unusually, a close interest in management and the details of the organisation. In many respects, however, despite the clarity of his leadership, he was more the exception than the exemplar.

Each Cabinet will, or should, contain widely acknowledged heavyweights, the ones who, in Churchill's vivid phrase about Joseph Chamberlain, 'make the weather'. That means dominating the political landscape and influencing policy across government. Leaving aside Prime Ministers, such as obviously Margaret Thatcher, any list of ministers with that impact in the past fifty years would include Barbara

Castle (though she never quite had the wider influence she believed she deserved), Roy Jenkins, Denis Healey, Geoffrey Howe, Nigel Lawson, Michael Heseltine, Kenneth Clarke, Gordon Brown (before he became PM) and George Osborne.

All were influential in defining the terms of the policy debates of their governments and in getting their way. It is revealing that all but Castle and Heseltine were Chancellors of the Exchequer with the power to influence policy across government. Castle's real period of achievement was mainly at the beginning of her Cabinet career in the 1960s (in helping permanently to change attitudes to drink-driving via the breathalyser, as well as over seat belts). Jenkins was probably at his peak in overseeing, and pushing, the liberalising social legislation of the mid-1960s – which has not been reversed and has influenced attitudes up to this day – rather than as Chancellor. Also nearly half of these ministers had their first post at Cabinet level, and never worked their way up as junior ministers. That is unusual, and is again at odds with what happens in the private sector, where executives progress upwards from post to post. Moreover, and this is crucial, many held their main post for four years, and in some cases longer.

There is a second category of those who make a lasting mark in a more limited way in the departments they have headed – Tony Crosland, Norman Tebbit, Kenneth Baker, David Blunkett, Peter Mandelson and Michael Gove. In some respects, members of this second group had a longer-lasting impact in their specific areas than the first group, whose influence may have been wider at the time but not necessarily later. The impact of Chancellors can be more short-term than might appear at the time as good economic times end.

Similarly, Norman Tebbit accelerated the pace of legislation affecting trade unions which has remained in force, while Kenneth Baker's changes to the national curriculum and to school inspection still set the basic framework now, even though current children may wonder, when they have a day off school, what Baker days are (to allow teachers to prepare).

The majority of ministers are less influential, or memorable. Any Cabinet will contain a mixture. As Norman Tebbit observed (in Hennessy and Shepherd, 2016, p87), 'a Cabinet of twenty-odd people is unlikely to have more than half a dozen real drivers, a lot of competent people – but people who drive reform are in short supply'. There is nothing wrong with that. All Cabinets include, and need, the 'sound men and women of government' who keep the wheels of administration turning undramatically and are seldom, if ever, considered as potential PMs – George Thomson in the 1964–70 era; Merlyn Rees in the Callaghan years; Willie Whitelaw, George Younger, Norman Fowler and Tony Newton in the Thatcher and Major governments; Jack Straw, Margaret Beckett and Alan Johnson in the Blair and Brown years. Straw aptly called his memoirs *Last Man Standing*. There are also some who aspire and never quite make much of a mark, and are quickly forgotten, through the swing of the electoral pendulum or bad luck. Only political anoraks will remember who was in a Cabinet for a couple of years before getting dropped. Or those who were moved rapidly from post to post, so rapidly that they barely had a chance to make a mark. Yet they had 'their exits and entrances', their aspirations for a time to make an impact and influence public policy before disappointment set in.

Most junior ministers are doomed never to rise higher

— either to occupy a number of junior and middle-ranking posts over several years if their party remains in government, or to depart after a couple of years. But some do prosper; there has never been a glass ceiling for junior ministers. Of the sixty-three non-Cabinet ministers in the Commons, including whips, appointed at the start of the first Thatcher government in May 1979, a third reached the Cabinet at some point over the following eighteen years. It took some nearly a decade, while others had risen and fallen by then, leaving office, generally never to return. And of her original Cabinet, only Geoffrey Howe was still there almost to the end. Of the similar number of non-Cabinet ministers in the Commons appointed by Tony Blair in May 1997, a dozen – or one in five – reached full Cabinet status over the Labour years. That was partly because some subsequent Cabinet members, such as Patricia Hewitt, Alan Johnson and Charles Clarke, only became ministers in 1998. And unlike the Conservatives, Labour then did not treat the whip's office as a potential training ground for future ministerial high-fliers. Of the fifty-six Conservative non-Cabinet ministers, including whips, appointed by David Cameron in May 2010, some fourteen have since reached the Cabinet, mainly after the end of the coalition in 2015. Some Cabinet ministers appointed since 2010 were not even junior ministers then, such as Boris Johnson, David Davis, Karen Bradley, Nicky Morgan and Gavin Williamson (the latter three were only elected to the Commons in May 2010, and started climbing the ministerial ladder later in the Parliament), let alone several of those appointed to the Cabinet by Theresa May since 2016 only to resign subsequently, mainly over Brexit.

Looking back two centuries, Gladstone began as junior

whip then became under-secretary – unlike his great rival Disraeli, whose first post was as Chancellor of the Exchequer. For a long time, this was more common than the more recent cases of those who started at the top – generally after a long period of opposition – such as Tony Blair and Gordon Brown in 1997, and David Cameron and George Osborne in 2010. Theresa May, who entered the Commons when her party was routed in 1997, has also only served as a Cabinet minister in one other post. Winston Churchill, Anthony Eden, Harold Macmillan, Alec Douglas-Home, Harold Wilson, James Callaghan, Margaret Thatcher and John Major all spent at least a brief period as non-Cabinet ministers, providing a useful apprenticeship to their later Cabinet service. As has been widely noted, one of the frequently made complaints against both Tony Blair and David Cameron is that they never really understood what it was like to be a departmental minister, let alone a junior minister, never having been one themselves.

There has been a tendency then to regard most junior ministers as worthy dogsbodies who will rise no further. It is too easy to dismiss the significance of non-Cabinet ministers. Some do it themselves, as Chris Mullin did in his entertaining diaries, as quoted at the beginning of this chapter, and civil servants sometimes look down on junior ministers as being necessary, but often tiresome. After two years 'in the lower foothills of government' Mullin left office, for the first time, after the June 2001 election, complaining in his farewell phone call with the Prime Minister (2009, pp203–4) about his 'utter lack of influence' in office. 'Every year since 1990 I could point to something that has changed for the better as a result of my intervention. All that stopped when I became a minister.' Tony Blair laughed, 'That's a great tribute to ministerial life.' But he returned to office two years later. This view has been countered by the late Malcolm Wicks, a contemporary of Mullin and minister in three departments over 1999–2008. He has set out (2012) not only the heavy workload of ministers but also what they can achieve to improve the way the state helps the public.

Nearly two centuries ago, in the second quarter of the nineteenth century, Macaulay dismissively wrote that 'a man in office, and out of the Cabinet, is a mere slave'. But that was in the era of the minimalist state. Even then (as Theakston records, 1987, p5), Aberdeen could tell the young Gladstone that becoming an under-secretary in the Colonial Office was 'a fine opening for a young man of talent and ambition and places him in the way to the highest ambition'. Reflecting a century later, in the 1930s, Duff Cooper said (in Theakston, 1987, p32): 'The life of a junior minister is not a disagreeable one, but it provides little in the way of training for the higher responsibilities to which it should lead.'

In his collection of essays, *The Charm of Politics*, the now largely forgotten Richard Crossman reviewed the memoirs of Sir Geoffrey Shakespeare, aptly entitled *Let Candles Be Brought In*. Sir Geoffrey was a perennial junior minister in the 1930s, serving in five departments under seven ministers over ten years after 1932 (Theakston, 1987, p33). He was, in Crossman's words 'the natural under-secretary', adding that every Prime Minister requires for the majority of the posts in his administration, 'honest unassuming career politicians who can read a departmental brief almost as though they had composed it and put a questioner off the scent without actually saying what is untrue; and accept without frustration the unimportance of their own activities'. Much the same could be said now about many, though not all, junior ministers, who are destined not to rise any higher. However, with a greater number of career politicians now than in the 1930s, more may have started with hopes of advancing higher. But it is both patronising and misleading to dismiss the contributions of those who serve just as junior ministers. Many, if not most, are quite realistic about their career prospects and are pleased to have served in a couple of ministerial posts, achieving some changes and improvements.

In reality, there is a balance. Some junior ministers find they have little impact and largely exist to answer letters and adjournment debates on behalf of their seniors. But others can credibly claim to have made a difference, usually in a specialist area. Can ministers increase their chances of making an impact by preparing for office?

# CHAPTER THREE

# Professional Politicians. Amateur Ministers?

'I was lucky. I became a minister in 2005 after seven years as a special adviser in Tony Blair's Number 10, dealing constantly with ministers and civil servants. As a spad I learned a huge amount about how Whitehall and Westminster work, and how they can be made to work… However maligned the office of spad may be, it is an excellent preparation – in many ways an apprenticeship – for ministerial office.'

– Andrew Adonis, foreword to *The Challenge of Being a Minister*, Institute for Government, 2011

'You know the people I'm talking about. They all go to the same schools. They all go to Oxford. They all study PPE. They leave at 22 and get a job as a researcher for one of the parties and then become MPs at the age of 27 or 28 – we are run by a bunch of college kids who've never done a day of work in their lives.'

– Nigel Farage, speech in Cambridgeshire 2014, quoted in Goodwin and Milazzo, p7, 2015

We live, we are told, in the era of professional politicians, who are remote, in it for themselves and disregard the public's interests. That is the populist mantra, not just in Britain but across the Western world, often expressed by those who have spent most of their adult lives earning their living from politics. But what does this mean for ministers? If elected representatives are increasingly drawn from the ranks of the career/professional politicians, then surely ministers will be more qualified to handle the burdens of office?

The picture is more complicated than when I first wrote about the rise of career politicians in the early 1990s (1993, p119). Then, I defined three categories: full-time politicians working in jobs directly linked to politics, whether as political researchers or advisers, public affairs consultants or lobbyists, full-time councillors or trade union officials; those in intermediate positions in jobs not regarded as long-term careers but intended to facilitate and finance political activity; and those in 'proper' jobs or freestanding careers wholly independent from politics. These criteria were inevitably subjective but, with whatever caveats one applies, there had been a decline from 80 per cent in 'proper' jobs among those MPs first elected in 1951 to just 41 per cent in 1992, while those who were already full-time politicians had risen from 11 to 31 per cent among newly elected MPs between 1951 and 1992. The trends are clear.

Peter Allen and Philip Cowley (in their chapter in Leston-Bandeira and Thompson, 2018) argue that there are more professional politicians now than thirty years ago, though they remain a minority. They offer slightly different definitions than my earlier analysis, which is that a career politician is one who seeks to sustain consistent and long-standing income from political life through a lengthy stint in office. Career politicians live for, but also off, politics. By contrast, they define professional politicians as those who have entered the legislature via routes that saw them work primarily around politics before standing for election – such as those who work for MPs, special advisers and those employed by think tanks. And they talk of a third, broader, group of the political class – elected politicians who are seen as being unrepresentative of the public at large. Taking a narrow definition, those with an occupational and professional background of professional politicians or political workers rose from around 3 per cent in 1979/83 to nearly 17 per cent in 2015, according to estimates by Byron Criddle in successive British general election studies (edited by David Butler, Dennis Kavanagh and Philip Cowley). Others who focus on occupations as instrumental to politics would put the figures much higher, but still a minority. The trend is clearly upwards, with more MPs now whose background is largely or solely in primarily political occupations, whether as special advisers, researchers to parties or MPs, working for lobbying firms or as full-time councillors of staff. Many of these are more familiar with the workings of Parliament than those who have had freestanding careers separate from politics.

Being a professional politician – defined as having worked in and around Westminster before standing for election as an MP – is unquestionably an advantage in gaining ministerial office. In the study quoted above, Allen and Cowley look at what happened to the very large cohort of MPs first elected in 1997 over the following thirteen years up to 2010. Some 36 per cent remained on the backbenches; 13 per cent became parliamentary private secretaries; 17 per cent became junior ministers or similar level shadows; 23 per cent were appointed to Minister of State and equivalent shadow positions; but only 12 per cent made it to the Cabinet or the opposition

Shadow Cabinet. However, those MPs with prior political experience before being elected did better. Fewer remained on the backbenches, and 64 per cent made it to the Cabinet or Minister of State level, nearly twice as many as the 1997 entry generally. And nearly three times as many of the professional politicians made it to the top level. In addition, professional politicians are also more likely to be promoted quickly. Over 90 per cent of those who reached Cabinet or Shadow Cabinet level gained their initial promotion in their first term in Parliament. And they were appointed to a higher level in their first promotions than MPs generally. So prior political experience is definitely an advantage in securing early promotion.

Not surprisingly, the greatest comment on the impact of former special advisers was in the 2010–15 period, when David Cameron and George Osborne and their shadows Ed Miliband and Ed Balls were all former spads, three to previous Chancellors of the Exchequer. The high point in terms of numbers was in the Major, Brown and Cameron premierships, and particularly in the Brown years, when nearly a third of the Cabinet were former special advisers (Jack Straw, Hilary Benn, David and Ed Miliband, Ed Balls, Andy Burnham, James Purnell and Andrew Adonis – though the latter two did not overlap as Cabinet ministers). In general, the number of Cabinet ministers who were former special advisers increases the longer governments go on. Since 2010, the list of former special advisers in the Cabinet, excluding the Liberal Democrats, has included not only Cameron and Osborne, but also Jonathan Hill, Damian Green, David Lidington and Matthew Hancock. But for all the high-profile names, a useful research note by Matthew Honeyman for the Constitution Unit (2013) points out that fewer than 5 per cent of special advisers since 1979 had gone on to be Cabinet ministers by 2013. The note concludes that: the fact that only a minority of Cabinet ministers were previously special advisers is a reminder that there is no one route to the highest offices in government. In the last two elections, there has been a sharp decline in the number of special advisers being selected as candidates then elected as MPs, one in 2015 and two in 2017.

A few civil servants have also crossed the line into party politics, generally via the transitional phase of being special advisers, such as David Willetts and Andrew Lansley. Sir George Young was also a civil servant in the 1960s. A more informal route into understanding Whitehall comes from politicians married to civil servants. Jack Straw met his wife, Alice Perkins, when he was a special adviser in the 1970s and she had a long career as a senior civil servant. They kept their careers apart – he never shadowed or headed a department in which she served – but, as he has admitted, he gained insights into how Whitehall and civil servants worked, which helped him later as a senior Cabinet minister for thirteen years. Oliver Heald, who had three different spells as a minister, has said (MR, in office 1995–7, 2012–14 and 2016–17) that he gained some idea of how the Civil Service worked with ministers from his wife Christine, who had been private secretary to the Home Secretary. Other examples are Peter Shore, Oliver Letwin and currently Rachel Reeves, whose spouses were, or are, senior civil servants, Shore's being a doctor and medical adviser and Letwin's a government lawyer.

Former special advisers and, of course, former civil servants do have insights into the workings of government not possessed by other new ministers – they have, in Andrew

Adonis's words above, served an apprenticeship. As such, they are often welcomed by the Civil Service as understanding from the start how Whitehall works.

A related argument, borne out by the fate of some of the former spads, is that while a period serving an apprenticeship in this way may prepare you for understanding how government works at the highest level, it also has downsides. James Ball and Andrew Greenway echo some of the points made by Nigel Farage above. They argue in *Bluffocracy*, appropriately part of a series entitled 'Provocations', and published in 2018, that many special advisers are products of an educational culture – notably via the Oxford PPE degree – which values fluency over expertise, resulting in superficial decisions and short-termism. The populist revolt in the UK, and elsewhere, has been a reaction to that culture. So while former special advisers may be technically proficient at working as ministers – and most of those mentioned above were effective operators within Whitehall – this does not necessarily mean they had good political judgement or were seen more widely as convincing and authoritative leaders. In a review for the *Times Higher Education Supplement*, Nick Hillman, a former special adviser, and a higher education specialist, challenged their view that the solution is to put experts in charge, questioning the nature of expertise and arguing that politicians, civil servants and journalists are expert in political matters and keeping the show on the road, and in intervening to balance competing demands. Moreover, the number of PPE graduates at the top of politics is still a small minority, with quite a few historians, students of English and in Theresa May, a geographer. Ball and Greenway (2018, pp43–4) quote a YouGov poll highlighting the contrast in the public's view of politicians' personal lives and their broader social and occupational background. A clear majority of voters are generally forgiving about politicians' personal lives and marital problems. But more than half think of someone as being unsuitable for office if they have never had a real job outside politics, think tanks or journalism.

The actual numbers hardly suggest that career or professional politicians, or former special advisers, are taking over government. Yet what matters is the prominence of many of them. The impression can also be much more influential than the reality. Andy Burnham, former special adviser, youthful Cabinet minister and Mayor of Greater Manchester, said sweepingly in a newspaper interview that 'all the current generation of politicians, myself included, typically came up through the back offices. We're the professional politicians generation, aren't we?' Up to a point. This exaggerated admission was only true of a minority of the Brown Cabinet even when Burnham served in it. But this view and Nigel Farage's claim are widely believed. No matter that Mr Farage has been a member of the European Parliament for twenty years, or three-fifths of his adult life, the myth or the caricature of the takeover of government by former special advisers and professional politicians has been very powerful. I discuss how special advisers work with ministers and civil servants in Chapter Seven.

However, since only a minority of ministers have been former special advisers, there is still the question of preparation for office for the vast majority of incoming ministers. Serving as a backbench MP is very different from being a minister. Becoming a minister is one of the few senior posts in public life for which there is little formal preparation, let alone training. A couple of decades ago, one might have said none. Ministers were assumed to have an intuitive understanding of what was involved merely by being politicians, or, otherwise, to sink or swim on the job. That shrewdest of parliamentary and ministerial veterans, Margaret Beckett, has summed up that view (in David Richards) that 'no training could prepare you for the pressure of ministerial life, only experience helps'. Similar attitudes exist in Australia, where Anne Tiernan and Patrick Weller (2010, p66) report a former Cabinet minister as saying:

> There's no course that teaches you how to be a minister. It is assumed that if you are elected, you can be an effective minister. There is no training course, and, unless you ask, no one volunteers to help, so basically it's what you glean from watching others and from applying what you think are commonsense principles to the sorts of things that you are called up to do.

Mike Penning, a down-to-earth Conservative, now a former minister, told an inquiry by the Public Administration Select Committee (PASC) in 2010–11: 'I would really worry if you had to do a course and pass a course to be ministers, because we're not clones, we're individuals. I'd have failed the course, whatever course you put me on.' Similarly, Liberal Democrat minister Norman Baker told the same committee that the skills of being a politician – how to communicate with people, how to prioritise your time and how to absorb information quickly – are the skills that an MP has to have, and a minister has to have the same skills.

No one is talking about courses or exams, as opposed to

guidance and help. Mr Baker epitomises the transferable skills/learn on the job view which neglects the big differences involved in being a minister. There is a very characteristic view, shared by other professions, that their role is unique, so there is no room for development. Practically no other part of the public or private sectors takes that approach any more. The Institute for Government report on *The Challenge of Being a Minister* (2011, p44) identified three key misconceptions about support for potential and current ministers. First, training and development would be threatening, since politicians believe their reputations would suffer with colleagues and the public if they were seen as needing help. Second, such support would be inappropriate, since comparisons with what happens in large organisations are spurious because of special innate and intuitive political skills. Third, such support would be inadequate, since those appointed ministers are already highly specialised and skilled, reflecting their existing abilities to perform in Parliament and the media.

Being an MP certainly supplies some of the necessary skills and experience, in understanding the political environment – and many ministers, particularly in the later stages of a government, have previously been parliamentary private secretaries. That varies enormously depending on the minister and how far they are willing to involve their parliamentary private secretary. A more directly useful experience is as a whip as an intermediary stage prior to becoming a departmental minister. David Waddington notes (pp166–7) that throughout the Thatcher years the whip's office had been used as a training ground 'for those who it was thought had the qualities to become departmental ministers'. Three dozen of those who served in the whip's office in the Thatcher and Major years went on to become departmental ministers, fourteen at Cabinet level, while two dozen made the same transition during the Blair and Brown years.

Sir Michael Fallon was one. He describes (MR, in office 1988–92 and 2012–17) that there was a policy in the late Thatcher era of

> having a whip's office split between older members who'd been around for a while and were going to spend five or six years in the office but weren't likely to be ministers, and then every year or two having a batch of younger members who were of possible ministerial calibre. In those days the whip's office elected their members and then presented them for approval to the Prime Minister.

Fallon notes that his two years in the whip's office gave him experience of two big departments, Education and Social Security, as well as Scotland, and geographic responsibilities, which changed from year to year.

> You learnt about departments. You got to know how good the junior ministers were. You went to the morning meetings, the ministerial 'prayer' meetings. You sat long into the night, sitting on a bench watching other junior ministers perform. You reported on them, you contributed to the annual review of their performance, and indeed of the Secretary of State. So it was quite a helicopter view of how well the department was coping in political and parliamentary terms. You understood more

about the legislative process than you did when you were just a backbencher, including the importance of getting things right in the chamber.

The annual performance review, on a Sunday evening, involved 'going through every member of the party, where they were in their careers, whether they were still ambitious, bitter, still supportive, and whether there was talent there that hadn't been spotted. Sometimes it was to say, "Let's give somebody a second look, not write him off." People can improve and be more supportive than they were to start with.'

Backbench MPs do not themselves gain any understanding of how big organisations like government departments are run and how complicated decisions on policy are taken. It is revealing that in the Ministers Reflect interviews, many of those asked about preparation referred not to their prior experience as a backbencher but to their pre-Westminster background in business, as a professional or in a leadership position on a local council. Several of the former ministers highlight the importance of this pre-parliamentary experience in helping tackle the challenges of being a minister – for example in local government (Paul Burstow and Bob Neill) or accountancy (Mark Hoban and Michael Moore). On the Labour side, David Hanson (MR, in office 1998–2001, then parliamentary private secretary to the PM, and 2005–10) is not unusual in talking about his lack of formal preparation but referring to his experience as leader of his local council, director of a charity, management training and, in the Commons, in the whip's office – 'a great training ground because I saw things that I hadn't seen as a backbench MP, the public-facing bits of parliamentary activity on statutory instruments, on a bill committee and in discussions with the opposition'. That gave him an understanding both of policy issues and of handling staff.

The PASC inquiry (2011) concluded that 'Undoubtedly Parliamentary experience does provide many of the skills that MPs need to perform well as a minister. However, other skills, notably those required to oversee a large and complex organisation, are unlikely to be developed during a member's career in the House.' Most MPs effectively run small businesses, employing a handful of people, like a corner shop retailer. That does not equip them for a senior role in large government departments involving complicated personal relationships and hierarchies. It is striking how those who have worked in big organisations of all kinds cite that as an advantage when they became ministers.

Since the late 1990s, potential ministers have been given help to understand what the role involves both beforehand and then when they have taken office. The word 'attempt' should be underlined, since there has been little coherence or consistency about what has happened. There are really two stages: before taking office and afterwards. At a general election, that means in opposition and then in government.

Going back to the mid-1990s, there have been various initiatives to prepare opposition frontbenchers for government. That is separate from, although usually in parallel with, the access talks which permit contacts between leading members of the opposition party or parties and Permanent Secretaries (as discussed below). My emphasis in this chapter is on preparations for being a minister, as opposed to work on policy. It is about understanding how a minister operates rather than what policies they might pursue in office. That underlines the limitations of experience as a shadow in opposition. This can obviously help in familiarising a future minister with the policy area and the immediate issues, though some of that can be in a vacuum away from the realities of Whitehall and public spending constraints.

Moreover, by definition, a shadow is not actually responsible for anything, and can only issue statements and make sound bites in order to attract attention. Stephen Hammond argues (MR, in office 2012–14 and 2018–) that 'no matter how much you want to pretend you're a minister in opposition shadowing, the reality, of course, is extremely different. A shadow minister really just does policy stuff and debates and things in the House and meetings. Nothing like the new burden of other things that come with office.' Sir Alan Duncan underlines the limitations (MR, in office 2010–14 and 2016–):

> I think shadow ministerial jobs are of almost no use whatsoever in training you to be a minister, because the quality of briefing is minimal and you are not really running anything. You are not running a department. All you are doing is posturing and issuing press releases and trying to win an election. What trains you to be a minister is having done something outside politics first, in actually running something.

In this case his experience in the oil sector was 'much more interesting', helping give a sense of corporate structure and lines of command. This underlines the distinction between developing the skills to head, or be senior in, a department and having worked out policies.

Being a shadow therefore addresses one part of being a

minister – having clear priorities – but does not of itself assist in understanding how to implement these policies. There are obvious advantages in having shadowed a particular portfolio when becoming a minister (as is highlighted in Riddell and Haddon, 2009, pp30–2). Sir Edward Heath, with his managerial view of government, was convinced that future ministers must specialise long before they come into office. There was not a complete transfer from opposition to government roles. And Heath's plans were disrupted by the death of Iain Macleod, the Chancellor, within barely a month of taking office. However, a series of Chancellors (Geoffrey Howe, Gordon Brown and George Osborne) came to office with clear priorities having shadowed the Treasury for four to five years beforehand. Similarly, in May 1997, both David Blunkett and Jack Straw had discussed education and criminal justice/ constitutional policies previously, which gave them a head start when they took office. Otherwise, however, there were big changes between the shadow teams and the post-election Cabinets, with around two-fifths of the new Cabinet in both 1979 and 1997 not occupying the same positions as in opposition. At both transitions, the Defence Secretary was different from before the election, but this did not really matter in view of the continuity of policy. In other cases – Energy in 1979 and Health in 1997 – the changes of personnel probably had more impact. Indeed, there was a striking contrast in the longevity in office between those Cabinet ministers who had shadowed the same post in opposition and those who were freshly appointed in May 1997. None of the newcomers lasted the whole Parliament, and all had left the Cabinet or had been moved by autumn 1999 at the latest.

In May 2010 the discontinuity was even greater, because

of the formation of the coalition and the inclusion of five Liberal Democrats in the Cabinet who had no previous experience of government. Some Conservatives were shifted around, producing the strange phenomenon that thanks to the pre-election access talks, some Permanent Secretaries were more familiar about Conservative plans than newly appointed Secretaries of State. Sir David Normington, for instance, then in the Home Office, had extensive discussions with Chris Grayling, the Conservative shadow spokesman, before the election about the party's home affairs priorities, including several not publicly spelt out in the party manifesto. Theresa May, the incoming Home Secretary, knew nothing about these private discussions. Damian Green, her Minister of State for Immigration, notes (MR, in office, 2010–14 and 2016–17) that he had

> what in retrospect was the huge luxury of doing a ministerial job which I had shadowed for five years. So that had two big advantages: one, I knew what our policy was and had thought it through in some detail, and secondly, so did the officials. So the conversation more of less went, 'Are you serious about this?' and I said 'Yes', and they said 'Okay fine, well there are a number of options.'

In all the general election transitions, lack of familiarity with Whitehall has been at least as important as lack of continuity from shadow to actual Secretary of State in creating problems for new ministers coming to terms with office.

Before the 1997 general election Labour held seminars at the then Templeton College, Oxford about the challenges of being a minister wrestling with the system. This was organised by Patricia Hewitt, formerly Neil Kinnock's press secretary, then working for Andersen Consulting, later Accenture, before entering the Commons and becoming a minister. This followed discussions between Jonathan Powell, Blair's chief of staff; Charles Clarke, his predecessor under Neil Kinnock; Hewitt; and the late Sir Nicholas Monck, a then recently retired Permanent Secretary. Margaret Beckett took her Trade and Industry team to the Templeton session and says (MR, in office 1975–9, 1997–2007 and 2008–9) it was very amusing, because

> I had a big team, of about six, some of whom were very free spirits in the sense of firing off press releases and stuff all over the place, and to see literally the almost physical shock on their faces when it was explained to them that when you were a minister, your departmental head and probably Number 10 had to sign off potentially on the content of any speech, or any press release. You didn't just go firing things off and making publicity for yourself. Everything had to go through the machine and everything had to be agreed across government, cleared with other departments and so on. The sheer stunned horror on their faces was quite funny actually! And not everybody fitted in well, because not everybody was prepared to accept that discipline. So they would kick against it and cause trouble and generally be a damn nuisance, but not for very long.

Patricia Hewitt (MR, in office 1998–2007) argues that the Templeton sessions had limited value, since many Labour shadow ministers found the discussion of management, strategy and organisational change irrelevant to their own experience as opposition politicians. Many saw their role as taking policy decisions and leaving implementation to Permanent Secretaries. She talks of being depressed that 'the Shadow Cabinet really didn't feel they needed any training or development'. She recalls a session when 'we took them through how long it would take to get from policy decision to implementation – and they simply couldn't believe it. It was kind of, "This is nonsense, we're going to be able to do it faster."' The Andersen team was

> just carefully talking them through the process: consultation, policy decision, briefing parliamentary counsel, getting the bill into Parliament. Then you've got secondary legislation, and somewhere along the line a bit more consultation, and then you've got to establish the new agency and frankly you're lucky if you haven't hit another election by the time you've done all of that! And, of course, it's true, but they didn't really like it.

Her explanation is that for many the thinking went

> 'Hang on, we're ministers. We're going to be ministers making decisions, implementation is somebody else's problem.' Of course, almost none of us had been in government. So they just thought all of that would be taken care of. They were such in an old policy mindset; you came up with a policy, you became a minister and that was that. And the most you would have to do was put a bill through.

Hewitt also points to a change in the role of ministers from when Labour was previously in government in the 1960s and 1970s: by the late 1990s, ministers were supposed to be less aloof and more engaged in the detail of securing behavourial change, which was often less about legislation than working with other parts of the public sector and outside bodies.

That underlines the big gulf between operating in opposition, where the focus is on responding to the media and making statements, and being in government, where choices have to be made – though, in practice, after May 1997 many of the habits of opposition persisted. Revealingly, Tony Blair, Gordon Brown and John Prescott, none of whom had any ministerial experience, did not attend the Templeton sessions. The general view was that the sessions did not fulfil earlier hopes. A parallel exercise run by the Fabian Society focused more on the constitutional and institutional background, and involved former Permanent Secretaries and academic commentators such as Peter Hennessy. The trouble with both sessions was that they did not really involve a sufficient number of shadows or special advisers. As with the Conservatives ahead of the 2010 election, there was a reluctance to include opposition special advisers for fear both of leaks and because of a reluctance by the leadership to give any indication of which of the existing political advisers might serve in government.

Ahead of the 2010 general election, the Conservatives worked closely with the then newly formed Institute for Government to organise breakfast seminars to brief members of their shadow team about how government worked. This was led by Francis Maude, himself a former minister, and by Nick Boles, about to become an MP, who ran their implementation team. This gave former ministers and current and former senior civil servants the opportunity to discuss the workings of Whitehall and, for instance, how the British government interacted with European institutions. A session with Michael Heseltine was reckoned to be the most popular, alongside one with three former Cabinet Secretaries. They were intended to be only the first base of the programme alongside development work with individual teams. Again this was distinct from the opposition's preparations on policy and its contacts with Permanent Secretaries, though advice was given by the opposition business managers (Sir George Young and Patrick McLoughlin, both with experience of government) about how to handle a bill. Caroline Spelman attended the IfG seminars, which she describes as 'semi-useful' (MR, in office 2010–12), but nothing really prepared her for the experience of government itself:

> I think more does need to be done on big changes of government. I mean my party had been out of power for thirteen years, so there weren't a lot of people knocking around who'd had experience of being in government. If you had been a special adviser, which is increasingly a sort of route into politics, it is a bit different.

An approach was made to the Liberal Democrats for similar preparatory sessions at the IfG, but, to their later regret, Nick Clegg turned this down for fear of leaks making his party appear presumptuous. The Liberal Democrats did discuss, and war-game, alternative scenarios for the possibility of a hung Parliament, including some policy priorities, but they were much less prepared, indeed hardly at all, for the demands of being ministers, which had still been seen as unlikely.

During the 2010–15 Parliament, the Institute developed a programme of working with the Labour opposition. This was focused on a number of shadow teams to assist them in understanding how to work together and how departments operated There were also a few sessions with either the Shadow Cabinet or groups of frontbenchers about how the transition process operated and Whitehall machinery. And, as before 2010, there were private discussions about the constitutional options in the event of no party winning an overall majority. But all this work proved to be redundant at 10 p.m. on 7 May 2015, when the exit poll showed that the Conservatives were heading, unexpectedly, for a small overall majority.

It is always hard for members of an opposition party – especially one that has been out of office for a long time – to prepare for life as a minister. Catherine Haddon and I concluded in our *Transitions: Lessons Learned* report (2011, p20) that there are limitations on what any opposition can do to get the right type of up-to-date insights. We suggested that the Conservatives

> were reliant, perhaps over-reliant, on advice from what one insider described as 'quasi-civil servants' from the big management consultancies and from retired Permanent Secretaries. This is clearly helpful to those who have never held office before – particularly concerning the nuts and bolts about how government works. The doubt is more about whether any opposition party can brief itself sufficiently on its reform plans before taking office. The involvement of consultants and former officials is no substitute for better and deeper contacts with the current Civil Service leadership.

Francis Maude (MR, in office 1985–92 and 2010–16) remains unrepentant about the usefulness of development sessions for shadows and potential ministers:

> I would make it compulsory, much less optional. I don't think I succeeded in getting David Cameron to say to shadow ministers, 'You must do this. Part of your job is if Francis says turn up to something, you turn up to it.' So I think there is a limit to what you can do, there is a limit to how much benefit you get from former ministers, particularly if you have long electoral cycles; they get out of date. I will be – the next time there is a new Conservative government coming in – I will be completely useless, because A, the world will have changed, and B, I will have forgotten or distorted it in my memory. So you remember things differently. I think there is a limit to what you can do.

These party preparations operate in parallel with access talks between the opposition and Permanent Secretaries. Begun ahead of the 1964 general election, these discussions are formally about letting Permanent Secretaries know about the opposition's plans and what they might mean for the machinery of government changes and the organisation of departments. From the Whitehall point of view they are also part of a reassurance exercise: to convince the opposition that the Civil Service is not partisan and is not committed to the ministers and ideas of the existing, and possibly outgoing, government, a suspicion often held by the opposition party, generally wrongly. There is also a getting to know you exercise so that shadow Secretaries of State can meet (often for the first time at any length) the senior officials in the departments they want to head. It frequently does not work out like that, since incoming Prime Ministers – even ones as certain of winning as Tony Blair in 1997 – do not necessarily appoint people to the roles they shadowed in opposition.

The emphasis is very much on policy and the organisation of government, rather than on preparing MPs to be ministers. As the late Sir Jeremy Heywood, the then Cabinet Secretary, told the Commons Public Administration and Constitutional Affairs Committee inquiry on 'Ministerial Effectiveness' in 2018 (questions 439 to 441): 'the Civil Service does not spend a lot of time working with backbench MPs or opposition MPs in preparing them for ministerial office – we do not see that as our role as a Civil Service; we work for the elected government'. He noted the work of the Institute for Government and the gap that existed. He added, 'as a general question, is there a systematic training programme or induction programme for people who might at one point become a minister? There is probably a gap in the market.'

Sir Jeremy drew a distinction with what happens when a minister is appointed. Departments have induction packs and briefings on the issues facing a department and the organisational structure of a department. He conceded that 'a large chunk of the training of ministers is going to be done on the job. The emphasis is very much on highlighting departmental priorities, and not on providing a more general background about how Whitehall works and the pitfalls of being a minister.' Attempts have been made to fill this gap more systematically since the last three general elections.

Chris Mullin records in his diaries (pp21–2) an induction

session at Lancaster House organised by Jack Cunningham, then a Cabinet Office minister, in September 1999, two months after he became a minister following a reshuffle. There was, he said, 'Lots of sensible advice. Control the diary. Don't take boxes home. Big problems don't necessarily demand big solutions. Keep your eye on the big picture.' Some of the advice, he noted, bore no relation to his own situation as a junior (and in his eyes, uninfluential) minister in the then Department for Environment, Transport and the Regions, who was cool towards, and distant from, John Prescott, the Deputy Prime Minister in charge. 'This, for example, from Sir Richard Wilson (the Cabinet Secretary). Your relationship with the Secretary of State is the key. Your clout will depend on whether you have his confidence. That's me out, then. Apart from team meetings three days after I was anointed, I've only seen my Secretary of State on TV.' Mullin adds that

> What was interesting was how Sir Richard Mottram and Sir Michael Bichard – and Sir John Kerr from the Foreign Office – eagerly sought to be in tune with the New Labour zeitgeist (my phrase) and to challenge the conventional image of the mandarin (not always successfully) though Bichard did like challenging civil servants' traditional approaches, arguing that they needed to think more outside their silos, were insufficiently focused on outcomes and tended to take it for granted that intellect equals creativity, which is often not the case.

The workshops organised by the Institute for Government and the Cabinet Office after the 2010, 2015 and 2017 general elections focused on practical questions about how to be an effective minister. These sessions featured, for example, Sir Jeremy Heywood, another experienced Permanent Secretary in Sir Chris Wormald and some former ministers such as Sir Hugh Robertson and Mark Hoban. The response to these sessions was positive, though attendance became patchier the further away they were held from a general election, since they were not regarded as a priority by departments and by ministers' private offices. Much depended on whether a lead was given by the centre. Neither Tony Blair nor David Cameron had much interest in development of ministers, so the key was the lead offered by the Cabinet Office. Francis Maude, at times a figure of controversy in his reform efforts, was fully committed to the development of ministers in office, as well as in opposition, and arranged seminars for ministers at the Institute for Government, similar to the one described by Chris Mullin. As in the pre-elections sessions, the star at these events was Michael Heseltine, even though he was more a figure of inspiration than a role model in describing the practical challenges facing ministers.

Lynne Featherstone (MR, in office 2010–15) stresses the value of the IfG session in directly influencing her work as a minister in the Home Office. She quotes the advice of Lord Heseltine:

> you are going to be swamped, you are going to have a tsunami of work cover you, you will run around, you will do orals (questions), you will do speeches, you will do all the duties of government, read all the papers. Five years will go and you will be a good little minister and you will have done nothing you ever wanted to do in

politics. My advice to you is prioritise ruthlessly, find
what you want to do and make sure you do it.

At the same session, according to Featherstone, Andrew
Adonis told the new ministers,

> trust your civil servants. If you don't direct them, they
> will keep your diary full, but if there is something you
> want to do, make sure that it is their priority and direct
> them, and they will go to the ends of the earth for you.
> Don't believe *Yes Minister*; don't believe *The Thick of It*.

Lynne Featherstone commented that 'actually, it has been a
bit like that'. She took the advice to heart: 'I went back to my
office and said to my civil servants in my private office, "I
want to do same-sex marriage." I just thought, well Michael
Heseltine says prioritise; this is what I want to do and I told a
couple of members of my private office. I said, "How do I do
this?"'

Such sessions also provided an opportunity for ministers
to swop 'war stories' about their own experience. In the coalition years, it was revealing that there were few differences on
party lines, and Conservative and Liberal Democrat ministers had more in common in complaining about poor drafting
of letters by civil servants, or being ignored by their Secretary of State. As with the pre-election preparations, Maude
would also make these post-election sessions compulsory:

> the Prime Minister needs to say, 'All new ministers must
> do it.' It needs to be run, this induction, by a minister – an
> experienced, seasoned minister like I was. 'You will do

this.' That is just part of what the role involved. I would do an annual thing as well. It doesn't need to be more than half a day actually. A lot of it is just sharing war stories.

Yet this post-election development work – and the more limited induction by departments – only partially make up for the lack of adequate preparation for most ministers before they face the shock of taking office.

# CHAPTER FOUR

# The Shock of Office

'No one can know until they are faced with it whether they can make decisions. And not just one decision, with the luxury of a day to think about it, but a box full of decisions and another box full. I'm sure there are ways of testing that, but certainly in the British system, prospective ministers are not tested for that.'

– Jack Straw, holder of several senior Cabinet posts 1997–2010, Ministers Reflect interview 2016

'It was a delight, but also a shock. I think I burst into tears, quite frankly, it was such a surprise. I was absolutely thrilled and delighted and felt incredibly privileged, but had done no preparation whatsoever.'

Susan, Baroness, Kramer, on appointment as a Transport minister, 2013–15, Ministers Reflect interview 2016

All ministers remember when and how they were told of their appointment. The circumstances are often bizarre, even comical, but all reflect an awareness that their lives had changed in far-reaching ways. The experience is frequently disorienting, as new ministers struggle to come to terms with a world with which they are often completely unfamiliar, and try and work out what they can do to make an impact. The incoming minister is only one piece in a large jigsaw of forming, or reshuffling, a government for a Prime Minister. So it is easy for the minister to feel lost – and uncertain.

One of the biggest challenges for an incoming Prime Minister, especially after their party wins office at a general election, is deciding whether to appoint their opposition team to government, and whether they should hold the same posts. As Jack Straw's quotation above shows, there is a large element of taking a punt. Of course, there are ties of patronage and loyalty as well as the power of other senior members of the leadership team who have their own allies – and for Labour before 1997 the Shadow Cabinet was elected, rather than chosen by the leader. Even Tony Blair felt obliged to appoint most, but not all, of his elected Shadow Cabinet to his first Cabinet under the then, subsequently dropped, Labour rules. As Straw notes (MR, in office 1997–2010), there has also been an assumption that 'if you've been good in opposition you're likely to be good in government, whereas the skills needed for the two are often very different. You can think of quite a number of examples of people who were brilliant in opposition but simply froze in the headlights in government.' That is one reason why Prime Ministers tend to have reshuffles a year or two into office, to drop those who had served as shadows but did not make the grade in the Cabinet.

Jonathan Powell, Tony Blair's Chief of Staff during his entire ten years in Downing Street, has drawn the parallel with Machiavelli's prince (2011, pp141–2), that the only power a Prime Minister has is patronage,

> so for him the choice of ministers is the way he exercises his influence, and unlike the prince he depends on their

continuing support for his survival. New Prime Ministers, however, have no management experience, and when we arrived in Number 10, there were no written rules on reshuffles, just lore handed down from one principal private secretary to another over the generations.

Powell noted the constraints on the number of paid ministers (discussed in Chapter One) imposed by the Ministerial Salaries Act – adding that 'So far, no government since the 1970s has dared to change it, although at the margin successive governments have found increasingly imaginative ways round it.' That is a euphemistic way of admitting the many ways that Tony Blair and his successors have sought to increase the payroll vote (or, rather, the unpaid additional vote) of MPs required to support the government in Commons divisions.

New ministers since 1997 have frequently noted the contrast between their position and that of the person appointing them. All four Prime Ministers since 1997 were never junior ministers, and the same was true of their Deputy Prime Ministers and the two most long-serving Chancellors. As Liberal Democrat Jeremy Browne remarked (MR, in office 2010–13), 'They'd never been on the shop floor in ministerial terms, and they don't actually know what junior ministers do. Cameron, Osborne, Clegg, Blair, Brown have never even really run a department if you don't count the Treasury as a normal department, let alone been a junior minister, whereas normally you have to go through it.'

Only a few, usually very senior, ministers are certain of appointment, and what post they will occupy, invariably after a general election. Sir Geoffrey Howe, Shadow Chancellor for more than four years at the time of the 1979 election, recalled (p121) how he was called by Margaret Thatcher to her study at Number 10. '"As you know Geoffrey," she said, "I want you at the Treasury." Anything else would have been a shock, but it was good to hear the actual words.' The outcome may always have been predictable, but, as Charles Moore recalls (2013, p417), there was a clash of head and heart: 'although in her heart she would have preferred Keith Joseph, she was not seriously reluctant to give Howe the job for which, she could not deny, he was now well qualified'.

Some new ministers have to adjust to not getting the post they wanted, or at the seniority they hoped. As noted in Chapter One, however, few turn down the offer of a ministerial post – although some reject the first post offered. In May 1979 (Moore, 2013, p429), Thatcher initially offered Michael Heseltine the post of Energy Secretary. He resisted. 'I've been rehearsing Environment for three years. That's what I want to do.' Thatcher's handwritten notes show she had intended to give Environment to Labour defector Reg Prentice, who got a senior non-Cabinet post instead, as the Prime Minister gave in on the spot to Heseltine. As she confessed to a private secretary, 'I don't like one-to-one confrontations with Michael'. There is very seldom any consultation about what job someone would like, or have particular experience for, or interest in, as Chapter Ten on reshuffles underlines.

There is often a disconnect between a busy and distracted Prime Minister appointing lots of ministers and the eager appointee. As Hutton and Lewis explain (2014, p177),

When the Prime Minister appoints you as Secretary of State, he'll certainly know who you are and what job he wants you to do. When he calls to appoint you, let him do the talking – if he wants you to do something, he'll say so. If not, just remember he's making another twenty similar calls that morning, and needs to get them all done before the lunchtime news.

The system of appointment can appear casual. Kenneth Clarke remembers (MR, in office 1972–4, 1979–87 and 2010–14) when, in May 1979, he was appointed to his first parliamentary secretary job, in Transport, working for his old Cambridge friend Norman Fowler, not only was there no induction or anything, but 'no one in Downing Street could tell me where the department was, let alone give me any other guidance as to what I was supposed to do'.

Patrick McLoughlin, a long-serving Conservative whip and minister, first took office at the tail end of the Thatcher era in 1989. It wasn't straightforward. First (MR, in office 1989–97 and 2010–18), when he arrived at the gates of Number 10 and said the Prime Minister wants to see me, the policeman said, 'that's what a lot of people say'. He wasn't on the list. When eventually he saw Margaret Thatcher, she said, 'This is one of the nicer parts of the reshuffle, where I can invite people to join the government for the first time.' She told him he was going to Transport as Minister for Roads. But, as noted in the Preface, when he arrived at the department, Cecil Parkinson, the Secretary of State, said he might have to change around the responsibilities, and asked him to do aviation and shipping. 'To which I said, "There are two problems with that: I've got the most land-locked constituency in the United Kingdom and I'm afraid of flying." Without a second's breath, Cecil said, "Excellent, you'll bring an open mind to this subject."'

The circumstances of appointment can be even more bizarre in the era of mobile phones, when people are not always at home standing by their landline phones. Bernard Donoughue records in his diaries (2016, p190) how on Bank Holiday Monday, May 1997, just after the election, he had been at Kempton racecourse when he was alerted that the new Prime Minister would soon be in touch. He moved away from where the course loudspeaker giving the names of the runners in the next race could be heard, so that Tony Blair would not guess 'how I was wasting my time at the races at this great and serious moment in the nation's history'. At 4 p.m. he was told to be on standby, but the call was put back every twenty minutes until 6 p.m., after the races were over. He was stuck, neither being able to go to the races nor being able to drive home in case the call came when he was on the M3. (Donoughue didn't find out until later that 10 Downing Street had, by mistake, sought and found Brian Donohoe, a Scottish Labour MP, who was the recipient of the most irrelevant prime ministerial phone call of the day.) Donoughue was to be an under-secretary at Agriculture. 'My heart sank, since I knew quite a bit about most policy areas but agriculture is the one I knew least about. It is also bottom of the Whitehall pile in departmental seniority.' He accepted, as virtually all ministers do – and two days later he recorded in his diary: 'One thing is clear. There is a world of difference between being a minister and not being one. I am lucky.'

Liberal Democrat Jeremy Browne was in a Tesco in his Taunton constituency getting a pint of milk when his mobile phone rang – as he peered down on all the newspapers with pictures of David Cameron and Nick Clegg on the front. 'It was the Downing Street switchboard putting Nick Clegg, or as they put it, the Deputy Prime Minister, through to me to say that I was going to be a Minister of State in the Foreign Office.' After ringing his mother, he got a call about forty-five minutes later from his private secretary saying, '"We're all in the office awaiting your arrival." I said, "I'm still in Tesco in Taunton! I'll come up tomorrow."' He then got the train up to London.

> My mobile phone rang again: 'It's the Downing Street switchboard, the Prime Minister would like to speak to you.' And the train was very busy and I thought I'm going to sound like a nutcase saying congratulations Prime Minister on the phone! So I rushed off to the loo, looking like I had some terrible illness. So my first conversation with the Prime Minister was in a First Great Western loo. Then as soon as we started talking we went into the tunnel, near Castle Cary, and he cut out. So I went back to my seat and he rang again, and I rushed off back to the loos with all the people round me thinking, gosh this man is ill, really isn't well at all! And I had a nice conversation with the Prime Minister in the loo.

Justine Greening (MR, in office 2010–18) also experienced the problems of being appointed on a train when she was promoted from Economic Secretary to the Treasury to, appropriately, Secretary of State for Transport. David Cameron's call to tell her 'promptly cut out because mobile signals aren't great on train'. But the next thing she knew she had got a job she 'absolutely adored'.

New ministers quickly find out that their departments already know more about their arrival than they do. After the phone call, or meeting with, the Prime Minister, an unknown person will immediately be in touch, their private secretary, arranging their welcome to the department. Arriving at their new department can be strange. Edward Garnier recalls (MR, in office 2010–12) that, after his appointment as Solicitor General, 'the first thing I had to do was go up to the department in Victoria Street. A rather dull office building, looking rather like a motel on an arterial road than a Law Officers' Department'. No grand imposing architecture there.

There are many accounts of the bemusement of new ministers coping with the flow of work, with parliamentary duties and with the Civil Service. Alan Clark (as in his diaries) was not alone in finding himself in an unfamiliar world. Ministers soon learn that the key relationship is with their private secretary, generally a younger official marked out for promotion. A good private secretary (and most are) can be a great asset, and support, in induction, for a junior minister when they start. As discussed in the previous chapter, departments are not good at providing formal support to explain how a new minister operates, although private secretaries can help informally. Their focus is much more on briefing incoming ministers on issues, which, of course, suits them. Liam Fox admits (MR, in office 1994–7, 2010–11 and 2016–) he had a problem with his private office in Defence in 2010 which was difficult to manage:

> I think there are very strong arguments for, as quickly as you can, recreating a whole new private office. Civil servants, whether they think they're doing it or not, have an affinity as to how things were done before, and often have an affinity to former ministers. And had I my time

over again, I would have changed more of my private office more quickly.

Jeremy Browne said that at the Foreign Office, he did not have 'an induction process that would be recognised by an HR department, but getting the relevant people from the directorates and talking me through all the relevant issues in the countries in quite a systematic and methodical way'. Stephen Hammond, initially a junior Conservative minister at Transport, stresses (MR, in office 2012–14 and 2018–) that

> the decisions you make in your first few days can set the tone for how your private office runs. You've got to take a view on how your private office runs. It's one of the things that's going to make you more effective. Some people take the office [as it is] and some people, I think, sometimes work on the theory of constructive tension that they're all out to get you … I think it's not a very good idea to throw all the pieces up in the air straight away. But, clearly, if after a month, there are things or people you cannot work with, I think that's acceptable to go to the Permanent Secretary and say we need to make some changes.

He believes the Civil Service 'occasionally do test their ministers in various ways. Inevitably it's quite difficult sometimes to change people's view of your priorities and what you want to get done unless you establish some of the rules fairly quickly. I think it is just the sheer extra hours you need to work.' Hammond also underlines the need to work out good processes, such as clear timelines about the papers in his red box, so he knew what to prioritise, then a weekly diary and media meeting, and then a monthly catch-up to check what has been done and what needs to be done.

Norman Tebbit (p166) vividly describes how well the relationship with a private secretary works as the interface between a minister and a department. 'A good private secretary (and over eights years in government mine were from good to superlative) is the minister's eyes, ears and voice within his department.' Jeanette Darrell, Tebbit's first private secretary in May 1979, was 'very good indeed … she was highly efficient and protective, organising everything I asked for and things I didn't with perfect efficiency'. Many of his friends asked him what it was like to be a minister. 'One thing, I told them, is that although when I was a child I never had a nanny nor a governess, I now knew what I had missed, saying I had acquired a governess called Jeanette.' One day when he was out of the office, one of his friends telephoned and spoke to her. When he arrived back, she stood 'rather menacingly beside my desk and asked, "What's all this 'governess' business, minister?"' Tebbit flannelled, to receive only a 'Hmph'. But Darrell got her revenge a couple of weeks later when he wanted to get out of a long-winded meeting. She walked over to him and said, over his shoulder, 'in an awful stage whisper, "Time for walkies, minister."' The matter was never mentioned again. Other ministers and private secretaries would certainly recognise the exchange.

Twenty years later, Patricia Hewitt experienced a different culture clash (MR, in office 1998–2007). After getting phone calls at about six in the morning congratulating her on her appointment, long before she went to 10 Downing Street to be told by Tony Blair that she was going to the Treasury, she walked along Whitehall to her new department followed by a camera crew. Arriving at reception, Hewitt said 'Hello, I'm your new Economic Secretary.' She then met her private office and asked for a computer. 'In fact, I said, "What I'd really like is a large screen and a docking unit", to which my private secretary said, "We've never had a minister with a computer before, what's a docking unit?"' That was 1998; a lot has changed.

Conservative George Freeman neatly sums up the relationship between the minister and the private office (MR, in office 2014–16):

> It became clear to me after a while – never having worked in Whitehall – that the private office viewed their role principally as the gatekeeper to the ministerial sign-off, authorisation and decision for the rest of the Whitehall machine. For the minister, the private office is the only bit of the machinery which is not just allowed but is actually supposed to be their transmission mechanism for their vision, mission and reform across the whole of Whitehall. It is supposed to be a two-way interface.

He thinks private offices are under more pressure from the machine to deliver what it needs and wants than to think about 'What does my minister want to get done across Whitehall and how do we help them do it?' His conclusion is that 'When I got up in the morning my private office was not "my" private office. It was the Civil Service's private office for setting my priorities, rather than for transmitting those priorities across the system.'

Most ministers are agreed on the absence of any real induction on their arrival – in the sense discussed in the previous chapter of preparation for how to handle the demands of the office as opposed to the usually detailed and voluminous briefing papers on policy questions prepared by departments. It is normally only a few weeks later that some sort of collective briefing on how to work as a minister occurs, and these sessions are usually short. Nicky Morgan, who like Patricia Hewitt started at the Treasury, says (MR, in office 2012–16) that her

> first few weeks were fascinating. But it's very difficult because the civil servants, your private office, will put on briefing sessions for you, but to be honest with you, at that stage you don't know what you don't know. You just have to get on with it, and hopefully be supported and watched by your private office and by others to stop you making mistakes which six months down the line you would know far better how to handle.

Conservative Caroline Spelman was stunned by office. She says (MR, office 2010–12) that becoming a minister in 2010 was

> nothing like I'd ever experienced before because I had not been a minister. And I went from never having been in government to being in the top job, the Secretary of State, without having shadowed that department, other than briefly for seven months, about seven years before. I was coming into government at a time of great difficulty, a time of austerity, and to implement quite substantial reductions in our running costs in a department that I hadn't studied.

Spelman admits that the first three months 'felt totally and utterly unsustainable', with no break between meetings:

> I think the thing that surprised civil servants is that we as ministers, particularly me with no ministerial experience, didn't actually know what was required of us, so one of the things the principal private secretary had to do in the early days and weeks was actually explain what we had to do, because no one had explained that to us. And they were quite surprised we didn't know that.

George Freeman, who occupied the novel position of Life Sciences minister, divided between the Business and Health Departments, echoes the theme of

> no training, no guidebook, no manual, no induction! You leave the Cabinet room with promotion ringing in your ears, cross the road, and walk straight into the department and start doing the job. Now, in some ways of course, the whole of your career has been a preparation for that moment, but it is quite a weird way to run an organisation.

He admits that comparisons with the long transition periods in the USA reflect very different systems. But,

> I have often wondered whether after a general election it wouldn't be better if the clutch plates of government and Parliament wait two months before they engage, for new officials to get to know ministers, set the priorities, have some awaydays, go through the policy history and the

heritage and what was in the manifesto, and the realities of the challenges facing government, and then bring the programme to parliamentary accountability. Meanwhile, Parliament could take some time to think about who would be good to chair committees and all that.

Calls for more phased transitions spread over a week or two – which occur in parliamentary systems such as Australia and Canada as well as in presidential ones – run against the strongly held belief of senior civil servants, as well as politicians, that incoming governments want to make a mark quickly and the media expect them to do so. But forming administrations and setting priorities when the leading players are exhausted after an election campaign is not necessarily sensible or good government (as discussed in the two Transitions reports by Catherine Haddon and myself, 2009 and 2011). The argument for a more gradual transition was reinforced in May 2010, when it took five days to form a government and another week to have a new administration fully in place, and meanwhile the world (or rather the financial markets) failed to collapse.

Almost all new ministers, and particularly junior ministers, remark on how different life is in government compared to opposition. Mark Hoban, who served in the Treasury and at Work and Pensions, says (MR, in office, 2010–13) that 'as a minister you just have to know everything. You are required to do everything that is in your remit, so you cannot pick and choose in the same way, so that there is a bit of a learning curve there but certainly in DWP, the learning curve was much steeper'.

At the top level, there is always the unexpected, as every

Home Secretary and Foreign Secretary can testify. Jacqui Smith (MR, in office 1999–2009) had the most dramatic possible reminder of her responsibilities after becoming Home Secretary at the end of June 2007, when there were two attempted terrorist attacks, in Glasgow and London, within days of her appointment:

> I think it was probably a good thing that it happened right at the very beginning. And the fact that, with the exception of the two terrorists themselves, nobody was really injured, meant that on reflection, it was a pretty good induction. Because what it meant was that very quickly I met the most senior counter-terror people, both in the police and in the security agencies. I got a feel for what happens when there actually is a live terror attack. I got a feel for what role a minister plays at a time like this – what value can you add? All of those things were very helpful. Politically and personally what it did was put me in front of people quite early on. I quite often say that the thing that people most often said to me about my public performance that weekend was 'You seemed very calm and reassuring.'

She notes that there is subtext here about her being the first female Home Secretary and doubting whether a woman could do it, so bring a man in. There have, of course, been two more female Home Secretaries since then.

For members of the government in the Commons, becoming a minister comes on top of duties as a constituency MP – as well as family ties. Most ministers insist on having Fridays out of London in their constituencies unless they are on foreign trips and the like, or, rarely in recent years, have parliamentary business on a Friday. That suits their departments too, since civil servants can get on with necessary work in the absence of ministers. The priority of constituency ties and duties did not matter so much forty or more years ago when ministers sometimes only visited their constituency – if it was a safe seat and outside London – once a month or even less frequently. A combination of political and social factors outside the scope of this book has meant that all MPs have to pay much greater attention to their constituencies.

An increasing number of MPs and ministers are mothers, and a number have given birth during their time in the Commons. It is now barely remarked on for ministers to take time off after they give birth and then return a few months later. Maternity and parental leave are relatively recent developments – let alone proxy voting for MP mothers with young babies.

Above all, ministers quickly realise that they need stamina. Being a minister is hard work. Relatively few can rival Roy Jenkins in being able to handle most business in office hours, while having a good lunch, and enjoying a vigorous social and cultural life. One of the biggest changes from the early 1990s onwards was the arrival of the alcohol-free lunch for most ministers, if not for all backbenchers. For most ministers, in the evening and early morning, there is the tyranny of the red box and the daily list of meetings and engagements. So next in importance to the private secretary is the diary secretary. Sir George Young, with his decades of experience, says (MR, in office 1979–86, 1990–97, 2010–12, 2012–14, 2016–) that you have to have a serious conversation with the diary secretary and you say nothing goes in the diary until I've agreed it. It seems fairly obvious, but sometimes the civil servants say, 'Well, the Secretary of State has always done this conference.' Then, if possible, keeping Fridays clear so you can do the constituency. And being sort of ruthless, I suppose, about priorities and if you can, delegating to poor old junior ministers.

Junior ministers see themselves sometimes as victims in this process. Chris Mullin recalls in his diaries (pp12–13) early on in his ministerial life being

besieged with invitations to address conferences organised by obscure but no doubt worthy organisations. Mostly these are the crumbs that fall down from the tables of my superiors and my first instinct is to reject the lot. However, they usually all come with notes from officials advising acceptance and, reluctantly, I concede. Before long my whole life will be eaten up by pointless activity. One such invite, originally addressed to Nick Raynsford, came with a note from his private secretary still attached. It read, 'This is very low priority. I suggest we pass it to Chris Mullin.' I wrote NO and waited to see what would happen. Sure enough, as I anticipated, someone was in my office within the hour, explaining why it was really of the highest importance.

In her first, most junior, job, Jacqui Smith had the same experience as Chris Mullin in having invitations sent down the hierarchy from the Secretary of State, via the Minister of

State, to her — a clear reminder of the pecking order. Almost all ministers agree that they spent far too much time meeting representatives of outside groups, always nowadays described as stakeholders, or making routine, and instantly forgettable, speeches to conferences.

Smith said that 'one of the shocks of ministerial life is the speed with which decisions need to be taken — the amount of paper, but reading and general information and submissions that you need to process and the speed with which you need to do it'. Similarly, Caroline Spelman says her life consisted of a

> lot of face time, not much downtime, and the only down-time you had was 'red box time', so it was kind of working time. There are very, very long days ... You might start on the red box at ten o'clock at night, taking two or three hours to do. I used to reckon I was doing really well if I got to bed by midnight, and quite often later.

She said this suited the civil servants very well, since they could do all their work during the daytime and then load up the box at night-time.

Nicky Morgan admitted that, as Education Secretary, she slept

> a lot less than I had done before. I mean it is a crazy system. People complain about MPs having outside jobs, but the ultimate outside job is being a minister — because it is fairly all-consuming, and, of course, you don't just finish in the evening, you then go home and do a box for

several hours. You've got to try and pace that, and try not to exhaust yourself, because that's the time when you become ill and then you lose perspective. So it's really important that you do balance all these things. Then, of course, you've got weekends, constituency, family, another box, massive box, six hours' worth of work every weekend arrives on a Saturday morning – it's a juggle. There's never a period when you're not working – or very, very infrequently, summer holidays, Christmas holidays.

The burden falls particularly heavily on women ministers such as Morgan and Spelman, who have children, as well as constituencies some way from London. They are also more candid than male ministers about these pressures. Spelman found the amount of sitting and face time 'very wearing' and, because she is quite sporty and is used to doing some exercise to try and stay fit:

in the end I took to balancing my red ministerial folder on the handlebars of an exercise bike in the gym at seven o'clock in the morning, to the great amusement of everybody in the department ... I was doing two things at once. I was exercising, and at my freshest part of the day, taking in the red folder of all the briefings on the day's meetings.

Vince Cable, who had had a demanding career in business, admits (MR, in office 2010–15) that being a Secretary of State was 'very hard work. It's by far the most difficult job I've ever had to do intellectually or physically. I'd normally go fifteen hours a day.' Even the ever resilient Kenneth Clarke admits 'the hours are colossal. I couldn't do it now. You have to get by with not much sleep and your family and everything do get squeezed out a bit.'

Every minister agrees that they need to focus on a few issues, or else effort will be spread too thinly to make an impact. Deciding on priorities is not always straightforward, though Secretaries of State obviously have more leeway than more junior ministers. According to John Campbell's magisterial biography (p266), Roy Jenkins said in an interview that he had learned from his study of Asquith (also a Home Secretary, then Chancellor) that to succeed as a minister 'you should concentrate on relatively few issues on which you think you can really do something decisive, not dissipate your energies over too wide a field'. But as Jenkins and many other Home Secretaries have discovered, they do not always have a choice. They have to devote their energies and time to unexpected and generally unwelcome events. Moreover, junior ministers seldom even have that as a theoretical choice.

Some ministers are appointed with an instruction to tackle a particular policy priority or manifesto pledge. That applies more at Secretary of State level, when a new minister is told by the Prime Minister to lower the temperature in an area which had been very contentious under their predecessor, notably in departments like Education and Health. In other cases, it is more self-selecting. Jacqui Smith, who had six different roles in ten years, says (MR, in office 1999–2009) that 'the only time in my ministerial career I really got guidance from the Prime Minister about what he wanted me to do was when I became Home Secretary when Gordon Brown and his team had produced a letter that said "These are my priorities for the Home Office.'" Earlier, when she first became a junior minister, Tony Blair said 'words to the effect of, "You used to be a teacher, we thought it might be a good thing for you".'

A related challenge is working out your relationship with your Secretary of State if you are a junior minister, or with junior ministers if you are an incoming Secretary of State. For a junior minister, much depends on relationships with Secretaries of State, how far they are willing to delegate. Sir Michael Fallon notes (MR, in office 1988–92 and 2012–17) the contrast between his first and second Education Secretaries, John MacGregor and Kenneth Clarke.

> Very different style. John wanted to know everything and see everything; he checked your homework. Whenever you went to him with a policy, he went through it with the civil servants. Ken was more trusting. They were both good bosses, but Ken delegated much more: 'This is your portfolio, these are the issues for you. If you get into trouble come back and see me.'

A generation later, in the Treasury, Mark Hoban regarded George Osborne as a good delegator, leaving him to develop some changes in tax relief. 'One of the challenges for junior ministers is that there are priorities that are set out by your boss but there are things you might want to do that perhaps aren't on his radar screen, perhaps slightly neglected, that you feel actually can be promoted and tackled.'

There is a learning process in which an astute Secretary of State learns from their earlier experience as a more junior minister. Andrew Mitchell had been a junior minister in the mid-1990s and was then Secretary of State for International

Development for the first two years of the coalition. In his first, junior role in the mid-1990s, he says (MR, in office 1992–7 and 2010–12)

> the trick about being a minister is to get some responsibility of your own. When I became a minister in social security I identified an area, which was the Child Support Agency, that was extremely difficult, very fraught, and there was so much detail that in the end the Secretary of State would not be able to micromanage it. So I found a niche for myself to deliver for my Secretary of State.

And when he was DFID Secretary,

> I tried to give my two ministers – who were both extremely good – areas to get on with ... The route to enjoyment as a junior minister is to find an area where you can drive forward the policy and where you're not always having to report to the Secretary of State. As a Secretary of State it is to know what you can devolve and to keep your eye on what really matters. It is a very different job being Secretary of State, a very different job.

Steve Webb (MR, in office 2010–15) was the one Liberal Democrat in the Department of Work and Pensions, and, despite ideological differences, he had a good relationship with Iain Duncan Smith, who allowed him a good deal of freedom in his area of pensions:

> The funniest thing is we'd have a weekly ministerial meeting and there would be the Secretary of

State, Conservative, there would be two parliamentary secretaries, Conservative, and the minister in the Lords – that's four. Some of these have parliamentary private secretaries, that's about even. You'd have the Tory whips, you'd have the Tory whip in the Lords. And it wouldn't be unusual when they ushered the civil servants out for the political bit of the meeting for it to be me and twelve Tories. Even when I had half a spad (special adviser) it would be the two of us and about fifteen Tories because mysteriously they seemed to grow at the same time.

Webb, of course, had access to the Quad (the small group at the top including Nick Clegg and Danny Alexander), which gave him 'leverage and influence beyond my rank. So in a strange sort of way I was in a far more powerful position as a Lib Dem in the coalition in the department than I would have been if I'd been a Conservative doing exactly the same job'.

**CHAPTER FIVE**

# Ministers and Civil Servants: the Two Cultures

'Politicians always have tensions with civil servants because civil servants are completely different. Politicians are small organisation people – they believe you get results by what you do yourself. You have been an analyst or a university lecturer or a journalist, or particularly a lawyer, and there is a very direct relationship. Civil servants are big organisation people. They think in terms of structures and hierarchies and mandates. When the Prime Minister said to me, "I want something done", my immediate reaction was "I need a person who does this." I did not think I was going to do it myself.'

– Lord Turnbull, former Cabinet Secretary in evidence to Public Administration Committee, Eighth Report, session 2009–10

'The Civil Service is not a conspiracy to stop ministers doing things. That's the crucial angle. By and large they will often warn you that something won't work. They're not always right, but it's very important that they are not seen as simply a bunch of boring do-nothings putting up objections for everything. It is worth trying to understand why they don't think it will work to see whether it's a valid reason and if there is a genuine concern that has to be tackled.'

– David Willetts, former Universities minister and former civil servant, in Ministers Reflect interview, 2015

Ministers and civil servants come from distinct tribes – with different backgrounds, attitudes, aspirations, ambitions and instincts. That does not mean they cannot work together. They can and do. But just as it is wrong to see ministers and civil servants as inevitably in conflict – even of the manipulative *Yes Minister* kind, so it is misleading to accept at face value the constitutional traditions of civil servants automatically obeying, and following the lead of, ministers. The reality is more subtle, and interesting.

Civil servants look to ministers for a lead, for guidance and direction, not least in standing up for their departments. The ministers who are praised, and admired, are those who provide that lead, who have a clear vision and objectives and are decisive, but who also listen and respond to advice. This is little or nothing to do with ideological preferences. Civil servants have views but are accustomed by training and temperament to work with people with whose outlook they personally disagree. More important are temperament and judgement – and respect. Civil servants want to be involved – a source of complaint sometimes about special advisers keeping officials on the outside – and to be trusted. There is a two-way process between ministers and officials, recognising differences of approach but trying to create a sense of mutual interest and dependence in a team.

Tensions can develop when a minister seeks to exclude civil servants, and even more when they blame them, directly or indirectly. When we interviewed officials for *The Challenge of Being a Minister* in 2011, they came up with similar lists of ministers who were disliked and regarded as ineffective – for much the same list of reasons. These included a failure to develop relationships with civil servants, reflecting personal insecurity, an inability to trust others, and a lack of self-confidence to open out to officials whom they had known before taking office. As reported (in Riddell et al, IfG, 2011, p16), civil servants are, in general, scathing about ministers who try to micromanage. As one senior official put it, with a somewhat world weary air, 'The main thing we've got to do is to convince them that we are competent – they ask us to do something, we deliver it.' Ministers naturally want to be sure that officials are competent, since they, the politicians, will be held accountable when things go wrong. It is a two-way process, and ministers, even those highly rated for their effectiveness, have complaints about the Civil Service. Some of the more substantial criticisms are discussed below, but many ministers have more day-to-day complaints about, for instance, the quality of correspondence and submissions, not just spelling mistakes and poor grammar but producing slabs of unusable prose.

The traditional constitutional bargain is that ministers take the credit when policies work, and the blame when things go wrong – while civil servants provide frank advice in private and avoid either public praise or blame. These conventions have become strained in various ways, as some ministers, and often even more, their special advisers, have sought to blame Whitehall, the bureaucracy and linked interest groups – what some Conservatives have called the 'blob' – for the frustrations they have faced in trying to achieve change. In recent years, there has been more blaming of civil servants by some ministers, and ex-ministers, and their advisers and allies – reflecting, in part, policy failures and deeply controversial policies such as Brexit. There has been tension in minister/Civil Service relations over the long-running saga of the implementation of Universal Credit, as well as over immigration. One of the unusual features was that the two key ministers involved in welfare reform, Iain Duncan Smith and David Freud, were both in the same posts for six years, while civil servants were moved much more often.

As Lord Freud notes (MR, in office 2010–16),

> You don't achieve anything at all without medium-term planning for between two and three years. That's an interesting concept because politicians don't do that and you stop the civil servants doing it by promoting them every two years! So you don't really have anyone, structurally, doing the strategic implementation over the two-to-three-year run down into anything serious. And, as you know, you can't do anything in less than two to three years. Nothing.

He says that, now with Universal Credit, key people are being held there, though it is hard to promote in post (one of the difficulties shown by the excessive turnover of civil servants). Lord Freud compares DWP officials favourably with former colleagues in the City: 'you certainly wouldn't get my former colleagues in the City working as hard and with the intensity just for the personal satisfaction of achieving the goal. They are remarkable people – absolutely no doubt about that.' In this case, some of the problems have been about the timing of implementation of such a complex project.

Brexit has been more complicated because of deep, and well-publicised, disagreements within the government leading in several cases to high-profile ministerial resignations. That has led to disillusioned ministers, former ministers and advisers blaming specific civil servants working for the Prime Minister. That can, in turn, trigger leaks and charges which further undermine the relationship. But this criticism, however vocal and strident, has so far remained a minority voice, and reflects the exceptional circumstances and deep disagreements involved in Brexit. A common charge from the pro-Brexit camp has been that Whitehall is pro-Remain. David Davis, the former Brexit Secretary, said after he resigned that, 'If you added up all the Permanent Secretaries who voted to leave the European Union, I suspect the answer would be zero.' What is more striking is how flexible the Civil Service has been in adapting to the profound, and unexpected, shifts in long-standing government policy and objectives.

Whatever officials' private views may have been, they responded immediately to the June 2016 vote in preparing for Brexit, just as they shifted in 1979 following the election of the Thatcher government. The problems have been more to do with ministerial divisions over policy than the attitudes of civil servants. It is striking that even committed Brexiteers who were interviewed, such as David Jones, who served in the Brexit department in 2016–17, praised civil servants (MR, in office 2010–14 and 2016–17). On his recall to government to join the new department, he says: 'I was hugely impressed by the professionalism of the Civil Service. The Civil Service is one of the greatest national resources of this country. The sheer professionalism of the officials who were taking on the biggest challenge that this country has had since the Second World War, and being quite prepared to deal with it, was so impressive.' His period in office was, however, before the arguments between ministers became so intense as to lead to resignations.

In part, of course, the constitutional bargain has masked the reality in practice of a complicated relationship of influence and accountability. The theory is that accountability goes up from civil servants via ministers to Parliament, where ministers answer on the floor of the Commons and to Select Committees. But it is not, and has never been, as straightforward as that. Civil servants are not merely anonymous creatures subservient to ministers. They have their own legal existence, or rather Permanent Secretaries do, as accounting officers responsible for financial probity and the good management of departments for which they are answerable to the National Audit Office and the Public Accounts Committee of the Commons. I will explore the implications later in this chapter.

Both extreme views of the relationship are wrong. Most civil servants do not try to undermine their Secretaries of State in a Sir Humphrey Appleby type way – of course, there are examples of this happening but they are not that common, and usually unsuccessful in the long-term. Similarly, the often lauded picture of civil servants confronting ministers with bold, uncompromising advice at variance with the latter's stated views is naive and can appear self-righteous. Of course, it is the duty of civil servants to warn if they think a policy is illegal, will not work or will be too costly. But the prime responsibility of officials is to help the government of the day implement its priorities.

The dilemma was well addressed in the tributes and assessments of the role of the late Sir Jeremy Heywood (Lord Heywood of Whitehall) when he was forced to retire in autumn 2018 because of ill health, and a few days later died, after more than two decades as one of the most influential, and respected, civil servants in Whitehall. Jonathan Portes, a former leading economist in the Cabinet Office and a friend and colleague of Sir Jeremy, summed up the challenge for officials in a piece for the *New Statesman*:

> The textbook description of the role of the Civil Service is to provide impartial, objective advice to ministers, who then decide. Meanwhile, the *Yes Minister* parody – the Civil Service whose primary interests are to maintain the status quo, and with it, their own power – still has a powerful hold over the public imagination. Neither is accurate. Civil servants who 'speak truth to power' by telling ministers that their pet policy ideas are crazy and unworkable don't get far. But simply nodding along and promising to deliver the undeliverable is not only a betrayal of the responsibilities of the civil servant but is what leads to policy disasters like Universal Credit. Being a good civil servant is about squaring the circle – analysis combined with persuasion, vision combined with realism. Nobody did, or does, that better than Jeremy.

Former ministers who worked with him also stressed his ability to produce workable solutions to difficult problems, answering many of the criticisms which appear in this chapter about the Civil Service's caution and lack of originality. Sir Jeremy was widely misunderstood and mistakenly criticised because of his influence – ministers and, in particular, successive Prime Ministers listened to him. As Rohan Silva, one of

David Cameron's political team wrote (2018), Sir Jeremy believed that government should be innovating to improve and 'had profound respect for the line between elected representative and unelected bureaucrat – and he only ever fought for things the Prime Minister also wanted to see happen'.

In its 2018 report on 'Ministerial Effectivness', the Public Administration and Constitutional Affairs Committee (p11) examined relations between ministers and civil servants – quoting Sir Amyas Morse, the long-serving Comptroller and Auditor General that, on the Civil Service's balance between impartiality and responsiveness, 'the ship has probably tilted in the opposite direction over a number of years where it is difficult for civil servants to feel they can stand up'. Matthew Taylor, a former senior adviser in Number 10 in the Blair years, is quoted as saying that civil servants 'self-censored rather than challenge their minister'. Faced with the prospect of challenging a minister's preferred policy, too often they decided 'it was better to nod sagely than look care-threateningly unhelpful'. Not being like that is what made Jeremy Heywood so respected and influential. Finding the balance between constructive advice and being negative is the big test for any senior civil servant.

Changes of government present a challenge for the Civil Service, however detailed the preparations. Trust has to be won and the doubts of new ministers overcome. Sir Brian Unwin, a senior Treasury official responsible for the management of the budget in 1979, recalls (2016, p154) how 'The cultural transition in the Treasury was a substantial one, and we did not find it easy to persuade the incoming Chancellor and Prime Minister that, although it was only a short time since we had been loyally serving a Labour government, we were now, as civil servants, on their side also.' There was a sense of professional pride in the Treasury officials to show that they had studied the Conservative plans and were well prepared for them. So despite earlier suspicions of a Keynesian bias in the Treasury, Sir Geoffrey Howe was relieved (1994, p127) by the sense of 'an extremely well-drilled wartime operations room'.

Thirty-one years later Mark Hoban made a similar point (MR, in office 2010–13). He started at the Treasury, where he notes 'how much care the Civil Service had taken to prepare for the incoming government, notably in his area of reforms to financial regulation' – partly reflecting the pre-election contacts between George Osborne's team and Sir Nick Macpherson, the then Treasury Permanent Secretary. Hoban says that

> this impression of an obstructive Civil Service, a product of *Yes Minister*, was completely blown away by this preparedness for our agenda and then a sense that if you gave clear direction, officials would go away and implement and do it really well in a very thoughtful way, come back with ideas, options. I was just really impressed by the professionalism of civil servants and the thought they put into our arrival.

That reflects a more general Civil Service desire to establish good relations with incoming ministers and to impress them, seeking to rebut the frequent claims by opposition parties that officials were personally or ideologically committed to the previous government. That can lead to an apparent excessive desire by civil servants to please new ministers by suppressing doubts and questions they may have about an incoming government's policies.

In a lecture at King's College, London, six months after leaving office in 2016, George Osborne stressed the complementary roles of ministers and civil servants.

> I am not someone who for a moment subscribes to the idea that somehow the ministers are all brilliant, and, if it were only for a better bunch of civil servants things would all be extremely well-run in the country. It's true that the Civil Service is inherently quite cautious and is not necessarily going to be the source of a lot of original thinking – but that isn't actually necessarily their job.

He treated the Treasury staff as part of a team, with their own parallel careers, rather than demanding a hierarchical relationship.

The overwhelming majority of those interviewed in the Ministers Reflect series praise the Civil Service. This begins with their appreciation of their private offices and private secretaries noted in the previous chapter. Steve Webb, the Liberal Democrat Pensions Minister in the coalition, catches the relationship vividly (MR, in office 2010–15). When he asked his private office what they were there for, they said, memorably, '"We're the roadies, you're the talent." You know, it's to enable you – they are to enable you to do your job and now that I'm stripped of all of that, I appreciate it ever so slightly more.' He viewed the Civil Service in general as 'very good, very supportive. They liked having someone who didn't just know a certain amount but actually had purpose.' Ministers praise the intellect and hard work of civil servants, and the non-partisan nature of the Civil Service. Politicians' fears before taking office that civil servants had accepted the approach of the previous government invariably disappear when new ministers discover that officials are keen to serve them – so the non-partisan nature of the Civil Service is praised and appreciated. But non-partisan is not the same as not having views related to departmental interests.

The Goats, outsiders, often businessmen brought into government (see Chapter Nine), generally view the Civil Service favourably. Lord Green of Hurstpierpoint says (MR, in office 2010–13) that the 'old image of the Civil Service as a bunch of Sir Humphrey Applebys is very unfair. These were intelligent hardworking people who cared about the work they were doing. And, of course, incorruptible. We take this for granted at our peril but that's a feature of British public life I was privileged to see close up and frankly I was impressed.' This is an extremely important point, and could not be said in many countries. The questions about the Civil Service are, with rare exceptions, not about their probity but derive from their often ambiguous relationship with ministers. Other Goats were more critical of Civil Service caution and lack of familiarity with the outside, business world.

Behind the general admiration of Civil Service support and brainpower, there is often criticism of a certain passivity, and a reluctance to put forward their own thoughts and views on a problem. Some Conservative ministers – notably Francis Maude but also others – are critical of the Civil Service. Oliver Letwin served as an adviser in Margaret Thatcher's Downing Street in the 1980s, and was the key policy co-ordinator during the 2010–15 coalition. He is strongly supportive of the Civil Service's values and approach as a whole, but

believes (MR, in office 2010–16) that since the 1980s, the Civil
Service had changed quite a lot:

> generally for the worse. And that I think was a consider-
> able worry to me all the way through my six years in
> government in a sense that in the late 1970s there were, as
> there always will be in a vast bureaucracy, all sorts of
> problems and gaps and difficulties. But you could more or
> less rely on it that not only the most senior, but also the
> most significant junior civil servants in the early 1980s
> would be able to think more or less straight and would
> speak and write recognisably in English. They would
> know the difference between something which was being
> said that had evidence behind it, and something being said
> which was an attempt to disguise the fact that someone
> hadn't got the slightest clue what they were talking about.

He exempts the Cabinet Office and the Treasury, who were
significantly better than the average, but there was 'a huge
amount of terrible guff, at humongous length coming from
some departments'. He asked for submissions to be written at
one quarter of the length. Initially he thought this didn't
matter, but then 'I discovered quite quickly it did really
matter, in the sense that people just didn't know what they
were talking about'. He blames the 'management speak' of
the 1980s – 'my sense was that the government in 2010 was
less good at getting down to nuts and bolts and finding out
why things weren't working and putting them right than it
was in the 1980s, which is a distressing fact'.

A number of other ministers also criticise not just the
capabilities of some civil servants but also, more specifically,

their drafting skills. Theresa Villiers cites (MR, in office 2010–16) the example of 'some correspondence that was drafted in quite a thoughtless way, which if I had not picked up on it and rejected it then I would have been sending out something that was misleading – not intentionally misleading, but the way it was drafted was sufficiently ambiguous that it would have misled people'.

An equally common criticism from ministers of all parties is that senior civil servants are, if anything, reluctant to give original or challenging advice. This may be because of a fear of getting on the wrong side of ministers and their special advisers after some of the tensions of the past twenty years, or a more inherent caution. Vince Cable says (MR, in office 2010–15) that, although he

> had a very high regard for a lot of the civil servants, some of them were frustratingly legalistic. It wasn't traditional Sir Humphrey-type but I was constantly being given advice that there are 'legal risks'. If it wasn't a financial problem, there was a 'legal risk'. But when you actually went into it, the legal risk of being sued successfully was probably one in a thousand. But that is a legal risk. Until I got wise to this I tended to kowtow to it but eventually I realised it was just people being lazy or unadventurous or not doing their job properly. But there was Civil Service inertia around a lot of issues.

Government lawyers argue that there has been a change in recent years from a 'don't do that' approach to advising on a balance of risk and looking for legally defensible ways around problems.

Many other ministers were frustrated at the risk-averse character of their officials. Lynne Featherstone complains (MR, in office, 2010–15) about

> just having to go through so many different hoops to get things done. And also civil servants are by their nature scared of doing something wrong. I found that just drove me insane. It is their job to be brave and experimental. But sometimes the level of caution and the number of people who would have to be involved and the lack of linear decision-making. And everything had to be checked before anyone got to see the Secretary of State.

Fellow Liberal Democrat Jo Swinson (MR, in office 2012–15) sometimes found the Civil Service to be

> really frustrating. But, equally, I sort of learned to love them in a strange way and you end up with a bit of a meeting of minds. And the challenge that they give in doing a kind of sense check or risk check. They can be too risk averse, my goodness. Civil Service lawyers sometimes really would have you do nothing. But sometimes it's a valuable point to put across and say, 'Have you thought about this consequence and that consequence?' and so on.

New ministers are often surprised to find that they do not appoint or control their staff in the way that a private sector executive would. Nicky Morgan says (MR, in office 2012–16) that the really weird thing about being a minister is that, on the one hand, you've got these civil servants, the people you're dealing with on a daily basis, you need them to be good, reliable and working hard, and that's what they do. But you're not really involved in appointing them or managing them. So it's very different from a professional environment.

When a couple of years later she was Education Secretary, she noted the paradox that 'you've got three thousand people working for you who are not really working for you. They're working for the department, and you just happen to be in the department for a period of time.'

Frustrations about not actually running a department were particularly expressed by ministers with a business background. Looking back on his time at the Energy and Climate Change Department, Greg Barker says (MR, in office 2010–14)

it's not clear what the responsibilities of ministers are, and the dividing line between management and policy responsibility. I felt that as a minister I carried the can for policy, but it was very frustrating, particularly as someone who had a partially commercial background, that I would be responsible for something if it went wrong, but often I wasn't responsible, or I didn't have the power really to ensure that it was delivered effectively. I had little say over the resource or the naming of particular individuals who were responsible for delivering that policy.

He was never consulted in the assessment of officials, or

asked for feedback about them. Barker is not alone in complaining at

> not being able to pick my own people for important
> policy work – you wouldn't expect a CEO of a new large
> company to come in and be told that it's up to them to
> deliver better returns for shareholders, but you can't
> change any staff or you can't mess with any of the senior
> appointments on the board, or the people in the market-
> ing department or the people in product development.

Permanent Secretaries are strongly resistant to ministers becoming involved in their personnel decisions apart from at the most senior levels, and in particular cases, the choice of private secretaries, though Barker notes a 'nudge, nudge, wink, wink' flexibility in practice. Civil servants can themselves be critical of the attempt to run big departments by ministers unfamiliar with the working of sizeable organisations.

Few of those interviewed accepted in full the critique of the Civil Service developed by Francis Maude, when he was Minister for the Civil Service during the coalition government from 2010 to 2015. Maude was unusual in that he both wanted to be responsible for the Civil Service and held the job for the whole of a Parliament, rather than, like most ministers, seeing a post in the Cabinet Office as a temporary stepping stone to a more senior departmental role. Maude was controversial within Whitehall, both among Secretaries of State, who resented what they argued was his interference in their departments, and among many civil servants, who disliked what they saw as the abrasive approach of Maude and his advisers. Yet, while many officials objected to his style and what they perceived as an anti-Civil Service approach, they accepted the thrust of a number of his criticisms and his specific recommendations for improvements.

The essence of the Maude case (MR, in office 1985–92 and 2010–16) is that in the eighteen years he was out of office, the Civil Service had deteriorated 'really quite a lot'. He admitted that this disillusionment was 'steep and distressing' and he saw the Civil Service as suffering from 'institutional complacency'. His critique differs from many who talk about politicisation, which he disputes – 'My concern with the Civil Service has never been that it's politicised.' Indeed, unlike some of his Conservative colleagues, he defends the idea of 'a permanent, impartial Civil Service' as an excellent one. He believes the Civil Service

> still has some brilliant people, some of the best civil servants in the world capable of doing amazing stuff. The thing that had got better, which most ministers would not see but was my kind of obsession, was the functions – finance, commercial, etc. – at least you had people who had some background in it, whereas thirty years before, it was generalist civil servants who were told 'Your turn to be head of finance'. So all this was a little better than it had been. I think the habit of giving very robust, candid advice to ministers had deteriorated a lot in those intervening years. The balance was different. Civil servants had got much less good in the intervening period at accommodating difficult people, the people who are a bit quirky, a bit maverick, maybe a little bit eccentric. The Civil Service contains a lot fewer people who are disruptive in the good sense.

However, despite his praise in general for an impartial Civil Service, Francis Maude says he was 'sadly disillusioned by the extent of sheer inertia, sometimes active obstruction, often just passive. The worst thing ever, which is you don't give advice, saying "Minister, this is a really stupid thing to do." You go along with it and then don't do it, and that is just intolerable and there was far too much of that.'

In his Speaker's Lecture in September 2017, he complained about the defensiveness of the Civil Service:

> all too often, the first reaction of senior civil servants when something wrong is discovered is either to cover it up or to find a scapegoat, often someone who is not a career civil servant and who is considered dispensable. There seems to be an absolute determination to avoid any evidence that the permanent Civil Service is capable of failure. Another indicator is that if a minister decides that a Civil Service leader is not equipped for his or her task, this has to be dressed up as 'a breakdown in the relationship', with the unspoken suggestion that this is at least as much the fault of the minister as of the civil servant. It can never be admitted that the mandarin was inadequate in any way.

He argued for creating a culture more friendly to innovation and removing, rather than promoting, underperforming officials; increasing the esteem paid to operational, financial and technical skills, notably in leadership positions; improving functional leadership at the centre of government in property, procurement, IT and digital, HR, finance and project management; and a strengthening of ministerial offices. Many of the changes on the operational side and the bolstering of functional leadership were overdue and were supported at the top of Whitehall, if not by many departments which opposed the centralisation of some purchasing and other activities. This is an important subject outside the scope of this book, but progress here is central to the efficiency of Whitehall in handling change and the development of big projects.

Maude sought to strengthen ministerial control over departments by changing their boards with the appointment by Secretaries of State of more non-executive directors from the business world. This was about administration and support in running a department, not policy as such, though, at first, Civil Service leaders were worried that it would undermine the position of Permanent Secretaries at the head of their departments. The impact varied across departments depending on the experience and personality of the Secretary of State. Jonathan Djanogly notes (MR in office 2010–12) that, at Justice, Kenneth Clarke understood how a board worked from his time as a member of a number of private sector boards and as deputy chairman of British American Tobacco. So, in Djanogly's view, Justice had

an effective non-executive board, which Ken Clarke valued highly. For a junior minister it's very easy just to be siloed into what you do and not to realise what's going on in your department, let alone other aspects of government. And to have an effective board is the way by which you can understand what's going on within the department and also the cost implications.

However, he does not think 'all Secretaries of State valued the board let alone attendance by their junior ministers'.

Vince Cable had experience of business though he admits he was less enthusiastic at first about the development of boards,

> because it just involved bringing in two or three people, a couple of whom were obviously mates of the Permanent Secretary. I didn't get a strong sense at first that this was going to make any difference, and I think they'd picked up that I wasn't really engaged with it. After the first two to three meetings, I took the view that I wanted to be more active and I got in some new people whom I felt more comfortable with. So towards the end, the board became a very important and active part of the governance of the department. But initially it wasn't and it was highly experimental.

Some of the ambiguities of the role of departmental boards and non-executive directors are brought out by Tim Loughton, who was a junior minister under Michael Gove. Loughton speaks (MR, in office 2010–12) of

> this new beast of the board, which was never well explained. We had no input into who was on the board. The Secretary of State had decided all of that, the outside external directors and everything as well. It was a rather muddy mix of what is their role? Is it to oversee the running of the department but not to oversee the running of policy?

In a review for a report on ministerial and Civil Service effectiveness in 2018, Professor Andrew Kakabadse of the Henley Business School noted in his written evidence that

> the emergent view from numerous civil servants is that most boards are less productive than they could be. The prime reason is the poor leadership from the chair of the board, namely the Secretary of State. The quality of chairmanship is reported as varying substantially. Certain non-executive directors report that they have hardly met their Secretary of State. Others state that the Secretary of State pursues their political agenda and attends less to board oversight, advisory or support function.

However, he quoted Permanent Secretaries as praising the contributions of non-executive directors as bringing both independence and lengthy external experience to government departments.

The recruitment of successful business people to serve as non-executive members of departmental boards has continued, though the overall impact is uneven and hard to measure. Not only has much depended, as noted above, on the attitude of the Secretary of State – some less interested and some more inclined to appoint those they already know – but also crucially on the view of the Permanent Secretary. Some non-executives have seen their main role as advising Permanent Secretaries and senior officials on the running of departments and on major change and transformation programmes – a plus but not in the way originally envisaged. And Permanent Secretaries have in their turn co-opted non-executive board members as advisers, especially when a Secretary of State is less interested in them.

Maude also proposed the expansion of ministerial offices, akin to 'cabinets' in the European Commission and in parts of the rest of the European Union as well as some Commonwealth countries. This involved expanding a core private office by bringing in other officials and some outsiders to provide expert advice. Gordon Brown had developed a very similar idea called a Council of Economic Advisers when he was Chancellor. This idea was adopted on a very limited scale in the coalition years in face of the worries of Permanent Secretaries that such expanded offices would cut ministers off from the main parts of their departments. Nicky Morgan was one of the first Secretaries of State to set up an extended ministerial office (EMO) at Education.

> I was happy to give it a go and actually I think it worked very well. You've got the private office of civil servants, you've got the EMO and I had probably by the end about six of them, who are people who really know their briefs. They were great for things like funding allocations, equalities, primary assessment, the school structure. They were all pushing in the same direction. They were the ones able to say, 'Hang on a second, how does this follow?' They would talk to each other, they all sat together so they could learn what the others were doing.

Liberal Democrat David Laws, who saw life from both the centre and a key public service department, says (MR, in office 2010 and 2012–15) that it depends hugely on who the people are who are recruited, and what the mindset of any Secretary of State is. There clearly is a very big risk that if you've got the wrong Secretary of State who hires the wrong people, who either aren't very good or are just doing a highly political job, that could be both a missed opportunity and also a risk that the Civil Service then gets the message they just have to serve up any old tosh that is going to be politically acceptable.

But after 2015–16, this experiment, known as extended ministerial offices, was quietly abandoned.

The Maude critique is not, of course, novel. In many, though not all, respects there are echoes of the criticisms which Sir John Hoskyns developed before and during his period as head of the Downing Street Policy Unit from 1979 to 1982, as well as in the criticisms of Steve Hilton and Dominic Cummings after their experience as advisers in the coalition years. The Whitehall experience of Hoskyns was just before the time Maude was first a junior minister in the Thatcher years. The Hoskyns case was that much of the responsibility for Britain's poor performance (he was thinking of the 1960s and 1970s) was due to the defeatist traditions and attitudes of the Civil Service and Whitehall, who are resistant to radical change. Hoskyns, notably in his book, *Just in Time: Inside the Thatcher Revolution* (2000), did not spare ministers either in seeing them as lacking talent, being unable to take decisions and being overwhelmed by day-to-day work and not thinking strategically. His solutions were greater interchange with the private sector (as has been happening), recruiting ministers from outside Parliament (as discussed in

Chapter Nine) and allowing ministers to set up 'cabinets' on the French and Continental European model, as noted above.

Among Maude's colleagues, David Willetts (MR, in office, 1994–6 and 2010–14), himself a Treasury civil servant in his twenties, was one of the most prominent dissenters. He rejected both the Maude analysis about the state of the Civil Service and his specific drive to increase Cabinet Office centralisation of certain functions such as IT purchasing. As noted at the beginning of the chapter, Willetts did not see the Civil Service as a conspiracy 'to stop ministers doing things'. He says that in the coalition Cabinet

> there were two schools of thought. There was one school that basically worked with the machine and worked with stakeholders to try to make things happen. That was by and large the approach of George [Osborne] and Vince [Cable, his Secretary of State at the Business department]. And there was a second set of ministers [by implication Francis Maude and his allies], who saw the Civil Service as the enemy, got into a state of conflict, often generated media headlines by virtue of the conflict, but were not necessarily achieving permanent changes as a result.

In particular, he said that the 'worst department of government by a long margin is the Cabinet Office: it is completely dysfunctional. And I speak as a former Cabinet Office minister under John Major. It's not accountable. It imposes absurd things on you. It then runs away when things don't work out and always blames you.' He cited an IT system that didn't work in the Department of Business, Innovation and Skills (BIS) but 'which had been imposed because of the Cabinet

Office's hatred of big companies since they thought they were being ripped off by them. So we had an absurd small company that couldn't deliver an IT system and then it didn't work.'

Maude's later Speaker's Lecture after he left office produced a strong response from Sir Jeremy Heywood and John Manzoni, the then Cabinet Secretary and Civil Service chief executive. Sir Jeremy said the Maude lecture had presented 'a wholly inaccurate portrayal of what is widely regarded as one of the world's most effective and efficient civil services'. They highlighted the continuation of the reform programmes Maude helped to create to improve commercial, financial and digital capacity. Reform in their view was 'deepening and accelerating'.

These exchanges – which reflect the tensions of the coalition years – reveal the frustration of some, but far from all, ministers with the performance of the Civil Service at a time of considerable change. The governing marriage has been buffeted. No one disputes that the Civil Service needs reform, and it is happening, albeit not as fast as many would like. But it is also about the impatience of a generation of activist politicians. The impatience is not new. It was heard twenty years ago when Tony Blair talked about the 'scars on his back' over reform of public services. An important feature of the coalition years was the presence of Liberal Democrat ministers with no previous experience of national government. Most were positive about the Civil Service. Lynne Featherstone says (MR, in office 2010–15) she found the Civil Service 'a joy', and she created a blog in praise of civil servants because she was so cross with Francis Maude. 'I thought he was denigrating them terribly.'

There are questions about whether ministers are trying to do too much, and, in some cases, too quickly. John Manzoni, the Chief Executive of the Civil Service, said in 2016 that government, via the Civil Service, is 'doing 30 per cent too much to do it all well'. That is a reflection of more activist politicians, keen to achieve change quickly, and inflated public expectations of what the state can, and should, do. On the other hand, almost all ministers share a frustration with the frequency of changes of civil servants, in part a product of the sharp cutbacks in overall numbers during the coalition period. Some incentives have been introduced to encourage officials managing major projects to stay longer in post.

Tensions also exist about the formal lines of accountability referred to earlier in the chapter. Civil servants are often not negative and resistant, but too willing to follow a ministerial lead even if they have doubts about the feasibility and value for money of a project – not least if it involves implementing a manifesto commitment. The eagerness to please new ministers can lead to a reluctance to point out problems with new policies. Statutorily, Permanent Secretaries as accounting officers are answerable to the Public Accounts Committee (PAC) of the Commons for the probity and value for money of budgets, which is examined by the National Audit Office. Permanent Secretaries regularly appear before the PAC to explain how money has been spent. This is in parallel with the accountability of Secretaries of State and other ministers for policy on the floor of the House of Commons, and Lords, and to other Select Committees. The two lines of accountability increasingly overlap as ministers cannot distance themselves from the delivery of projects they implement.

Permanent Secretaries have the option, indeed the duty, to

seek a ministerial direction from a Secretary of State if they believe a spending proposal or decision breaches a series of criteria: regularity, that is beyond the department's legal and statutory powers, or agreed budgets; propriety, that is high standards of public conduct in running a project; value for money, that is whether an alternative course would be cheaper or offer better outcomes; and feasibility, that is if there is doubt about the plan being implemented accurately, sustainably or to the intended timetable. If a Permanent Secretary believes one of these dangers is likely to arise, they should write to the Secretary of State expressing their concerns and seek a direction. In response, a Secretary of State instructs the Permanent Secretary to implement the decision, in effect becoming accountable for the decision. In the past, directions could remain secret for years. But since 2011, departments have been required to disclose the existence of a direction by the time they publish their annual accounts and the National Audit Office and the Public Accounts Committee must be informed. According to the Institute for Government's regular monitoring of directions, recent ones have been published on the GOV.UK website relatively soon after they have been issued.

Nearly seventy ministerial directions were published between 1966 and the time of writing, of which about a quarter have been since 2010. Brexit has introduced a new dimension since departments may need to spend money in preparation for Brexit before the relevant legislation has passed allowing them to do so. This is permitted by the issue of a technical direction. Ministerial directions include well-known affairs such as taxpayer support for the Pergau Dam in Malaysia (illegally linked to arms sales); the urgent request for support for Kids Company; an increase in special advisers' severance pay; and a series of proposals on EU exit preparations. Roughly two-thirds of directions are on value for money grounds.

What is striking is the number of controversial projects that do not feature on the list. Apart from some relatively narrow examples, or where a direction provides public reassurance that members of the public will be protected, Permanent Secretaries tend to regard seeking ministerial direction as a sign of failure, a lack of confidence in government policy – which risks a potentially serious breakdown in their working relationship with a Secretary of State. There is a reluctance to seek a direction on a major manifesto commitment of an incoming government since that can be seen by new ministers, and their advisers, as appearing to challenge their authority. Conversely, the private threat of a ministerial direction can be, and has been, used, or implied, as a means of persuading ministers to revise their plans. But, obviously, that has to be employed sparingly. This underlines the complexity of the relationship between civil servants and ministers, and the general reluctance of the former to challenge a clear political lead and mandate. As the Institute for Government has argued (in Guerin et al., 2018), there is a strong case for strengthening transparency around the decisions made by ministers and the advice they receive from civil servants in the early stages of a project. Ministers would be expected to justify their decisions even after they have moved on from the particular post – since problems often only appear at a later stage.

The traditional view of the ministerial/Civil Service relationship has also been questioned by academics, most recently and succinctly by Patrick Diamond in his book *The End of Whitehall?: Government by Permanent Campaign* (2018). He argues that the long-standing Whitehall approach has been replaced by what he calls the 'New Political Governance', which is centred on permanent political campaigning, ministerial advisers, personalised appointments and a partisan governing machinery. The traditional Whitehall model or 'paradigm' originated out of the Northcote-Trevelyan reforms of the 1850s (or at least what they were seen as representing) and the Haldane report on central government of 1918 – emphasising the principles of non-partisanship, neutrality, parliamentary accountability, bureaucratic permanence and mutual trust between politicians and civil servants. Diamond, who served as a special adviser in the Blair Downing Street, argues that the mutual respect that underpinned the governing marriage in the post-war era has been uprooted over the past thirty years. Mutual trust has broken down as civil servants are openly criticised by some ministers and advisers, and Whitehall's policymaking capability is undermined. Diamond argues that the convention that civil servants were loyal to the government of the day, not the political party comprising the government, has been turned on its head and officials are now beholden to the governing party's agenda and now have less influence on policymaking.

This critique is widely shared in the academic world. There have been unquestionably significant changes in recent decades with the arrival of more influential, politically appointed special advisers, while the institutional memory and capacity of the Civil Service have been undermined, contributing to serious errors in the execution of policy. But there is a great danger of oversimplification and of confusing the language and behaviour of some politicians and advisers at one particular time for a lasting trend. Patrick Diamond has identified the most significant developments but relationships have varied from administration to administration, and, indeed, within administrations depending on the personalities of those at the top.

Moreover, not all changes have been sustained. Francis Maude was to some extent the revolutionary advance guard of new methods of governing – and David Cameron was content for him to lead the challenge to traditional attitudes in Whitehall without himself as Prime Minister becoming closely involved. Indeed, when Maude moved on from the Cabinet Office in 2015, some of the changes were sidelined. The tone and mood of the debate over Civil Service reform altered – although the largely agreed changes to the specialist functions have continued. Moreover, most of the top officials, the Permanent Secretary cadre, have broadly the same background as in the past. Admittedly, more senior officials have spent part of their careers outside the Civil Service, but they have then moved into Whitehall well before being promoted to the top. An assertive and occasionally overbearing 10 Downing Street has waxed and waned over the years. Tensions obviously exist within the governing marriage and have been exacerbated by the debates over Brexit. But relationships between ministers and civil servants have always been complicated and at times ambiguous.

# CHAPTER SIX

# Departmental Baronies

'Departmentalitis stems from a preoccupation with the department to which the minister is assigned, to the exclusion of all other considerations including the fortunes of the government as a whole. If you are a minister afflicted with departmentalitis you will regard Parliament as existing only to further the interests of your department. You will show no interest in debates or question periods not related to your own department's activities. If you contract departmentalitis you will ruthlessly pursue your own department's interests even if another department has a better case: quite simply, your department must win. You will often not be interested in, let alone care, whether your department's activities impinge adversely on those of a colleague.'

– Gerald Kaufman, *How to be a Minister*, 1980, pp14–15

Outsiders tend to view central government as a monolith, a large impersonal and indivisible structure with one face and voice. But it isn't. Whitehall – and, of course, most civil servants do not work in SW1 – consists of nearly two dozen separate and distinct departments, often spread throughout the United Kingdom. As the quote from Gerald Kaufman above shows, the first loyalty of many ministers is to their department, where they spend most of their time surrounded by officials determined to protect and advance the interests of the department. It can appear almost tribal, like support for our local football team.

The key focus is on the Secretary of State, and not on other ministers. Oliver Letwin, who has past experience as a policy adviser in the Thatcher years, and then as policy coordinator under David Cameron, notes (MR, in office 2010–16) how, leaving aside the Treasury,

> departmental civil servants in my experience don't really pay any attention to anyone except the Secretary of State. They are totally focused on the Secretary of State, and, in fact, legally speaking, I suppose the rest of the ministers don't exist. If there's a junior minister that matters, the junior minister matters because he or she has the confidence of the Secretary of State.

That reinforces departmentalism. Jack Straw similarly talks (MR, in office 1997–2010) from his experience of the Home Office and the Foreign Office of 'Secretary of State worship – everything was focused on the Secretary of State'. Jeff Rooker, a Labour minister in the Commons and Lords for eleven years, stressed in evidence to the Public Administration Select Committee (2011, question 47): 'in most of the departments I was in, you wouldn't have known any hierarchy between parliamentary under-secretaries and Ministers of State. You are either in the Cabinet or you're not, and the person running the department is the person who decides what roles the juniors should have.'

A related phenomenon to Secretary of State worship is

Permanent Secretary worship, particularly in defence of a department's traditional ways of operating and against incursions from the centre and other parts of Whitehall. That applies less than, say, forty or fifty years ago (when it featured both in Roy Jenkins' early days at the Home Office and in the Crossman diaries), but there are still stories in some of the diaries and memoirs of the Blair era of Permanent Secretaries vigorously defending their patches.

Most revealing are the comments of those who moved between departments. Kenneth Clarke served in eight departments, heading five, over his long career. Looking back to the 1980s and 1990s, Clarke says (MR, in office 1972–4, 1979–97 and 2010–14) that

> departments were very different from each other in those days. No two government departments were run in the same way, and some of them did depend on the working methods of the Permanent Secretary, if you happened to go somewhere where there was a powerful Permanent Secretary. But they each had their own culture and could have quite a different feel, when you went in.

For him, the Treasury

> was the best department I ever worked in, because the intellectual quality of the people was undoubtedly higher, almost universally across officials, than any other I was in. I could run it like a debating society, because the then Permanent Secretary (Terry Burns) encouraged it. What I liked about it was that you could get a group of officials around the table and they would all join in and

the most junior guy at the table, just out of school I used
to say, no doubt just come out of university with a reasonably good degree, he or she would argue with the
Permanent Secretary or with me, with the same vigour as
anybody else. And we would all clarify where we would
go. It was a very stimulating atmosphere, which I used to
compare with something like a High Table at an Oxbridge
College. The mood I picked up from it was similar. I
used to say they were just like an Oxbridge College –
frightfully bright and not one of them capable of running
anything. They had policies and ideas – they were
brilliant.

The Home Office was, according to Clarke, a total contrast, 'staid and traditional and very hierarchical. You had to
be a very senior official indeed to be ever allowed to attend a
meeting with the Secretary of State. The main aim of the
senior officials was to make sure that the Secretary of State,
didn't do anything very rapidly. And if you agreed to do anything, they would go slowly.' He notes that then, in the 1992–3
period, 'policy advice was given only by the Permanent Secretary even when other officials took a different view'. He
says the quality was much more variable at Health and Education than at the Treasury and the Home Office. 'There
were some astoundingly good people but the average level
was not as high'. He describes 'The Health Department as
quite resistant to change. You can declare war more peace-
fully than you can reform a healthcare system. And the Health
Department was very geared to minimising the row with its
various clientele and lobbyists and interest groups.' The Education Department 'had this rather giant, self-perpetuating

bureaucracy feel about it. It was the only one which had its own political culture.'

Alistair Darling had a similarly broad experience of Whitehall in the Blair and Brown years, in six departments, and heading five. He again stresses (MR, in office 1997–2010) that all departments are different:

> they've got their own ethos, they have their own language. The Treasury is very, very good. They get some of the best civil servants. I think the Treasury sometimes can be guilty of looking down on the other departments in Whitehall. In fact, they are equally good and they certainly know their subjects very well. I was never in a bad department – the quality of civil servants in this country is very good.

Like Clarke, he underlines the importance of the Permanent Secretary relationship: 'The Permanent Secretary is very important because he or she sets the tone for the entire department. And the Permanent Secretary should be just that, someone who will say, "This is what you want to do, we can do this, and here are the obstacles you have to negotiate" and so on.'

From a more recent perspective, Justine Greening, who headed three departments, also notes (MR, in office 2010–18) that each was different:

> so the way you managed it had to shift. They're all different beasts. Transport: there's a massive operational piece there. Irrespective of whether you've subcontracted some franchise out, when it goes wrong it ends up

on your desk. And it's an investment department, so it's about how you do a portfolio. DFID [International Development] is a massive spending department, so again it's a portfolio question. But there is a huge dose of foreign affairs in there that you can't really quantify. So it's a very different series of calls around what good looks like. Then Education was entirely different again. I could control DFID through the business cases of investment largely, because that principally is a route into discussions around diplomacy, the Foreign Office, etc. But once you get into a department like Education, where most of the grants are block grants given to schools, then it's a very different beast to try and get a clear line of control through.

The differences partly reflect their roles as either largely policymaking or implementation departments, and their place in the Whitehall pecking order. No one disputes the primacy of the Treasury and the Foreign Office. The term 'Rolls-Royce' is invariably used. Jim O'Neill (Lord O'Neill, who served in the Treasury at the tail end of the Cameron period and then briefly under Theresa May), said (MR, in office 2015–16) that, 'having spent nearly twenty years at Goldman Sachs,' he found during his short period as a non-executive director at the Department for Education that it

seemed very bureaucratic and hierarchical, and I just assumed that that's what every government department is like. So being appointed as a Treasury minister was refreshing. I found the culture of the Treasury really good. I think maybe again it was something to do with my style. But for the things I was trying to do, my engagement with different parts of the Treasury was fabulous, particularly with younger people that seemed ambitious and eager to come up with ideas. The best compliment I could give them is that it often reminded me of Goldman Sachs, except people had a better purpose.

Mark Hoban, who moved from the Treasury to Work and Pensions, notes (MR, in office 2010–13) that

> where DWP was very good was telling you how you could implement and deliver something and what the levers were. Whereas the Treasury, because it was not a delivery department, was much more theoretical and intellectual, which was right for the purpose but there were real strengths in DWP – the intellectual capacity to think about how a policy should be designed, but also the experience to say this is how it should be delivered in practice.

In more managerial terms, Liam Byrne contrasts (MR, in office 2005–10) the 'kinetic energy' of the Treasury with its momentum of the Budget, and the Home Office as 'basically Britain's risk management business'.

The Foreign Office gets similar praise as the Treasury but also a recognition that it is somewhat detached from the day-to-day political battle. Sir Hugh Robertson had been Olympics minister before moving to the Foreign Office. He says (MR, in office 2010–14) that, at what was then the Department of Culture, Media and Sport, everybody knows everybody else. The directors and the ministers are quite close; the ministers are very, very close. You see each other the whole time. We all had offices in a row, so we always used to walk past, stick our head round each other's doors. The Permanent Secretary, if he hadn't seen me for a couple of days, just used to put his head round the door. You then get to the Foreign Office, which is this massive, rather grand monolith. The ministers are never, ever there together. The whole thing is much more structured and old-fashioned. The civil servants call you 'Minister' or 'Sir', the Permanent Secretary, the Permanent Under-Secretary as he's called, is a very grand figure at the top of this big diplomatic network. I tried to pop down and see him in my second week to ask him a question, and the door was barred. Eventually civil servants got in touch with each other and an appointment was fixed ten days later, and then there was a sort of 'I'll go down and see him' and they said, 'You can't do that. He has to come to you'. The whole thing was sort of wonderfully stage managed – a bit Gilbert and Sullivanish!

Robertson sees these contrasts as just very different ways of operating – 'the small, intimate nature of DCMS was fun in all sorts of ways; the slightly more formalised way that the Foreign Office did other bits of it made life as a minister much easier, because everybody knew where they were – there was a structure and an order to it that wasn't always there in a small, more informal department.' Alistair Burt, who has moved in and out of government, notes (MR, in office 1992–7, 2010–13, 2015–16 and 2017–19) that the 'Foreign Office is a complete Rolls-Royce department. It is full of very bright people, all around the world. It operates completely differently to Health because it does not have the same policymaking issues, and it does not have the back-breaking effect of running the world's fifth largest organisation with all the difficulties this involves.' Burt praises the quality of the officials at Health at a senior level, but notes the frustrations – with the division between the department and the NHS – of getting things done – 'the slowness of getting change'.

Jack Straw moved from the Home Office to the Foreign Office in 2001 – and notes that

> culturally the Home Office thought it was a cut above most other government departments; it had some bright people in it. What was striking when I got to the Foreign Office was that the quantum mass of really bright people was higher than in the Home Office. And also they're a different breed in that they're much more political with a small 'p', because when members of the diplomatic service are abroad, they are presenting the government of the day publicly, in a way no home Civil Service official does.

There is also a profound difference in the functions of the two departments, which affects what ministers do. Straw points out that in the Home Office he was being

> asked to make binary decisions: 'Are we going to do this? Are we going to do that?' And they were decisions by me; they were in respect of 'Do we deport this person? Do we declare them persona non grata? Do I

put a telephone tap on or don't I? Do I give them a warrant or don't I? Do I do this, do I do that?' These were straightforward exercises of the power of the state at the rough end of the power of the state, which is the Home Office, because ultimately it's about the state being able to lay hands on people. However carefully it is covered up, that is its job. And there was lots of legislation, changing the rules. In the Foreign Office there are internal decisions you are making, but a lot of the time you are asked for a steer about how we should deal with another country, or agreement about a negotiating brief. You are trying to influence events which are happening elsewhere, with actors who aren't open to you. You can't get the House of Commons to say, 'We're not going to do this, we're going to do that' in the Foreign Office; it's not the way it works. That is a very big distinction in terms of the nature of most of the decisions you are asked to take.

Jeremy Browne (MR, 2010–13) moved in the opposite direction from Jack Straw – from the Foreign Office to the Home Office – and at a lower Minister of State level. 'It's a bit like going from an Oxbridge senior common room to going to work for a local council. It's just terribly hard not to lapse into cliché when I say it's less rarefied.' It was partly to do with the buildings, the old, Victorian Foreign Office and the very modern Home Office. It is also a matter of style and tone – 'the Foreign Office is sort of unashamedly intellectual and the Home Office, maybe it depends on the particular character of the Secretary of State, was not so keen on that.' He describes a wide-ranging discussion in the Foreign Office, in which people competed with each other to show how clever they were, but with no action points at the end, and compares it with the less expansive and more defensive style of the Home Office, where 'success constituted getting to the end of the week without being blamed for anything'.

Damian Green notes (MR, in office 2010–14 and 2016–17) that the Home Office had an image of itself as a department apart, and that it took pride in that. He says that always having been regarded as 'a complete graveyard, the calibre of people there is very good, and as an institution, it's very good at coping with crises'. He compares it with the Ministry of Justice, where he also served as a minister at the same time, and which

> works at the speed of the judiciary – it is very slow and laborious, and took an age to get everything done and with much less of a self-image because it's a new department. The Home Office is a department for saying 'no', essentially; it's what any interior ministry is: 'We want to stop you committing crime. We want to stop you from coming in if you're an illegal immigrant. We want to stop you from behaving in a disorderly fashion ...' You would go to Cabinet committees on, for example, deregulation – a huge thing, everyone's in favour of deregulation – unless you're the Home Office, and you say, 'Fine, if you deregulate something else, that means more people will get drunk so there'll be more crime.' You'll realise that whatever you want to liberalise, the Home Office will always have an argument for why it's a bad idea, because somebody will exploit it to commit a crime or do something antisocial. I think it's inherent in the system;

interior ministries will always be slightly antipathetic to other parts of the government machine.

At the opposite extreme from the great, historic and powerful departments of state like the Treasury, the Foreign Office and the Home Office, and the big organisations like Health and Work and Pensions, is the Law Officers' Department. Edward Garnier, who was Solicitor General for two years, highlights the contrast with other ministers (MR, in office 2010–12):

> Being a law officer is not like being a political minister in the other departments. If you're the Secretary of State for Health, you have an intensely political and economic, but managerial role. The Law Officers' Department is not traditionally a policymaking department. It doesn't do or introduce legislation. Often, I used to describe our role as being like the lawyer in the cupboard – the government opens the cupboard and says, 'What's the answer to this? Thank you', and puts you back in the cupboard and shuts the door.

He also drew the comparison with submarines, which are 'most effective when unseen, unheard and operating quietly. Their presence – and the knowledge that they are about – is sufficient to persuade government ministers to behave, for the machine generally to understand and behave by the rule of law, etc.' Dominic Grieve, the Attorney General at the same time, describes the department (MR, 2010–14) as 'the in-house lawyer in government. You are there to support your colleagues, not to obstruct them. If they understand where you are coming from, then you're going to be able to help them and provide them with advice as to how to get round problems.'

Much of the Whitehall machinery consists of trying to reconcile the different viewpoints of departments. Some of this involves the write-round system, in which policy proposals and announcements are circulated around departments. Vince Cable saw this system (MR, in office 2010–15) as 'very, very frustrating. You're trying to do something in a hurry and you have to get something cleared with all of the government ministers who have the right to object to it. I suppose it's a safeguard, but it did mean that when you were trying to do things, they were blocked.' Stephen Timms, who served in several positions, including as Chief Secretary to the Treasury, during the Blair and Brown governments, argues (MR, in office 1998–2010) that examples of cross-government working were 'probably fairly isolated. I think generally cooperation between different government departments is quite difficult, and that's why they keep on reorganising.'

The classic mechanism for reconciling differences between departments and producing an agreed position is the Cabinet committee system. Its value depends on whether you are at the centre or in departments. Oliver Letwin says that during the coalition years 'the main issues were about differences of view being resolved in an orderly and amicable way. For that purpose Cabinet committees were very, very useful things, because you could have the formal debates and you could also have informal discussions outside them, and then they'd crystallise in the formal debates.'

Similarly, Nick Clegg stresses (MR, in office 2010–15) the

importance of the committee system during the coalition –
though decisions were rarely changed in the Cabinet itself:

> That seems to be in keeping with both single-party and
> two-party government. I can probably count on the
> fingers of one hand the instances where I felt that Cabinet
> discussions changed the trajectory of policy in a big way.
> But that was not the case in Cabinet committees. Again,
> it soured a bit towards the latter part of the coalition. But
> there was a purple patch for deliberative, generally good-
> humoured, generally rational policymaking in the first
> two and a half years or so. In the early days, Cabinet
> committees were some of the most enjoyable meetings I
> experienced in government. I often found myself adjudi-
> cating between really quite interesting debates amongst
> Conservatives. It was a bit odd but, at its best, the debates
> didn't fall along predictable party lines, and they covered
> everything from social care to knife crime, from NHS
> reform to changes in the curriculum. But then it soured
> and the meetings fell hostage to some political posturing.
> But, for a while, it was a really interesting experiment, a
> very heterogeneous bunch of people thinking surpris-
> ingly thoughtfully and objectively about policy.

For fellow Liberal Democrat Lynne Featherstone (MR,
2010–15), Cabinet committees were 'an absolutely, excruciat-
ingly awful part of government. A bigger waste of time I
have never been to in my life. Papers arrived the night before,
your civil servants write your lines for you, if you have had
the chance to look at it, you were very lucky. I just thought a

complete waste of time'. Another Liberal Democrat, Paul
Burstow, agreed (MR, in office 2010–12):

> inter-ministerial meetings [were] pretty pointless,
> because every minister was so busy and came with the
> brief they'd been given by their officials. And occasion-
> ally we would have a conversation where it was clear
> other ministers had a genuine interest in the subject and
> were able to step away from their brief. And then you'd
> have a good conversation and sometimes you might even
> get to somewhere different to the seemingly predeter-
> mined, pre-discussed outcome for the meeting. As a
> piece of process they're not very good other than rubber
> stamping the internal processes of cross-government
> negotiation between officials.

A similar view was expressed by former Labour ministers
from the Blair and Brown eras. Jim Knight said (MR, in office
2005–10) that 'it was hard not to think that a lot of the Cabinet
committee work was a waste of time, and it was just a box-
ticking exercise because the decisions were being made
somewhere else'. John Healey described (MR, in office 2001–
10) Cabinet committees as

> an administrative arrangement that is designed to give
> the political stamp to civil servants' ability to sort out dif-
> ferences and difficulties in advance. There were very few
> Cabinet committees where, in my experience, really
> serious argument and debate took place, where decisions
> that haven't been essentially prepared in advance were
> taken. The best committees and the best ministers were

those that didn't simply see it was their duty to turn up with the lines to take from their departments and simply argue their narrow departmental corner. Some Cabinet committees were chaired in a way that tried to minimise that.

It was not just seasoned politicians who were sceptical of the committees. Stephen Green, Lord Green of Hurstpierpoint, says (MR, in office 2010–13) from his long experience in banking and business that his

> abiding impression of these ministerial meetings is that they are not the productive part of ministerial life. I can't remember a single meeting where it wasn't the case that at least three out of twelve people had sent their apologies and another three would turn up late and a further three would leave early. It was very rare that you had any real, meaningful discussion. The real value of them often was in the five minutes before, and perhaps in the five minutes afterward, when you could have a quick chat with somebody who you'd otherwise not meet from one week to another, or if you did it was only at some formally structured meeting that the private offices have put together and with the civil servant taking notes.

The reason, he suggests, is

> because the agenda was always too crowded. Typically, they [the meetings] were one hour long, starting five minutes late. There was often quite a full agenda of papers that were a bit too long and you're asked to agree

something. Either it's blindingly obvious you should agree to it, or it doesn't really matter whether you do or don't agree to it. And if you have a departmental position that doesn't like it, you will have been given the brief to say our bit. But the chance of having a real discussion about what's a good idea, in this or that particular situation, was close to zero.

These doubts cover both an unusual period of government, the coalition, and times of one-party government, both before and after. Oliver Letwin underlines the difference, saying that in 2015, once you moved into

a majority administration with a very clear programme, there didn't seem much point in having prolonged policy discussions, because we knew perfectly well what our policies were – except in the National Security Council, where obviously we had to respond to changing scenes. But in the whole domestic agenda, it was pretty clear what we were trying to do. Indeed, George [Osborne] and I each had the view that in his case the Economic Affairs Committee, and in my case the Home Affairs Committee, were simply useful as clearing houses for papers, enabling officials and ministers to make regular agreements where there were mild differences between departments. But I never called a meeting of the Home Affairs Committee and he never called a meeting of the Economic Affairs Committee; the last thing we wanted to do was have a meeting, because we had quite enough meetings.

This contrasts with the meetings of these committees that had to be held 'to settle genuine policy issues inside the coalition'. So instead, after 2015, there was a focus more on implementation, and there was a problem there with Cabinet committees:

> They're great for resolving policy differences, if you get them right. But they're really not very good at trying to find out what's happening on the ground and trying to put it right if it isn't what it should be. In fact, no use at all. The number of people that come to Cabinet committees with all the relevant facts on a sheet in front of them is, in my experience, very limited, so our idea was: let's have some groups that are trying to get X or Y or Z to happen, where we were quite clear on what we want to happen but not all clear (a) whether it is happening and (b) if it isn't why it isn't, or (c) once we have discovered why it isn't, what to do about it.

So a series of mixed ministerial and official implementation task forces were set up, serviced by the central Implementation Unit and similar units in departments, to overcome problems of departmental coordination.

A frequent assumption of civil servants is that their already over-burdened Secretary of State is only interested in issues of direct concern to the department, and everything else can be brushed aside. Some Cabinet ministers have wider interests, however. John Whittingdale only served as a Secretary of State, at the then Culture, Media and Sport Department, for a year after chairing a Select Committee and much earlier working for Margaret Thatcher as an adviser. He recalls (MR, 2015–16):

that one area where the workload prevents you operating as you should, is your responsibilities as a member of government outside your department. Write-rounds are the best example; they are happening all the time. The department will tell you if there is a departmental interest and you'll be advised to put in something saying, 'I think this is a marvellous idea, but on this particular small point I have this reservation.' What the department didn't ever take into account was that I have views about policy.

That was summed up by the official comment on a paper on the world economy – 'we have no interest in that'. His solution was to involve his special advisers working with those of sympathetic ministers in other departments to spot issues in which he might be interested.

Away from broader cross-government issues, one attempted solution to the silo approach in much of Whitehall has been to create joint ministers with a foot in two departments. But the verdict is, at best, mixed. Philip Hunt, Lord Hunt of Kings Heath, who worked for a time both at Defra and the old Department for Energy and Climate Change, said bluntly (MR, in office 1998–2003 and 2005–10):

It's a nightmare; it doesn't work. First of all, departments don't really work together. So even if you have a joint minister, what effectively you are is a minister in one department, and then a minister in another department; and there isn't, I think, a mechanism whereby you are treated differently because you straddled between them. You can't have two private offices – you probably ought to make it work better but it won't really work. So you have one press office, so where is it based? That becomes your home department.

Hunt based himself at his more comfortable office with better views, at Defra, and otherwise popped into DECC.

Damian Green, who had posts in both the Home Office and the Ministry of Justice, is more positive (MR 2010–14 and 2016–17), while acknowledging the difficulties:

> You have two bosses. You have two sets of demands on your time, and all the things that ministers have to do that go beneath the radar – visits and speaking at dull conferences and so on. There's just twice as much of that. But most of all you are trying to work to two bosses who may well have two different agendas, and indeed there is an inherent tension between the Home Secretary and the Justice Secretary, whoever it is. So it makes it more difficult. But in a sense it makes it more satisfying because you can compare and contrast. I tried to make a reality of the fact that you are minister for both policing and criminal justice, and one of the things I was seeking to do, and one of the frustrations of not being able to do it any more, was actually trying to make from arrest to sentence and beyond, rehabilitation or whatever, one whole process.

He points to blockages in the system and different technologies – 'it sounds like organisational, banal things, but one of the things you can do as a minister is to transform the system if you can get all that sort of basic stuff right ... So there are insights and satisfactions available from going across two

departments, but basically it's more difficult; I would not rec-
ommend it.'

Apart from practical issues about having a joint private
office which moved between the two departments, Green
says he would

> occasionally get flatly contradictory advice; the two
> departments would just be advising people in two differ-
> ent ways … There was one point where I was required
> to write to myself as one minister in a department to
> myself in another department demanding that something
> happen, which I was tempted to do just to see how the
> system could cope with it – and then refuse my request as
> well.

Some ministers have seen opportunities in the ambiguities
of double hatting. Nick Boles, who was Skills minister jointly
at the Education (DfE) and Business Departments for the
second half of his four years in office, described (MR, in
office 2012–16) the experience of being a joint minister as
'great':

> This is a secret, and I suspect this isn't how it's meant to
> work, but I worked out that the beauty of being Skills
> minister across two departments was that neither Secre-
> tary of State was my boss completely. They might be my
> boss on some stuff, but not on other stuff. It wasn't like
> the stuff was completely separate, because the way it
> worked is that adult skills and apprenticeships were in
> Business, and 16–19 skills and apprenticeships were in
> Education. It was made more so by the fact that my two

bosses were both friends of mine who were elected at the same time as me, younger than me. They were not inclined to throw their weight around and tell me what to do.

He was helped also by his close relationship with both the Prime Minister and the Chancellor when he came up with the idea of the apprenticeship levy. He denied 'actively playing off one [Secretary of State] against the other, but I did absolutely make maximum use of the freedom of manoeuvre that the joint appointment gave me'. More broadly, Boles argues that if you interpreted joint appointments as having an office in two departments,

> it can become a huge waste of time. I used to refuse to go to DfE except for the weekly meeting (of ministers). The idea of having two offices and a private office all moving when the buildings were 150 yards apart, I just thought all that was nonsense. It can become a sort of pro forma, perfunctory, classic Whitehall bollocks. But if there's real substance in it [the joint appointment] that you can make more happen, then I think it's worth doing.

Ed Vaizey, a long-serving Digital and Culture minister, agrees (MR, in office 2010–16) that 'the biggest problem in government is working between departments', and he believes that the only way for them to work effectively together is 'on the basis of good personal relationships between ministers ... I think every minister should be in two departments, this should just be a rule, by and large, that particularly junior ministers should have some kind of link with another department'.

A novel answer (at least in British terms) to the departmentalitis question has come from Harriet Harman (MR, in office 1997–8 and 2001–10):

> all Secretaries of State ought to be together in one building. When you are all in opposition, you are all on one corridor, all working really closely together, and that facilitates decision-making. Then once you get into government, you're all separately locked up in different departments, and that interferes with the momentum of government. There is a lot of discussion that it takes a long time to do everything. One of the reasons it takes so long to do everything, and for ministers to get agreement, is because we are all separated in different departments. So much time is wasted and so much money is wasted because of the friction between departments. I think it would make a difference if ministers were working together rather than in warring baronies. There was, originally, the suggestion we should take over the Treasury building, next to Number 10. I can't remember how many ministers were supposed to be there, but all Secretaries of State. I think that should have happened. The whole establishment is for single departments, but there is virtually no policy which is a single departmental policy. One department will take the lead, but it will need other departments. They are all interconnected. The machinery of government, the way it is set up, works against governance in that respect.

Harman's proposal is similar to what happens in New Zealand and Australia. The executive wing of the New

Zealand Parliament Buildings in Wellington is commonly known as the Beehive, after its design – this is where the Prime Minister and other ministers have their offices. Ministers spend most of their time there separate from their departments. In Australia, also, ministers spend most of their time in the Parliament building rather than in their departments. That achieves the aim of ensuring they talk to each other, and to their personal advisers. The danger, as emphasised by civil servants in both countries, is that ministers become detached from their departments and permanent officials, and listen mainly to the growing group of political advisers. That can have two effects: first to produce decisions and new initiatives without sufficient input from officials about practicality and feasibility; and second, and in a contrary direction, to reinforce the tendency of departments to go their own ways without sufficient political leadership and direction.

It is partly a matter of size. Scotland post-devolution has a unified government without separate departments, but even now its responsibilities exclude large parts of social security, defence and foreign affairs, and the executive in Edinburgh still has limited tax-raising powers. Jim Wallace (Lord Wallace of Tankerness) served as Liberal Democrat Deputy First Minister from 1999 to 2005 in the Edinburgh coalition with Labour, and then as a Lords minister in the Westminster coalition, as Advocate General for Scotland. He maintains (MR, in office 2010–15) that 'In many respects, government in Scotland was easier; not that decisions were any easier, but the lines of communication are so much shorter. You didn't have to do write-rounds – that's an exaggeration, but you could get things done, agreed. Far more quickly. You didn't have to go through the other team's process.'

Although his period as a minister was short, Chris Huhne had studied Whitehall for a long time, as a journalist, businessman and opposition politician. His view (MR, in office 2010 12) is that

> the real problem with Whitehall is that it inherits an awful lot of structures which are not necessarily appropriate to what it actually needs to do. I'm reluctant to say that, therefore, we should tear everything up by the roots and start again, because the very process of changing institutions is so painful for so many people that they then spend the entire time in which they are changing institutions worried about their position and in defensive mode. And that's actually worse than the problem. So I'm quite conservative about changing boundaries and traditional departmental areas of responsibility. But I think we could be much more effective at cross-departmental working. I think that has to happen at a ministerial level, where the Prime Minister, the Chancellor and the key ministers want the same objective and are trying to deliver it and make departments work across boundaries. It has to happen at the senior Civil Service level mirroring that so that it's followed through and Permanent Secretaries know that playing the game of one department fighting another department, as usual, is not going to be something that is career-enhancing but which is actually something which the Prime Minister will see as being a problem.

Prime Ministers often like to address the problems of departmental clashes and apparent ineffectiveness by changing the machinery of government. Harold Wilson was addicted to this. Edward Heath experimented with super-ministries (the Environment and Trade and Industry). Wilson in his second period as Prime Minister split these. Margaret Thatcher eliminated some smaller departments, though she divided the mammoth Department of Health and Social Services. John Major was more cautious, though setting up the Department for National Heritage (later Culture, Media and Sport) in 1992 and merging Education and Employment after considerable preparatory discussion in 1995. Tony Blair created for his Deputy, John Prescott, a super-ministry covering the Environment, Regions and Transport which was later dismantled. Otherwise, his changes were generally in response to problems like the 2001 foot-and-mouth outbreak or the growth of terrorist threats. During his premiership the old Lord Chancellor's Department in stages evolved: first, into the Department for Constitutional Affairs; then, after 2007, into the Ministry of Justice, taking over prisons and parole from the Home Office. Gordon Brown has perhaps the record for creating and abolishing a department, Innovation, Universities and Skills, within two years, and then creating the Department of Energy and Climate Change primarily for his protégé, Ed Miliband, though a new, separate Pensions Department was also considered.

To summarise a long debate, the widely accepted conclusion is that the initial disruption and the costs of changing ministerial boundaries are generally high and best avoided unless there is a long period of preparation and debate. Moving the boundaries between departments may solve one problem but often open up another, shifting the areas of tension and difficulty. David Cameron was cautious until the

Brexit vote in 2016 led to the creation of two new departments, one to handle Brexit itself and other International Trade, while the Energy and Climate Change Department disappeared in July 2016 when Theresa May became Prime Minister. None of this, of course, in any way removes or reduces the rivalries between departments, and particularly the big departments of state.

# CHAPTER SEVEN

# The Shadow of Number 10, the Treasury and Special Advisers

'I was just constantly reminded of the quote from an American politician that every time I climb another rung up the political ladder, power seems further away. I was just astonished by the extent to which Number 10 and the Treasury and the Cabinet Office stuck their nose into departmental affairs. I had made speeches in opposition about Downing Street, under Gordon Brown's Treasury, meddling. The reality was far worse than any of my rhetorical flourishes. I had just no idea of the extent to which they micro-managed and nosed into departmental affairs. I was absolutely horrified by it.'

— Nick Harvey, Liberal Democrat Minister of State for Defence 2010–12, Ministers Reflect interview, 2015

No minister, however junior and in however obscure a role, can forget 10 Downing Street and the Treasury. This is not a book about Prime Ministers, their power, and rise and decline. But it is impossible to ignore the impact of the Prime Minister, and his or her advisers, in affecting the lives of ministers and what they can, and cannot, do in departments. And in most cases, that has also meant relations with the Treasury.

The style and approach of the centre has varied, but the past forty years has been marked by a number of strong, and often ultimately fractious, partnerships between Prime Ministers and Chancellors leading government – Margaret Thatcher and Nigel Lawson from 1983 until 1989; Tony Blair and Gordon Brown from 1997 to 2007; and David Cameron and George Osborne from 2010 until 2016. They all had their particular styles, and relations between Number 10 and the Treasury waxed, and usually waned, but they set the tone and direction of government for ministers. Departments have to negotiate and manoeuvre with both.

Historians can debate when and how the centre became more assertive – and it has, in practice, depended heavily on personalities. James Callaghan at the end of the 1970s was always seen as a traditionalist. He is quoted by Bernard Donoughue, the then head of his Downing Street Policy Unit, as saying (in Weller, 2018, p130): 'Callaghan, when we pressed him to interfere and make a department do this or that, which we foolishly thought was the right thing to do, would say: "That is for the department. That is for the minister. Back him or sack him."' Some see this period as a golden age of Cabinet government and ministerial responsibility for their departments, but it was also a period of major strains for the government system and for the UK generally.

Margaret Thatcher unquestionably drove governments, for most of the time in conjunction with the Treasury, but sometimes, and on some issues like the poll tax, not. Like most Prime Ministers, her greatest power was in appointing and shifting, or dismissing, ministers – in that way, she could get people committed to reform in the key departments (as discussed in Chapter Ten on reshuffles). The power of the reshuffle can, by definition, only be exercised occasionally. In between, there is what Nigel Lawson has described as a mutual veto, in which a Prime Minister can usually stop a Secretary of State from doing something. Similarly, a Secretary of State can, for a time, frustrate a Downing Street initiative – but only for a time since, ultimately, a Prime Minister can, and will, remove an obstructive minister. That explains many of Thatcher's most important reshuffles – in 1981 and in the late 1980s, when, in her eyes, insufficiently energetic ministers were dropped or shifted and were replaced by those seen as more likely to take forward her desire for change.

Tony Blair believed that reform could only be achieved if it was driven from the centre, by his special advisers and by the likes of the Delivery Unit (under Michael Barber from 2001 to 2005) focusing on implementation and monitoring of particular priorities in public services. Ministers were summoned regularly for stock takes, to explain what they had done and where they were going. And the Blair Policy Unit was a regular source of initiatives, notably in the areas which were seen as his interests rather than Gordon Brown's. Peter Mandelson had a unique perspective on how Tony Blair worked with ministers (MR, in office 1997–8, 1999–2001, and 2008–10):

> The Prime Minister did like to operate bilaterally with ministers through stock takes, examination of performance and discussions in groups rather than formal committees. He was a driver and agenda-setter, an educator and a progress chaser, and a quality controller. That's what Blair was. He had a very clear hierarchy in

his head as to what was important, what needed to be dealt with at any particular time. On Sunday, at Chequers, he would write down an assessment of his own government – possibly half a dozen different policy areas and subjects where he thought things were not going right, were being mishandled, poorly thought through, inadequately delivered or presented. When that was issued on the Sunday evening to a dozen or so people – who included senior civil servants but, in the main, his policy, political and media staff – these people jumped. If it needed meetings the next day you would go in, and you would indeed sit on a chair or sofa and you have different areas of government activity interrogated by him. Sometimes he would want to see more people, sometimes he would want to see ministers. Most of the time he operated through the Number 10 policy staff and the private office, but he was definitely hands-on. The idea that he could simply wait a couple of months for a paper to be presented to a Cabinet committee and discussed, possibly inconclusively, was not acceptable to him, and he was right not to govern in that way. But the casualty of it was the formal Cabinet committee system, which, when it worked well, did have an ability to collectivise decision-making and secure collective responsibility, but was inevitably much slower.

All Prime Ministers tend to need, and want, senior allies, whether ministers or advisers, who act on their behalf to coordinate and implement policy. Sometimes they are described, usually in an exaggerated way, as enforcers. These people are often grand figures who are widely respected and, while loyal to the Prime Minister, independent of him or her. That applied in very different ways to Willie Whitelaw in the first two Thatcher terms and to Michael Heseltine in the final phase of the Major government. Alternatively, they can be closely associated with the Prime Minister, as with Peter Mandelson both at the start of the Blair government and a decade later at the end of the Brown government. These arrangements tend to be very ad hoc, as in royal courts of the past. That was certainly true of Oliver Letwin, who says (MR, in office 2010–16) that he was

> somewhere behind a political version of a Cabinet Secretary, a special adviser and a Mr Fix-It. So my role was bizarre ... I wasn't aware of any job description, and in fact I didn't really have any very clear mandate at all. I regarded it as my job just to make sure that so far as possible, the show stayed on the road. Whatever it was that David Cameron wanted done on Wednesday, I tried to do it. And then I moved on to Thursday.

As Letwin emphasises, much depends on personal relationships and on circumstances. He did not regard his role as essential in any way:

> Everybody has their own style. Besides which there's a difference between coalition and majority governments. During coalition I was fulfilling another role, which was just continuous discussion to try to make sure that things didn't blow up, and I think somebody would have needed to do that, but it could have been all sorts of people ... I do not think it was in any way essential to have a senior

minister doing what I was doing in a majority administration: it just depends on the Prime Minister of the day
and how they operate and who they get to do what.

However, like all courts, it is not always clear whether the
voice comes from the top man or woman, or an adviser on
their own initiative. Few ministers are as robust, or cavalier,
as Kenneth Clarke, who reports (MR, in office 1972–4,
1979–97 and 2010–14) that, in his final phase after 2010,

> at first I found all kinds of Number 10 apparatchiks were
> turning up in the department, having meetings with my
> officials and discussing policy. So I got them all thrown
> out and said if anybody wants to come over from Number
> 10, to have a meeting with my officials, I shall happily
> chair a meeting and I can put it together and we can all
> discuss it.

Most Secretaries of State, however, prefer a policy of cooperation with Number 10 rather than confrontation. Alan
Johnson, who headed five departments in six years also notes
(MR, in office 1999–2010) the tendency of the Number 10
special adviser

> to come and talk to you on behalf of the Prime Minister
> – and some of them were better than others. I took the
> view that if there was a disagreement, if they were telling
> me that the Prime Minister wasn't happy with something,
> then the Prime Minister had to tell me that himself. When
> I was at Education, we had responsibility for adoption
> agencies, and we were introducing equality legislation

about same-sex couples being able to adopt, and there was a big row. It comes back to the Catholic Church. Catholic adoption agencies were refusing to comply, and were very upset about it. I had not just the special adviser from Number 10, but also a minister coming to tell me, 'You can't push this through, the Prime Minister is against it, a lot of your Cabinet colleagues are against it.' I talked to Cabinet colleagues and didn't find anyone against it and in the end, when I spoke to the Prime Minister, he said, 'I've never been against that.' Now, you know, maybe Tony changed his mind or he was being disingenuous.

Mark Prisk, a Conservative who handled business and housing during the coalition years, says (MR, in office 2010– 13) that these interventions could be frustrating. 'The centre – whether that's Number 10 or the Cabinet Office, changes its mind, changing arrangements at very short notice, a failure to plan ahead, chopping and changing and therefore distracting people from getting on with the job.' Hugo Swire, who served as a Minister of State under David Cameron in the Northern Ireland Office and the Foreign Office, complains (MR, in office 2010–16) about interference by Number 10:

You get all these young officials who suddenly become grander than the Prime Minister. They all end up getting infused by the power of Number 10. So they'd say, 'Minister, Number 10 don't want that', and I'd say, 'Hang on, who at Number 10? Number 10 is a building! So who at Number 10? Is it coming from the Prime Minister? In which case – fine. Is it coming from Ed Llewellyn or Kate

Fall (chief of staff and deputy chief of staff), in which case I will ring them? But who at Number 10?' And invariably it was some teenage scribbler giving themselves huge power. I used to check with Kate and she'd say, 'No, that's not what he means.' Because somebody had put themselves in a position whereby they were speaking with great authority without any rhyme or reason at all ... This cloak of Number 10, it was very tiresome whenever they interfered. I mean either trust your ministers to get on and do it, and if they're doing it, day in, day out they should have a feel for it, or sack them.

The same complaints were heard when Nick Timothy and Fiona Hill were joint chiefs of staff to Theresa May up to the 2017 general election.

Edward Faulks, Lord Faulks, who came from a successful career as a barrister to serve for two and a half years as a Minister of State for Justice (MR, in office 2014–16) talks of becoming frustrated about the governmental decision-making process:

because you would be prepared with the consultation, you had worked it up, you thought you were in the right place, you had the Secretary of State entirely on your side, and then you were told, via your private office, that Number 10 wasn't ready to go or had reservations. You never actually spoke to an individual or knew who had the reservations. I am perfectly certain it wasn't the Prime Minister, who had a lot of other things to do, but you felt it was somebody in Number 10 who didn't think this was going to play very well ... Towards the end I was finding it increasingly frustrating. We had a bank of announcements to make – of course the referendum came into it and all sorts of other things – that we couldn't announce. I developed probably inappropriate prejudices that there was some 25-year-old PPE graduate in Number 10 who was saying, 'This is not a good idea', and I thought that was not necessarily good government.

The power of Number 10 is particularly understood by those who worked there or in the centre for a period and then moved to a department. Peter Mandelson talked (MR, in office 1997–8, 1999–2001 and 2008–10) of them seeming to be

> not just of different parts of the kingdom [but] almost different countries. To go from the centre of government to a department, any department, requires a major gear shift. You're no longer a member of the hub; you're a spoke. You're a spoke on equal terms with all the other spokes. You're competing for your policy agenda, the Prime Minister's support, buy-in from other departments in the way that collective government operates.

Similarly, David Hanson, who was Tony Blair's parliamentary private secretary in his second, 2001–5 term, and a minister before and afterwards, argues (MR, in office 1998–2001 and 2005–10) that when he was in Number 10 looking outwards, 'you think you're the centre of the universe, everything's happening and people are deciding and talking about things. But when you're outside, Number 10 is a bit distant. It only took an interest in us if things were going wrong.'

Ed Balls had been closely associated with Gordon Brown for almost a decade and a half when the latter became Prime Minister and Balls became Education Secretary in mid-2007. Like many before him, Balls did not find it easy to assert his independence from his former mentor and boss. As he recalls in his memoirs (*Speaking Out*, 2016, p 203),

> For any Cabinet minister, the relationship with Number Ten is hugely important, whether discussing big announcements with the policy unit or handling problems with the media team. I worked hard at establishing a partnership with Downing Street, but made clear that I saw it as our job and our job alone to set the strategic direction or issue public lines.

Moreover, Balls acknowledges that for him

> it was made more complicated by the inevitable change in my relationship with Gordon. I was used to talking to him in person or in a rather relaxed and discursive way on our mobiles, but with him at Number Ten suddenly surrounded by a vast operation and a hundred things to do, and me similarly busy in a different department, the conversations we had ended up being more functional and business-like, and neither of us got out of them what we were accustomed to. Nor was sitting with Gordon in the back of an armoured Jaguar in the middle of a police convoy, crawling through central London on the way to a school visit, conducive to relaxed conversation.

And between 2007 and May 2010 Brown sought on a number

of occasions to bring Balls back to Downing Street on either a full- or part-time basis as an adviser. Balls wisely refused.

The Department for Education had, according to Balls (2016, p200), been used to being pushed and pulled by competing agendas from Downing Street and the Treasury, 'which is never conducive to civil servants feeling empowered and in control'. So he was determined that 'we were not going to be told what to do by Number 10 or Number 11'. However, it took time for him to get civil servants to tell him what they thought and their ideas. 'We got there in the end, but it took weeks of me saying to senior civil servants, "Stop asking me what I think and start telling me what you think, because that's what matters to me".'

Relations with 10 Downing Street differ in part depending on what position a minister occupies, as well as on individual personalities. Jack Straw, who had four senior positions over thirteen years, says the relationship varied between posts he held.

> In the Home Office – and bear in mind my relationship with Tony [Blair] was very close – he had every reason to trust me, and vice versa. I was doing what he was primed for. He'd approved of my approach to this, so he trusted my judgement on it. With some exceptions, basically he left me to get on with it, and I made sure I did.

He also worked closely with the Number 10 Policy Unit and Alastair Campbell: 'At the Foreign Office, it was different. If you become Foreign Secretary, and this must be true for any combination of Foreign Secretary and Prime Minister these days, you've got to accept that the head of government is

going to take a close interest in foreign policy, and the closer
you get to war, the closer will be their interest.' But here there
were divisions of interest, with Blair taking the lead on
Afghanistan and Iraq, and Straw on India/Pakistan relations
and on Iran, though there were differences on the latter.

> Leader of the House was a different job; there you've got
> to handle all the whips. And as for Justice, Gordon
> [Brown] left it to me basically. There was constitutional
> stuff which he was very keen on to begin with. He might
> well have pursued it had it not been for the financial
> crisis. But he knew that I knew all about this area and that
> I was on top of it.

This description applies to many other relationships
between a Prime Minister and a departmental Secretary of
State. It is a mixture of functions and personalities. Whereas
Prime Ministers increasingly dominate the big foreign policy
decisions, they often find relations with their Chancellors
frustrating, since even a strong PM usually cannot also run
the Treasury and write the Budget. Moreover, disagreements
between a Prime Minister and a Chancellor can frustrate or
undermine an initiative by a departmental minister backed by
10 Downing Street. When, for example, Margaret Thatcher
persisted with the poll tax or community charge despite the
opposition of Nigel Lawson, the Treasury reluctantly had to
provide a lot of money for the transition in the late 1980s, but
not enough to compensate all the losers, especially at a time
when house buyers were paying out more in mortgage interest payments. The Treasury never disguised its belief that the
poll tax would fail, and it was duly brought in and replaced,

all in the course of a single Parliament. In the second Blair term, disagreements between 10 Downing Street and the Treasury over public service reform – in particular over the NHS and tuition fees for higher education – had a major effect not only on how decisions were taken but also on the extent of reform.

Patricia Hewitt realised that she had to navigate between Number 10 and the Treasury. She learned this lesson when she was a Minister of State at the Trade and Industry Department before she became Secretary of State after 2001. She recalls (MR, in office 1998–2007) that

> when I was at DTI as a junior minister, it became blindingly obvious to me that the department had a real lack of confidence, coupled with resentment against the Treasury, because it was always interfering or being arrogant or whatever. And I just thought, 'Look, it is what it is, the Treasury is the senior department, you're just stuck with that fact in our system of government, they're the macro department, we're the micro department', and I sort of coined the phrase that 'We have to be the supply-side partners to the Treasury'. And once Tony appointed me, that's what I said to all my officials. I said, 'We are going to work with the Treasury. They may be difficult, but we are going to work with them.' And that's what I said to my special advisers … They knew to keep in touch with them [the Downing Street and Treasury special advisers], so we were managing that relationship all the way through. And it worked very well.

In other cases, it depends on how interested a PM is in the

work of a department. Some Secretaries of State can feel they are operating largely on their own – and junior ministers certainly can feel remote from a Prime Minister – apart from occasional social meetings and brief exchanges when voting in the division lobbies of the House of Commons, until the day of a reshuffle comes along.

One of the biggest developments of the past thirty to forty years has been the growing influence of special advisers, not just in 10 Downing Street but throughout Whitehall. At the time of writing there were about ninety special advisers working across the whole of government, of whom just over thirty work for the Prime Minister, and, outside the Treasury, there are usually no more than a couple per department. In one sense, this is a pretty small number compared with even the much larger total of senior civil servants. What matters, however, is the advisers' influence, and access to the Secretary of State, and some have been as, if not more, influential with their ministerial masters as any civil servants. It all depends on the personalities involved. But the growth in the number of advisers since the early 1980s has changed the influence/power balance of advisers to ministers and reduced the previous control of access by the Civil Service. The existing two advisers per Secretary of State, one for policy and one for primarily media and party work, is now embedded and accepted, not least by many civil servants, since advisers are seen as doing party work which the Civil Service cannot, and should not, do.

Contrary to *The Thick of It*, many departmental special advisers get a positive assessment from ministers. Greg Barker was very critical (MR, in office 2010–14) of the Conservatives' promise in opposition to reduce the number of special advisers as part of cutting the cost of politics (including also the plan to cut the number of MPs). 'It was a totally huge error, particularly when you have an area like DECC [the Department of Energy and Climate Change] that is super-technical and specialist. I think you must ensure that you have proper, efficient delivery of policy, but through a process that reflects the values of the minister.' This was reinforced by the unanticipated creation of the coalition, which complicated political relationships between ministers. DECC was headed by Liberal Democrat Secretaries of State. Barker says he had 'a very good working relationship with both my Secretaries of State and their special advisers. There was a slight creative tension at times, but we both knew the score. I didn't take direction from the Secretary of State's spads on anything political, that was clear.'

Similarly, Stephen Hammond stresses (MR, in office 2012–14 and 2018–) the value of special advisers. Most Secretaries of State had two advisers – one more concentrated on policy and the other more on the media:

> So there was a balance in making sure that working with the guy who runs the media, talking about where you're going on visits and what else you can do when you're there, not just what the Civil Service is suggesting. Also working with them to place the sort of articles you might be writing not from a government point of view but sometimes from a political point of view as well.

Hammond says he would probably pop into the spads' office at least once a day.

Very different views of the special adviser system emerge

from two ministers who worked with each other for two years: Andrew Mitchell as DFID Secretary of State and Sir Alan Duncan as one of his ministers of state. Andrew Mitchell shares the view (MR, in office, 1992–7 and 2010–12) that the Conservatives were wrong in opposition to be 'very much opposed to the special adviser system. We thought it was politicising the Civil Service. I'm absolutely against politicising the Civil Service, but I am very much in favour of the special adviser system.' Mitchell had

> two extremely effective ones. They were good because they'd worked for me in opposition and knew precisely what we wanted to do. And therefore the civil servants trusted them to give a good steer, and the civil servants would go to them saying, 'We're working this up, what will he say? Will he understand this? Will he think this works?' And they could tell civil servants the answer. And they would get it right and the civil servants knew they would get it right. So they were useful and also respectful to the civil servants and they didn't try to boss them around.

By contrast, Sir Alan Duncan is more critical. He says (MR, in office 2010–14 and 2016–) that

> special advisers can be a curse or a blessing. They have a unique capacity to corrode government by souring relations between ministers and feeding the newspapers. And so there is a fundamental issue about whether special advisers should ever tell a minister what to do. And a lot of them think they can. You know, 'I am my master's

voice so I tell a junior minister what to do.' And I made it clear at the very beginning to the special adviser. I said, 'If you ever, ever, ever think you are more important than I am, I will go straight to the Cabinet Secretary.' And I said, 'Don't even test it.' So I laid down the law, so they kept away from me, really, which is fine. But they are a bad breed in many cases. They get themselves up because they are right there next to the Secretary of State, so they think they are the bee's knees and have got the power.

Special advisers can also have a crucial role not only within a department but also in working between different Secretaries of State – matching the network of private secretaries – for the essence of Whitehall is the existence of distinct and often competing departments. And, also, they keep in touch with both the centre – via the Prime Minister's special advisers – and with Parliament.

# CHAPTER EIGHT

# Parliament

'The most useful training you have is being a backbencher, in terms of being in the House of Commons, because I appreciated when I was a minister, especially in times of crisis, whether it was the 10p top tax rise or the 75p pension or the banking crisis, the House of Commons still matters. How you perform there, how you behave, how you react to your own backbenchers who are also in opposition matters an awful lot. The first ten years in Parliament between 1987 and 1997 were a huge training. I think that is more important than anything else.'

– Alistair Darling, Cabinet minister 1997–2010,
in Ministers Reflect interview, 2016

'In my view civil servants constantly failed to understand the significance of Parliament to you as a minister. A slight feeling that Parliament was a bit of a distraction from the really important work. I had to explain more than once that actually my accountability was to Parliament and to MPs.'

– Jacqui Smith, minister 1999–2009,
in Ministers Reflect interview, 2016

Ministers differ in their attitudes to Parliament. Some regard it as central to their lives, others as almost peripheral. That might seem strange, since all ministers are members of the Commons or Lords – and have formal obligations in answering questions, taking legislation through and appearing in front of Select Committees. Many civil servants also regard the Westminster side of a minister's duties as secondary to their work in Whitehall, and some ministers too can become cocooned inside their departments. In both cases, that in part reflects longstanding views about the largely formal, almost ritualistic aspects of parliamentary questions or taking a bill through a Commons committee.

One of the main complaints of ministers of all parties, however, is that civil servants do not really understand Parliament. This is not primarily a matter of procedure or mechanics, or of briefing ministers for appearances before Select Committees. All departments have parliamentary units dealing with the Commons and, of course, bill teams when they are handling legislation. It is more a matter of attitudes and appreciating the roots and priorities of ministers as parliamentarians as well as members of the government. The implications of the overlap of the executive and legislature are often neglected or played down in an era of twenty-four-hour news and omnipresent social media.

Similarly, politicians' views are much more than the constitutional doctrine of ministerial accountability to Parliament, though that underpins the importance of the Commons and Lords to ministers. It is more about political realities – almost a form of insurance – that it is unwise for ministers to ignore, or appear to ignore, their fellow MPs. They may need support from their backbench colleagues when they run into trouble, as invariably will happen sometimes. This chapter is mainly about ministers' relations with the Commons. The next chapter addresses the parallel, and very different, topic of Lords ministers.

Jack Straw and Alistair Darling, who survived the full thirteen years of the Blair and Brown era in the Cabinet, both stress the importance of keeping in touch with, and paying attention to, the Commons. Straw (MR, in office 1997–2010) always had a reputation of being a good House of Commons man, and not just in his year as Leader of the Commons.

> I was very conscious about the need to spend time in the Commons. So I didn't have my diary packed with lunch appointments. I mean partly because I wanted to keep my weight down and I went to the gym in the Commons a long time before it was trendy! This was both because I needed the exercise but also because the locker room is a great place for gossip and stuff amongst a particular cross section of members who keep themselves fit I used to have lunch in the tea room regularly ... and, even when I was Foreign Secretary, I would make sure I was in the House one evening a week. I thought that was absolutely essential, because I was really conscious of the fact that, whilst my position at Blackburn, unless something absolutely extraordinary happened, was there as long as I wanted it, my position as a minister could come to an end at any moment. I think one of the reasons why it didn't was precisely because I was conscious of the fact that it could.
>
> I never, ever regretted spending time in the Commons. I used to pick things up and I'd have a little red book – which I still have – and people would raise things with me on both sides, and I'd scribble them down. I'd get

back to the office and I'd pull out the page and say, 'Will you get on with that?' and it made a phenomenal difference. And you'd find things out.

In his advice to a minister entering government for the first time, Straw emphasises paying attention to the House of Commons, and to 'not do what a lot of my colleagues did, which was to disappear into their red box, in their ministerial suite of rooms, only to reappear when they got sacked'.

Darling stresses (MR, in office 1997–2010) the need to complement the formal times going to the Commons for questions, statements and second readings with the more informal:

> I think the most important thing is to make yourself available to your own colleagues, and one of the best places to do that is the tea rooms. But in the lobbies you meet your colleagues and because it takes about twenty minutes to vote, and the lobbies are more like rooms, we mill around. You talk to people and they can come up to you and they don't have to make an appointment and they can say, 'What you're doing is bad' or 'Why aren't you doing this?' or people are telling me, 'It's different to what you say' – and this is absolutely invaluable ... You never, ever put down one of your colleagues in the House of Commons, even if you think they're a complete clown; you just don't do it. I'm not dewy-eyed about it. I'm not what you might call a 'House of Commons man', but it makes a hell of a difference.

Darling reckons that the reception he got when there were

serious problems, such as HMRC's loss of data for millions
of people, was 'infinitely better than it might have been
because people thought I was straightforward'.

A busy minister, however, can easily become detached
from Parliament. Indeed, the Ministers Reflect interviews
reveal a division in attitudes. It is easy enough to become
absorbed in departmental work. Liam Byrne admits (MR, in
office 2005–10) that he

> probably spent too little time in Parliament. I was a pre-
> dominantly departmentally focused minister. Again, in
> retrospect, I should have spent more time in Parliament.
> I went to Parliament when I had a job to do, like the polit-
> ical management of a lot of our immigration reforms,
> [which] was quite tricky. I should have spent more time
> on that, but, again, the jobs I had were so big. At one
> point I was doing three ministerial jobs when I was at the
> Home Office. It was a bit mad really.

Vince Cable, who remained at the Business Department
throughout the coalition years, says (MR, in office 2010–15)
that

> we got quite remote from Parliament – that was one of
> the slightly surprising things about the job. We had our
> BIS questions once every four weeks – at quite long
> intervals – and I can't remember that in the five years we
> ever dropped a ball in those questions. It was always very
> professionally organised and we always did well. But I
> think in a way that tells you we weren't put under a lot of
> scrutiny. I can't remember, except for tuition fees, ever

having difficult statements to make. The people who did give us a harder time were the Select Committees, but only really around privatisation. On every other issue it was actually quite bland. So we didn't engage very much or worry very much about Parliament.

Instead, Cable says, it 'was much, much more about the media. Every day I would be having three or four conversations with my special adviser about radio, television and what we were trying to say. I was quite active in the media, and that was how I communicated, rather than through Parliament.'

It is revealing that a number of the Liberal Democrat interviewees played down their parliamentary commitments – in part, it seems, because they were preoccupied by the unexpectedness, novelty and probably temporary nature of their ministerial posts. Chris Huhne says (MR, in office 2010–13) he spent 'as little time as I could possibly afford' in Parliament:

I would be in the lobby, I would talk to colleagues and people would see me in the tea room and I would also generally one evening a week go and have dinner in the dining room on the late vote evenings. So I was accessible to colleagues, and I think that's very important. But in terms of actually spending time on the government benches, as little as possible. Very little happens in the Commons that is of any use if you're defining your job in the way I defined my job to try and get the change the Department for Energy and Climate Change is committed to. The only exception is if there was a particular ally, a friend, who needed support and then I would go in and sit on the benches by them if they were going through some ordeal. But, in general, the amount of time you actually spend in the chamber is pretty wasted.

Similarly, David Laws also found (MR, in office, 2010 and 2012–15) 'the Parliament thing quite a light commitment … It can feel to some people a quaint sort of second order, different planet type of thing. When you are in Parliament, you think the world is revolving around you, but when you are in departments, you think that Parliament is just this irritating thing where you have occasionally to vote and be accountable.' Laws, unusually, never had to lead on any bill, and says he had 'to spend little time there [in the Commons] and that was a blessing, because being locked in committees looking at bills for months on end could really have taken up a lot of time'. Laws also admits that – apart from Nick Clegg and Danny Alexander – he had 'surprisingly little contact with other (Lib Dem) ministers. The connections, the sense of being a team, wasn't as great as it might have been.'

Steve Webb, Pensions minister during the whole coalition, is revealing in the tone and language he uses (MR, in office 2010–15):

Obviously, there's the parliamentary side of things. And you're the department's man in Parliament. So legislation needs taking through and you're the one who is going to have to do it. So there is the link with Parliament, but very much you live in the department. Parliament isn't exactly an irritation, but you spend very little time in it. You go and vote, you do oral questions, you take legislation through and that's basically it – Select Committee appearances and so on.

Much also depends on which department a minister is in. The Foreign Office is very detached from Parliament. Hugo Swire says (MR, in office 2010–16) that 'the lack of understanding of Parliament, even in the Foreign Office, was woeful'. He sees this as part of a problem of communicating to officials

> what the myriad demands on a minister are. I used to make this point about Parliament, which is so important: correspondence, answering questions and going to see parliamentarians on committees and so forth, are vital. As ministers, we derive our mandate as MPs, [and] as MPs we derive our mandate from our constituents, but ultimately we are drawn from Parliament and are responsible to Parliament.

The poor understanding of Parliament by officials is 'because they're sitting over there in their ivory tower and this may as well be a million miles away … I was always open to talk to officials about being a minister and being an MP. I was always trying to persuade them to cover and just sit in question time to see what we had to do.'

This sense of being distant comes not just from officials but also from ministers, depending on the department in which they are serving. Liberal Democrat Jeremy Browne notes (MR, in office 2010–13) that the Foreign Office, apart from Europe, 'can operate a bit detached from politics. Being a Foreign Office minister felt a bit, some of the time, like I was on a sabbatical from being an MP.' In contrast to being a Home Office minister, which he went on to be for a year, Browne points out that 'the Foreign Office does no

legislation, apart from a bit of Europe, which wasn't me. I
didn't sit on a single committee for two and a half years. I
hardly spoke in the House of Commons. I did a few Westminster Hall adjournment debates on what the fashionable
domestic issues were in my portfolio'. He covered Asia and
Latin America but these seldom came up in questions. Browne
admits that he 'would forget whether Parliament was sitting
or not. They [officials] would say we've scheduled for you to
meet the Ambassador of so and so, and I suddenly realised
that was all in a recess, the sort of Whitsun recess when I
could've been in my constituency. But I hadn't really thought
that in three weeks' time Parliament wasn't sitting.' That lack
of engagement was reinforced by his ministerial visits overseas, typically up to a week away because of the distances
– and then fitting in constituency obligations.

By contrast, for Browne the Home Office, with its heavy
load of legislation with hours in committees, 'I relished less.
I quite liked being in Parliament, some politicians don't like
Parliament at all. I do quite like Parliament but hours and
hours and hours in some committee … There is quite a contrast between scoping out the implications of the rise of
China to the regulations on dog leads.' He was struck by how
the Home Office took its tempo from the House of Commons.
'So when the House of Commons was not sitting it was
noticeably a more relaxed pace. Whereas when it was sitting,
there would be lots of urgent questions which the Speaker
was accepting. And there was a sense of constantly being a bit
under siege from parliamentary scrutiny.' Like Swire and
Browne, Hugh Robertson spent part of the coalition years in
the Foreign Office. He says (MR, in office 2010–14) that

one of the things that the Civil Service, bizarrely, doesn't do terribly well is Parliament. It doesn't understand it, and it doesn't understand the importance of a three-line whip. I sometimes thought that if the Department for Culture, Media and Sport didn't get it, the Foreign Office was worse. They just about understand there's a Foreign Affairs Select Committee but they don't get urgent questions or anything like that.

Both then, and later, he went back to the FCO teaching for young diplomats to try and tell them more about how ministers handle the Commons.

At the Home Office, Damian Green says (MR, in office 2010–14 and 2016–17) that the one thing that most struck him about the attitude of his own officials was

how little knowledge or, and worry about, Parliament there was. It was one of the messages that I spent a lot of time getting through – to the extent of giving talks to civil servants – that Parliament is hugely important for a minister. This is almost the only medium in which you can lose your job in about half an hour, and a lot of officials don't get that at all.

It also depends on the nature of a minister's post. Jacqui Smith draws an important distinction (MR, in office 1999–2009) about the nature of a minister's involvement with Parliament, reflecting on their seniority. In her jobs as junior and middle-ranking ministers, she realised that

all of a sudden you are not spending the time with your

colleagues in Parliament that you were spending previously. Your relationship with Parliament becomes much more about individual MPs and their issues, perhaps meeting with them or whatever. It becomes about legislation. It becomes about periodic oral questions. And that's largely it. One of the reasons why I liked being Chief Whip was that it got you back into the politics of Parliament again, in a way you probably don't do very much as a junior minister – which is surprising because you spend quite a lot of time there.

Smith had to do countless adjournment debates at the end of a day's proceedings, particularly at the Department of Health – 'I used to call that job the salt mines!'

John Whittingdale (MR, in office 2015–16) was in the unusual position of moving from one side of the accountability relationship to the other, with just a general election in between. Seen from the chair of the DCMS Select Committee, he viewed an effective Secretary of State as being in command of the brief when appearing in front of MPs. 'You are there for two hours usually, and you are examined in detail on every single policy without your brief and that is very tough.' When he became Secretary of State at DCMS after the 2015 general election,

I found myself on the receiving end; actually I was fine, but my officials went into overdrive. They kept putting huge expanses of time in my diary for Select Committee briefing, hours and hours, and I said, 'I don't need this. I've been doing this for years!' and I took it all out of the diary and I hardly did any prep. But I rested on ten years of knowledge of the brief. So that is an area where the experience was just hugely helpful.

Interestingly, Permanent Secretaries invariably set a lot of time aside to prepare for their committee appearances, generally in front of the Public Accounts Committee.

Much also depends on the size of a government's majority and, just as during the Blair years, the Conservatives and Liberal Democrats together had a comfortable working majority, so the demands of Parliament were less than at other times. If you look back to the last Wilson, and then Callaghan, governments in the late 1970s, and at the final years of the Major government in the mid-1990s, when there were either minority administrations or precarious Commons majorities, ministers not only had to spend more time at Westminster to vote but also had to pay much more attention to MPs, if only to anticipate, or head off, problems and possible revolts. Most ministers still believe that they should spend time talking to their backbench colleagues. Mark Hoban says (MR, in office 2010–13), however,

> I was quite surprised that there are some ministerial colleagues who seem to spend more time in Parliament than in their departments, which I think is slightly odd. But I think it's very easy to lose touch with what's going on, and I did try to make sure I would eat in the tea room in the evening and stuff like that. But the intention of going across to the House for lunch did seem to disappear.

Ben Bradshaw, a Cabinet minister for the last year of the Brown government and a minister in several departments, stresses (MR, in office 2001–10) how he spent most of his time

reading submissions, preparing for parliamentary scrutiny, oral questions, debates and Select Committee hearings. Having done the job of Deputy Leader of the House, it instilled in me how important Parliament was and how important it was to take Parliament seriously, which was another thing which sometimes the civil servants needed really drilling into them. Some ministers would turn up to Select Committees of the chamber badly prepared. I used to treat Select Committee hearings like my final exams. Parliament really matters.

Oliver Heald had three different ministerial lives under John Major, David Cameron and Theresa May, and emphasises the importance of keeping in touch (MR, in office 1995–7, 2012–14 and 2016–17), saying that when he was Solicitor General

you're very much accountable to Parliament, and it's important that you should always put your cards on the table with Parliament and go down there and make statements. Then, you have a role with your party. Because you are the front of house, you have to make sure that you're keeping in tune with colleagues and that you're not captured by the Civil Service and their thinking, and not really keeping in touch with party thinking.

He made sure he kept time in his diary for breakfast in the tea

room, working in the House and tea and a drink with colleagues, meeting a different group on each occasion.

Iain Duncan Smith recognises (MR, in office 2010–16) the
difficulty of balancing being in charge of a busy department
with the demands of Parliament. 'It's very difficult. You
rapidly begin to lose a sense of Parliament, because it's just
so busy and the department is always demanding your time,
and if you're conscientious, you have to do it. If you're not
conscientious, you don't care, you just hand it back to them
and say, "Get on with it", but I couldn't do that really.' Unlike
several other ministers he believes his private office did
appreciate the significance of Parliament for him, particularly
when they saw him having to go to the despatch box on difficult moments, such as answering questions at short notice.
'For all ministers and Secretaries of State, it is really important to keep in touch with this place [Parliament], because it
eats you alive if you're not careful. But it's very difficult to
keep in touch because your department demands your time.'
He stresses the pressures of Urgent Questions, which have
been granted more frequently by Speaker Bercow, while
pointing to 'ups and downs with Select Committees. We have
had a few rough moments with committees, but it's their job
to be rough with you. I never felt that I had to be overly polite
to them, so we used to give as good as we got sometimes, but
generally I think they were OK.'

The Civil Service can take quite an adversarial view of
Parliament, almost as much or more than ministers. This
works in two ways: first, in seeing their minister as the public
champion of the department in almost a gladiatorial sense;
and, second, in viewing the institution itself negatively as a
challenge. Harriet Harman, now the most experienced

woman MP, who undertook a number of ministerial roles, says (MR, in office 1997–8 and 2001–10) that

> the attitude that you go into questions with as a minister, from your department with your civil servants sitting there, is: how can you thwack down the backbenchers that are asking you questions so that they don't annoy you or cause you difficulty? Question [time] really ought to be seen as an opportunity to listen to what the opposition say and to listen to what your own side is saying ... I think there is too much of an adversarial approach to Parliament from the Civil Service, seeing Parliament as an obstacle, something that is there to be a problem when you try to get your legislation through. I think they should have embraced more the notion that you are putting it into the public domain in Parliament, and Parliament can improve it, instead of driving the business of the House through. Often, backbenchers on one side or the other side will be right, and the warning signs won't have been listened to. And then you go back to the department and they say, 'Minister, you really put them in their place.' It's short-term gratification, but we should be listening more.

The lack of understanding can apply to new ministers as well as to civil servants. Jo Swinson (MR, in office 2012–15) was like almost all Liberal Democrat ministers new to government. She was prepared to an extent by having been Vince Cable's parliamentary private secretary for two years, but she concedes that there were a whole load of things she had not seen – such as ministerial briefing meetings and submissions

– 'if you've not been in government you just don't have a clue'. She concludes that while 'there's a gap in Parliament understanding the Civil Service, I found absolutely the exact same in the Civil Service in terms of Parliament – there's a real need for much better understanding on both sides'.

Various initiatives have been launched to try and bridge the gap between departments and backbenchers. Tim Loughton recognises (MR, in office 2010–12) the problem of trying to stay in touch, and says he was one of the first to do what has now become commonplace and organise 'sort of surgeries for backbenchers who had any queries on constituency issues or children's policy or whatever. Now there are tea room surgeries regularly held by most ministers, usually run through parliamentary private secretaries. You can book a slot to go and see the Home Secretary to raise whatever you want to raise, which is good.' He talked to Labour MPs partly because children and social care was not as party political as education reforms. He believes it was crazy to ignore real experience on the other side – 'so I was very keen to try and transcend party political boundaries. The private office is always very nervous about that sort of thing.'

These dilemmas are even more acute in the House of Lords, where virtually no one outside the House, particularly including Prime Ministers, let alone civil servants, understands how it works, and therefore what qualities are needed in its ministers.

# CHAPTER NINE

# Of Goats and Lords

'It's not altogether surprising that the record over a very, very long period, going back to John Davies, of businessmen in government is not particularly good. And that's for a number of reasons. One, I think we don't understand the model of the way the government makes decisions. Secondly, we believe rather naively that all ministers are working to a common agenda with a common purpose. And in fact, they are not colleagues at all, they are frequently competitors, and there is little in the way of esprit de corps in politics, in government. And, finally, we have a habit of telling the truth, which is known in the world of politics as a gaffe.'

– Paul Myners, Treasury minister in the Lords, 2008–10, in Ministers Reflect interview, 2016

Prime Ministers have sought to broaden their choice of ministers by looking beyond the House of Commons to experts elsewhere. This would be quite normal in other Western democracies, where leading businessmen, academics and local government leaders serve as ministers and as leaders of departments – though the top posts still tend to be held by long-term politicians in all these countries.

In the UK, it is different. Outsiders rarely serve as the heads of departments, but are brought in to provide expert advice and support in subordinate ministerial positions. The record has been mixed because of the frequently ambiguous nature of their appointments. In order to become ministers, they are nowadays made members of the House of Lords, since it is much harder to arrange by-elections to get people into the Commons – and the constitutional conventions lay down that ministers are directly accountable to one or other House. Yet there is frequently a tension, to put it mildly, between their roles as departmental ministers and as parliamentarians required to be active and accountable in the Lords – a conflict rarely recognised by the Prime Ministers who appoint them. So they are hybrids, recruited for their expertise but requiring political and parliamentary skills which they did not previously possess in order to succeed, indeed even to survive.

The story is really one of outsiders becoming, or at least trying to become, insiders since, as the Public Administration Select Committee argued in its 2010 report (Eighth Report, 2009–10, p3), 'The Westminster system of government was never designed to support substantial numbers of appointments made from outside Parliament. The practice is better suited to countries with a full separation of powers, with corresponding checks and balances.' Leaders in other countries are also constrained by operating in coalitions, and, like the UK, affected by the increasing professionalisation of politics. The number of Lords ministers of whatever origin is always going to be a small minority. We are not talking of altering the basic understanding that the majority of ministers should be elected members of the House of Commons to ensure the democratic character of any government, in contrast to those up to the early 1900s.

The search for outsiders is not new, even though it gained public and media attention in 2007, when the terms 'Goats' was devised in response to Gordon Brown saying he wanted a Government of All the Talents, an intended policy of recruiting new ministers with no previous political or party connections. The much publicised Goats, and a succession of generally short-lived Trade ministers in the Lords from a business background, may, in retrospect, be seen as less significant than the changed composition and role of Lords ministers generally since the late 1990s. The fall in the number of hereditary peers after 1999 has been matched by an increasing proportion of life peers. Many more among the twenty-odd Lords ministers now play a significant role within departments, rather than just acting as their parliamentary faces. This chapter will examine the broader experience of introducing outsiders as ministers and the specific issues of Lords ministers.

There are several reasons that Prime Ministers look beyond existing members of the Commons and Lords, who are seen as having too limited experience for what running a government now requires. The UK has narrowed its pool of potential ministers to a much, much smaller group than in almost any other country where being an existing member of the legislature is not required to qualify for most posts. Moreover, the professionalisation of politics has narrowed the range of experience and skills available, though this point should not be overdone, since a majority of MPs, and hence potential ministers, still come from business, the professions or the public sector rather than more specifically political jobs. This is a contentious point since, as noted in Chapter Three, the more professional/career politicians supposedly have skills that their predecessors did not. The question is not just whether the skills of, say, a former special adviser hoping to be a successful politician are the same as what would be required to be an effective minister (as discussed by Ben Yong and Robert Hazell, 2011, p14). It is also about whether the narrowing of experience – fewer with 'real world' business or manual worker backgrounds – limits the skills available and required of ministers. A related question is whether current politicians are seen as having the required 'authenticity' and breadth to command public confidence. The polls cited in the first chapter suggest that they do not.

Moreover, the longer a party is in power, the smaller the pool of potential ministers becomes, since more people have already had experience of office, have resigned or been sacked and are unlikely to return. This point can be overdone since, even towards the end of Labour's thirteen years in office in 2010, around 45 per cent of Labour MPs had never held ministerial office. Party managers would argue that once you had deducted those temperamentally unsuited for office, the ethically questionable and persistent rebels, the pool of unused talent was much smaller. And, of course, the unacceptable and unappointable in the eyes of one ruling group can, as we have found, become the leaders themselves a few years later. This is despite the tendency of recent Prime Ministers to increase the number of ministers. Furthermore, as discussed in Chapter Ten on reshuffles, there has been a welcome trend recently to bring back some ministers who had previously been dropped.

Whatever the reasoning, Prime Ministers have decided they need to look outside the existing members of the legislature. World wars have seen outsiders brought in: a group of industrialists by Lloyd George in 1917; Ernest Bevin as Minister of Labour in 1940 (with an unopposed by-election arranged for him). Harold Wilson made Frank Cousins, a leading trade union leader, Minister of Technology in October 1964 (again a special by-election was arranged), though he was in office for less than two years. At the same time, Wilson appointed Alun Gwynne Jones, a former army officer and journalist, as a Foreign Office minister with responsibility for disarmament, joining the Lords with the title of Lord Chalfont. C. P. Snow, a scientist, civil servant and writer about power and bridging the two cultures, became a junior Lords minister. None of the Wilson appointments was seen as a success. Later in the same decade, the Conservatives under Ted Heath recruited John Davies, a former Director-General of the Confederation of British Industry in order to use his business experience in government. He eventually found a safe seat and served as Trade and Industry Secretary for a couple of years. He lacked a feel for politics but remained active in various ministerial and shadow roles until he was diagnosed with terminal cancer in 1978. Margaret Thatcher promoted to the Cabinet both Arthur Cockfield, a distinguished former civil servant and businessman, and David Young, a successful property entrepreneur and then chair of the Manpower Services Commission. Cockfield was initially at the Treasury and then Trade Secretary before becoming a European Commissioner who championed the single market, while Young handled unemployment and then the promotion of enterprise. Both were seen as effective ministers in their areas of expertise, though without wider political influence.

Tony Blair reached out much further to bring in outsiders, generally in junior and middle-ranking roles and all as ministers in the Lords. This was in addition to appointing a group of existing peers, notably women, with Labour links as ministers in May 1997, as discussed below. David Simon, a former chairman of BP, became Minister for Europe, though he found the experience frustrating and left after just over two years. By contrast, David Sainsbury, the former chair of the Sainsburys supermarket chain, lasted more than eight years as a Trade and Industry minister specialising in science, universities, research and innovation, and built up a high reputation for understanding the issues. The Blair years also saw the appointment as Lords ministers of Gus Macdonald, Charlie Falconer (in a variety of roles over a decade, though ending as Lord Chancellor in charge of the new Ministry of Justice) and Andrew Adonis (at Education and then Transport). Paul Drayson, a successful businessman and substantial donor to Labour, became, first, a defence minister, and later, responsible for science and innovation just under a year after being made a peer. The key point about all these, and Cockfield and Young, is that they performed substantial departmental roles.

Gordon Brown says in his memoirs (2017, p203) that he sought to make outside appointments work by casting them in a new way. Revealingly, in this section, he does not mention the Goats description widely used at the time. The innovation in the five outsiders appointed as ministers in the Lords in July 2007 is that all but one had no previous public political links to Labour, unlike the earlier Blair appointees. Four were clearly experts in their areas – Ara Darzi on the NHS; Mark Malloch-Brown on the United Nations, Africa and the developing worlds; Alan West, a recently retired First Sea Lord, on security and defence; and Digby Jones, a former

Director-General of the CBI, on business and enterprise. The latter lasted just sixteen months in office before leaving, complaining that his time in office 'had been one of the most dehumanising and depersonalising experiences a human being can have. The whole system is designed to take the personality, the drive and the initiative out of a junior minister' (evidence to Public Administration Committee, Good Government, Eighth Report Session 2008–9, HC 97).

Darzi and Malloch-Brown left after two years and a month and West lasted the whole life of the Brown government, until May 2010. Shriti Vadera, an investment banker who served in three departments over two years and three months, was always more of a personal adviser to, and fixer for, Gordon Brown. He once phoned her in the autumn of 2007 and asked what the banking community thought about the developing financial crisis. She said she did not know, since she was in Africa. Why was she there, asked a bemused Prime Minister, only to be told he had appointed her as an International Development minister. She was soon moved to the Business Department.

Other outsiders made Lords ministers during the Brown years included Stephen Carter for nine months in 2008–9 as Communications minister. He had had a successful career in advertising and as a communications regulator before an undistinguished nine months as Downing Street chief of staff. Paul Myners came in from the corporate world to the Treasury to help with managing the banking crisis from October 2008 until the 2010 election. Mervyn Davies, a former senior bank executive, served as Trade minister for fifteen months. From more conventional political backgrounds, Peter Mandelson returned from the European

Commission to head the Business Department from the Lords, while Glenys Kinnock, a former MEP, was made a peer to become a Foreign Office minister.

David Cameron and Theresa May have continued to bring in outsiders, though on a more modest scale. Successful businessmen, and women, were favoured as Trade ministers, such as Stephen Green, formerly chair of HSBC, serving in government for just over three years; Ian Livingston, former chief executive of BT, for eighteen months; Mark Price, formerly managing director of Waitrose, for seventeen months; and Rona Fairhead, former chief executive of the *Financial Times* and ex-chair of the BBC Trust, from September 2017. James Sassoon also served in the Treasury for two and a half years at the start of the coalition government, having previously been an investment banker, a civil servant and an adviser to the Conservatives at the end of their years in opposition. The other true Goats, with previous political ties, were Paul Deighton, who had run the London Olympics Delivery Authority, served as Commercial Secretary to the Treasury dealing with infrastructure, for two years and four months, to be succeeded in the same post for sixteen months by Jim O'Neill, who handled the Northern Powerhouse and relations with China; and Ros Altmann, who served as Pensions minister for fourteen months in 2015–16 after a long career in personal investment and retirement issues. An interesting, and long-serving exception was David Freud, who after a career in journalism and banking, had become a welfare expert, becoming a life peer in 2009 and then serving for six years from 2010 as Welfare Reform minister. Paul Marland became a life peer in 2006 after a long career in business and served as a minister in two departments (Energy and Climate

Change and Business, Innovation and Skills for three years). John Nash already had Conservative connections and was a party donor after a career in finance/private equity, with a close interest in education reform, before he became a Schools minister in 2013. His successor in autumn 2017, Theodore Agnew, has a similar business and party background as well as, like Nash, having promoted academy schools. Other people with long-term Conservative connections were appointed ministers and peers at the same time, such as Jonathan Hill and George Bridges (both of whom had worked for John Major in Downing Street), Francis Maude (after he left the Commons at the 2015 election) and Andrew Dunlop and Ian Duncan, both with Scottish political roots.

This list – only covering ministers who were brought in from outside Parliament to take office – raises a number of intriguing questions. Why did so many of the pure Goats have such short periods in office? In some cases, they were given specific tasks to do and left office when these were completed. For instance, Ara Darzi was specifically commissioned to look at the organisation of the hospital system in London and review staff and patient experiences. Once he had finished his review, he returned to his hospital duties – he had anyway been treating patients and operating part-time all day Fridays and Saturdays. He finished work at seven o'clock on Saturday evenings and then a red box would appear on Sunday. Similarly, Stephen Carter had been asked to do a review of digital policy, preparing the way for later action on superfast broadband. Once he had finished the Digital Britain report, he resigned.

In other cases, however, there clearly appears to have been frustration at the experience of being a minister, and a recognition that the role had a time limit. Stephen Green (MR, in office 2010–13) said at the beginning that he would not do less than two years and no more than three. 'Not less than two, because you shouldn't do anything for less than two, and not more than three because it is quite a gruelling job to be frank – in particular the travel.' All his predecessors and successors as Trade minister served for shorter periods. Several of the Goats interviewed in the Ministers Reflect interviews pointed to the big differences between the business and political worlds. Green, who came from heading a large global bank, noted that 'if you had been a CEO or a hands-on operating manager, the trick you have got to learn is that being a minister is more like being a chairman than it is like being a CEO'. Paul Myners, a former chair of household name public companies, noted (MR, in office, 2008–10) how ministers made decisions more frequently and at a lower level of importance than you would expect business people operating at the top of large corporations. 'I was struck by the number of files that came to me on which I was having to make decisions. And the speed with which decisions had to be made. I was struck by the number of letters I had to write.'

Similarly, Ian Livingston (MR, in office 2013–15), previously chief executive of BT Group, found the way decisions were taken 'strange and difficult', and counter to what would have happened in business – 'if you had a month to do something it would be done at official level for thirty days and then overnight by the minister. Rather than actually give the minister time, everything was overnight.' Livingston felt that having worked in a large organisation like BT was a big help, but there were huge differences in being a minister:

The running of the organisation bit, the trouble is you didn't have the levers that you were used to having. Your ability to change people and process in a way you could in business was different. So it could have been a bigger help if I had been able to exercise the levers. It's a cliché but there's quite a lot of truth in it, the minister is the chairman and the civil servant the chief executive. So it was a bit of a change. You had a lot of the accountability but not quite some of the capabilities to get it delivered.

David Freud, however, stresses (MR, in office 2010–16) the advantages of coming in from the business world. 'Having been in business means you can deliver things in a commercial context, and I think it's tough for politicians and indeed for civil servants who have not had that experience.' He sees that as a weakness of our system in contrast to other countries, where the division between the private and public sectors is far more permeable. In France, there is close interchange of personnel, as the Macron government shows, while in the USA, senior business executives are appointed to Cabinet positions, but these are very different constitutional systems. Freud adds: 'We have precious few people who've done what I've done, coming in from a business background with a set of capabilities, i.e. can negotiate with industry. That is a fundamental problem for this country. We find it very hard to do really big projects as a direct result.' Freud's solution is to put the people in charge of the implementation, not the policy, for the three major change programmes in the Lords on the frontbench. 'You are the minister for implementing X. But there would be two changes. They would have powers to build a team. And the reason they're in the

Lords is that they've got a public place where they can be held to account which isn't so adversarial as the Commons.' The building of a team is not quite as much of a challenge to the Civil Service as the words imply, since the changes to the running of major infrastructure schemes in recent years have developed more of a project management approach.

Paul Myners said that he and Mervyn Davies 'used to meet occasionally for coffee and tear our hair out or laugh out loud at some of the complexities of working in government. And it's not an easy task.' They had to acknowledge the very different way in which politics operates.

Few of the Goats had much feel for the political, let alone the parliamentary, side of their posts. Successive Prime Ministers must be held responsible. They – particularly Blair, Brown and Cameron – were looking for members of the executive who would address gaps in skills and experience in their administrations. They did not realise, and certainly did not explain to new Lords ministers, about their parliamentary responsibilities, largely because none of the Prime Ministers had the faintest idea how the Lords worked and the demands it imposes. There was also little induction or preparation. Ian Livingston, who moved directly from BT to become a minister, notes (MR, in office 2013–15) that there were two things he had to get used to: one was becoming a minister, and the second was being a member of the House of Lords, being at the despatch box and speaking in debates. However, he had the good fortune of a short transition period between the announcement of his appointment and taking over from Stephen Green:

Most MPs have plenty of time because they have been a backbencher for four, five, six, seven, eight, twenty years or whatever and then when they move to the frontbench they've seen it all before. I was doing it within a month or two and I had seen other ministers whose maiden speech is in a debate. I see them answering their first question and they've never seen it before and they don't know what to do. And you never get a second chance to make a first impression.

Paul Marland says (MR, in office 2010–13) that, in view of his business experience, the easy bit was running a department. He says officials 'by and large' loved having someone prepared to make a decision and give clear instructions since they did not have the skill set to do it and were not trained to do it:

That was like falling off a log for me. And also empowering the Civil Service was a very easy fit because you were used to managing people. The difficult bit was standing up in the House of Lords and performing and having to learn a sort of university degree in three weeks [on the detail of policy]. It is almost like being in the Globe: you are in a pit and you have got a whole lot of things which you are not used to doing. You are not particularly trained as a public speaker and you are not particularly trained as an orator. Not knowing what the first question is and then not knowing what the other twenty are going to be is an ordeal. So you take the view, I am going to run scared from this or I am going to really win this battle. So I decided I was going to win this battle and create a sort of persona in the Lords of a bit of fun but also having complete knowledge.

Jim O'Neill, who came from Goldman Sachs and is an accomplished media performer, confesses (MR, in office 2015–16) that when he was considering whether to accept a ministerial post, he talked to two people who understood him really well who told him that Lords questions and commitments would test his patience. One said, "you will hate the House of Lords", and that's why I left. That is something that's got to be changed – the ministerial duty in the House of Lords is just ridiculous.' He pointed out that he had to be around for every possible vote. 'So you have to completely abandon any personal life – most weeks on Monday, Tuesday, Wednesday. You know, for somebody who doesn't have political views, and I don't, it was boring and an inefficient use of time. How there is not modern technology for those who are in the Lords is just ridiculous.'

These views of Lords ministers, both politically committed and uncommitted, are revealing about the problems of bringing in outsiders who feel much more comfortable in taking executive decisions than developing political, let alone parliamentary, skills of patience and persuasion. Joyce Anelay (MR, in office 2010–17) is an acute observer of changes in the Lords. She came from the charity and welfare world, and the voluntary side of the Conservative Party to become a working peer in 1996, and notes that her many years in opposition in the Lords made her

> more prepared for government than others might have
> been – particularly I think those who've had real success
> in business, particularly entrepreneurial people, because
> they're used to making a decision and saying 'do this' and
> it's done and then they move on. In government you

have to invite others to work with you to achieve something and you can never move on because there's always the next stage.

Other Lords ministers adapted and enjoyed the Lords by participating. Like Paul Myners, Mervyn Davies adapted:

I loved the intellect of the House of Lords. I loved the questioning – it's a different style to the House of Commons. I loved the group of people that I came across, whom obviously I had never met before. Most of my friends were on the other side. I was just in awe of them. So my admiration for the House of Lords just went through the roof. I saw how hard they worked. I saw that whatever subject came up, there was somebody who knew a lot more about it than I did.

Alan West (in evidence to the Public Administration Committee, 2009–10, question 95) noted the pressures of being a minister:

It was like doing an A-level a night on some of these things, which were not to do with security [his departmental responsibility]. When I find I am answering questions on female genital mutilation, drug testing on gorillas, this is something I had not quite expected to do. It has been very good for my brain. I can actually learn poetry again now. That is not quite what I had expected.

Paul Myners said Gordon Brown told him that his primary role – at the worst point of the banking crisis in autumn 2008

— was 'to be able to speak with the bankers eye-to-eye and not to be intimidated by them, and not to be drowned in data and industry terminology'. The Prime Minister had said: 'You will have to go to the Lords but it won't take up much of your time and I will make sure that is the case.' That was not the case, because this was a very hot subject and therefore lots of questions were being put down in the Lords: 'I was given no preparation for the Lords at all and I found the whole experience quite difficult.'

The political and parliamentary side is easier in the Lords than in the Commons because there are so many non-politicians there already and they are more understanding about newcomers. Nonetheless, as the previous paragraphs underline, the adjustment for new ministers can be tough and demanding. This applies not only to the Goats picked from outside politics but also to peers quickly elevated to ministerial office who may have been party members for many years but who have no professional political experience. This argues for at least a short induction period, allowing intended new ministers a month or two to acclimatise and be given some preparation before starting the job. But such time seldom seems to be available when governments are formed and reshuffles undertaken.

The scepticism of official Whitehall is reflected in the view of John Hutton and Leigh Lewis (pp191–5), who point to the failures:

> Most of those brought into government as Goats in recent years have spent their lives getting to the top – be they captains of industry, highly decorated generals or self-made millionaires. They tend, by definition, to have

acquired pretty large egos – if there were a recognised international ego measurement scale most would be in danger of falling off the end – and they are used to having those egos seriously flattered. What they are most certainly not used to doing is following other people's orders or, much worse, toeing the party line. They are accustomed to calling a spade a spade, not indulging in long-winded euphemisms, still less ducking the question. Now all of these are fine and valued qualities; were it not for the fact that they are not always so in the rather ambiguous world of government.

The lack of essential political skills explains the short tenure of many, though not all, such outsiders who often leave office complaining about the political world. In doing so, they undermine the contribution of those Goats with specialist skills who have stayed the course long enough to make a difference and be valued.

Should the Goats of the Brown years have to be made ministers, as opposed to policy tsars? This is separate from the question discussed below of whether ministers have to be members of the Commons or Lords. The term 'tsar' is largely media-driven, with the help of Whitehall press officers, and is intended to convey the impression of government activity and priority for an issue. The term covers everything from specialist adviser (as distinct from a political special adviser) to ambassador or champion/coordinator of policy on an issue. Some are appointed formally with a status and role in a department, others informally. In some cases, the most significant aspect is the announcement of a famous name rather than what follows afterwards. In essence, it is about power and the distinction between advising and taking decisions. Ara Darzi told the Public Administration Committee (2007–09, p27) that, when approached by Gordon Brown about becoming a minister, 'I asked the Prime Minister whether I should be appointed as an adviser, and he was very reluctant to do that. His explanation at the time was that you needed to be a minister to make things happen and, in retrospect, I could not agree more with him.'

Another running issue is accountability. How can outsiders be made accountable to Parliament? That is a further argument for making them peers as opposed to just policy tsars who can be hidden within departments. When Lords Adonis and Mandelson were heading big policy departments, Transport and Business, at the end of the Brown government, there was a debate about whether they should be directly and regularly answerable to the Commons collectively – for example in Westminster Hall – rather than just questioned by its Select Committees, as both were. But this was opposed at the Commons end since MPs did not want to encourage more Secretaries of State heading departments being appointed to the Lords. This procedural hurdle does not seem to be an insuperable obstacle to the appointment of a few more ministers outside the Commons with substantive departmental roles. A mechanism for accountability can be found. This is leaving aside more radical proposals for allowing ministers in charge of a particular piece of government business, especially a bill, to appear in either House.

Perhaps a more interesting question is whether the Goats – who have generally served for two years or less as ministers – should become permanent members of the Lords as life peers, or just serve as long as they are in office. There is a procedure for peers to retire, though that is voluntary. An alternative is to appoint people as ministers without being a member of either House, as happened in the nineteenth century, in wartime and, occasionally before devolution, with the Scottish law officers. The challenge is ensuring account-ability, hence the preference for appointing to the Lords.

All governments require ministers in the Lords, to carry through business. Indeed, in 1900, Lord Salisbury was one of nine peers in the Cabinet. That reflected the weight of politi-cal forces in his government which anyway enjoyed a commanding majority in the Commons. Peers were big figures in government and held major offices of state. The number, and prominence, of peers in any Cabinet fell sharply during the twentieth century, though Attlee in 1945 and Mac-millan in 1957 still had five peers in their Cabinets. But by the mid-1960s, it was usually only two or three – the Leader of the Lords, the Lord Chancellor and perhaps one other Secre-tary of State, typically Lord Home and then Lord Carrington in Conservative administrations. Margaret Thatcher typi-cally had one Secretary of State in her Cabinet, first Lord Carrington, then, not at the same time, Lords Cockfield and Young. The number of peers has shown little change in abso-lute terms since 1900 (while falling as a percentage of the total number of ministers) since governments have had to take their business through the Lords.

The key has been the change in the character of these Lords ministers. Up to 1958, and the introduction of life and, equally significant, female peers, all members of the Lords were hereditary and service as minister was a form of occa-sional, not very demanding, public service. Until the late 1990s, most Conservative ministers were hereditary peers, whose role was largely parliamentary. Only a minority, Lords Carrington and Home, carried weight in Whitehall, apart from, at below Cabinet level, Irwin Bellwin on local government and Lynda Chalker, after she lost her Commons seat in 1992 and became a peer, on overseas development. Labour ministers were generally older life peers and former MPs, whose role was largely to act as spokesman for their departments. They rose from being whips which in the Lords also means representing departments at questions and taking through legislation to being junior and middle-ranking ministers, only very rarely reaching the Cabinet. The quality was mixed and civil servants watched nervously from the officials' box to see how their peers performed, a bit like jittery parents at their children's school plays. Would they remember their lines? Exceptions were some Leaders of the Lords, such as Willie Whitelaw after 1983, and Lord Chancellors, like Lord Hailsham and Lord Mackay of Clashfern.

That changed in the 1990s, initially during the Thatcher and Major years but most clearly in the Blair era. First, and most significant, was the appointment of a new, and distinctive, team of Lords ministers in May 1997 – younger, talented and, above all, female – who were clearly identified with Labour (unlike some of the later Goats) and had substantial careers before entering the Lords. These included Margaret Jay, Tessa Blackstone, Helene Hayman, Liz Symons and the late Patricia Hollis, later joined by Valerie Amos and Janet Royall. Unlike most of their predecessors they all played substantial departmental, as well as parliamentary, roles alongside the two businessmen turned ministers in David Simon (briefly) and David Sainsbury (for a much longer period). The impact of this formidable group was quite a challenge to the culture of the Lords and to the club-like assumptions about the Lords of many of the Conservative hereditary peers who had been ministers in the Thatcher and Major years.

Second, the removal of nine-tenths of hereditary peers after 1999, leaving just ninety-two, also changed the balance of peers available, especially for a Conservative government. Most of the Conservative ministers in the Lords since 2010 have been life rather than hereditary peers, many from the voluntary side of the Conservative Party, supportive think tanks and from local government. Some like Joyce Anelay or Tina Stowell worked their way up via the whip's office to become junior and then more senior ministers, the latter becoming Leader of the Lords.

Tina Stowell points out (MR, in office 2011–16) that there are two types of departmental ministers: first there are 'experts that arrive in the department and are there because they are bringing an external expertise. Then you've got generalists that go into departments and what tends to happen when the policy is divided up and portfolios are established is that the generalist House of Lords minister usually gets the worst, mundane bit of policy.' Leaving aside the occasional Goats/experts, the key distinction is between those who are primarily spokesmen and those with substantive policy roles. Stowell recalls her broad role in her first year as a junior whip: 'The scary thing is that you are suddenly thrust into the spotlight. I was only understudying for ministers. I wasn't a spokesman.' She reflects the experience of many other Lords ministers in saying that the first time she had to repeat a government statement (originally made in the Commons) it was about feed-in tariffs, something which she knew nothing about, and she had little time to prepare since it was an urgent question.

> Some of the government whips that first take that on, they're not experts, they're generalists, and they aren't even political either. So it's a huge amount to ask them to do and they get very, very little support from the relevant departments. I can't begin to describe how low down the pecking order you are in terms of anybody caring about making sure that you are briefed. It's pretty grim actually.

As discussed in Chapter Eight, she is scathing about the Civil Service's attitude to Parliament.

Joyce Anelay agreed on the difficult position of Lords whips, working in two or three departments. 'It's difficult for them to get that kind of status where the department really feels they're working to them ... they're not rooted in their department and it is much more difficult for Lords whips to feel they get a very good service.' Ian Livingston similarly complained about the level of support for Lords ministers. 'You can't get away with winging it in the Lords because they know and they will react. They really respect you if you know your subject. They don't take prisoners if you don't. And so it's almost that you have got the input less but the requirement higher.'

Despite these frustrations, in her later roles both as a departmental minister, and particularly as Leader of the Lords, Tina Stowell had a more substantial departmental and policy role, notably in taking through the legislation allowing gay couples to marry. That involved skillful handling of the

House. 'As Leader of the House of Lords, you are effectively a broker – between Number 10 and Whitehall and the House of Lords, an honest broker.' Her biggest message to her ministerial team was 'the most important thing is to show that you take the House of Lords seriously'. Indeed, the most successful, and respected, ministers were those who are modest, recognising that many peers will be greater experts than they will ever be.

Overall, however, looking at the succession of usually short-lived Goats from outside politics as well as the changed background and role of Lords ministers generally, the attempt to broaden the talent and recruitment pool of ministers has been pretty modest. There has not been a great infusion of outside talent, as opposed to a desirable strengthening of the ministerial teams in the Lords and some outsiders performing specific short-term tasks, such as Trade ministers. In particular, the impact of Goats has been limited – in their own eyes as well as of others. The exceptions, such as Lords Sainsbury and Freud, remained in one post for several years. The Public Administration Committee argued (2009–10, p21) that:

> Where ministers with non-parliamentary backgrounds have not been successful, it has tended to be because, in Jonathan Powell's words, they 'can't do the politics'. There are many reasons why this may be the case. However, it does not help that, as Lord Darzi said, no one tells incoming ministers 'what being a minister' or 'being a parliamentarian' actually involved, and that these competences have to be learnt on the job.

Ben Yong and Robert Hazell argue in their report (2010, p85) that 'there will continue to be occasional outsiders – those who are not from Parliament, but who have relevant technocratic experience or skills. Such appointees may usefully complement a ministerial team appointed from Parliament.' But they stress the need for hybrid candidates who have both technocratic and (transferable) political skills rather than making purely technocratic appointments. They point (p44) to the parallels with the problems faced by external appointments to the Civil Service: unclear expectations and a predisposition towards setting new recruits to fail; poor organisational fit; a lack of standards with which to evaluate performance; and poor retention rates.

Outsiders – and I would add, the Prime Ministers appointing them – should be made fully aware of the responsibilities of being a minister in the Lords, and particularly the parliamentary role. As with other ministers, induction and training can help, particularly support and acclimatisation before new ministers face the Lords.

# CHAPTER TEN

# Reshuffles

'I decided to reshuffle the Cabinet. There's a kind of convention
that it should be done every year. It's clear that governments
need refreshing and there is a need to let new blood through.
Also, a prime minister or president is always engaged in a kind of
negotiation over the state of their party that requires people's
ambitions to be assuaged ... If you don't promote someone, after
a time, they resent you. If you promote them, you put someone
else out, and then that person resents you.'

– Tony Blair, *A Journey* (2010), pp593–4

'Reshuffles have a negative impact on the effectiveness of the
government. Even the most able minister needs time to become
familiar with a new brief ... Ministers should be left in post long
enough to make a difference. Secretaries of State should be left in
post for the length of the Parliament and more junior ministers
for a minimum of two years. This will not always be possible, but
we would like it to become the norm.'

– Political and Constitutional Reform Committee,
'The Impact and Effectiveness of Ministerial Reshuffles',
Second Report of Session 2013–14

Reshuffles are one of the few means which Prime Ministers

have to try and change the direction and appearance of their governments. But they are frequently bungled and counter-productive, and are indirectly related to the performance of ministers, either in the past or the future. They are all about the political balance of a government, and seldom take account of executive experience. Even though Prime Ministers invariably hate carrying them out, they tend to undertake reshuffles almost every year for reasons of party management.

As noted in Chapter One, British ministers have shorter tenure than most of their opposite numbers overseas or than senior corporate leaders – and this goes to the heart of the argument about the impact of ministers and their performance. When I was Director of the Institute for Government and wanted to discuss reshuffles with a visiting delegation from Germany, it was very difficult to get the concept over to them, because they simply did not understand what we were talking about. For them, someone was appointed at the beginning of the four-year term, following often lengthy negotiations over the formation of a coalition and the allocation of portfolios, and that was it, barring illness and mishaps. That was partly true during the UK coalition government of 2010–15, when there was less turnover than before, or since, and no changing of Cabinet portfolios between parties. David Cameron made a virtue of keeping reshuffles to a minimum. In an interview with *The Sun* a year after taking office (quoted in The Political and Constitutional Reform Committee, p7), he said: 'I'm not a great believer in endlessly moving people between different jobs. We had twelve Energy ministers in nine years. And the Tourism minister changed more often than people got off planes at Heathrow. It was hopeless. I think you've got to try to appoint good people and keep them.'

Of course, many ministerial changes are not voluntary. Scandals, rows and mishaps occur. During the 2010–15 coalition, there were six departures at Cabinet level: five as a result of scandals and unacceptable conduct. Since the 2015 general election, the pace of forced departures has accelerated, with a regular flow of such incidents, as well as policy disagreements. Whatever the reason for the departure, the consequent ministerial changes have ripple effects, because the replacements, and their replacements, come from the same limited pool of MPs in the Commons. That alone undermines the good intentions of trying to leave ministers in place. Alan Johnson, who held five Cabinet posts in six years, including just seven months heading Work and Pensions, said (MR, in office, 1999–2010) that the Labour government had far too many reshuffles. 'Some were caused by scandals or resignations or whatever, but that can't excuse the regularity; it was almost an annual reshuffle.'

Then, as Tony Blair noted in the quotation at the beginning of this chapter, there are expectations that there will be a reshuffle every year, often in the summer or early autumn. The motive is usually presented in terms of refreshing the junior or middle ranks of a government, and strengthening previous areas of weakness. In essence, it is about trying to balance hopes and ambitions. Hilary Armstrong, who was government Chief Whip to Tony Blair from 2001 to 2006, has offered a shrewd insight into why reshuffles occur (PCRC, written evidence):

there are always external forces which either demanded a mini-reshuffle, or even changed the date of a reshuffle. Government is not like a company. The role of a minister is much more about leadership qualities, being able to take decisions, having a clear strategic view of direction and being able to motivate others. It should not be about the detail of operational activity. That is the role of civil servants.

As has been apparent so far in this book, there are clear differences in the views of ministers, between those, like Hilary Armstrong, seeing reshuffles as taking decisions and setting strategies and those who see them as much more involved in implementation/delivery. She argued, fairly, that 'ministers are far more subject to public scrutiny and media challenge than most company executives. They have that day in and day out – not just when there is a catastrophe – and some people are worn down by that.' Reshuffles, she acknowledged, are 'always difficult. Determinedly not having reshuffles annually, and refusing to lose ministers under attack in a way that would probably not have been true in the past, also has its difficulties ... Democracy is not tidy and streamlined; government appointments and changes are a product of that untidy system.' There speaks a realist.

The aims of such regular reshuffles have often been unclear and, at times, inconsistent. In evidence to the PCRC inquiry (p8), John Major acknowledged conflicting objectives, in which case he gave priority to the promotion of the most able to replace ministers who were underperforming. This was put ahead of the other aims of bringing a regional and political balance to the government. Similarly (PCRC, written evidence), it is not straightforward to 'make decisions on ministers' performance and on matching talents and experience' because of competing priorities:

As much as possible, I tried to match talent and experience to individual posts; but, upon reflection, I can see
this was often subordinated to the wider issue of giving
the best young talent the greatest possible experience at
parliamentary secretary and Minister of State level, in
order to prepare them for the Cabinet. As I look back,
this may not always have been the right decision in the
interests of good management of a portfolio and the best
service by ministers to the public.

In other words, ministers get moved around too often for the
interests of good government.

This reflects the familiar, constitutionally and tradition-
ally imposed constraints of a limited choice, predominantly
from among existing MPs. Current ministers have to be
shifted sideways, or moved slightly upwards, to fill vacancies
from those departing, with the gaps at the bottom taken by
backbenchers. In his guide to reshuffles (2012, p6), Akash
Paun notes that the scope for a rational, appraisal-based series
of changes is

constrained by the sheer limitation of numbers in the
Westminster system. Even for a government with a comfortable majority, the ratio of potential ministers to jobs
is relatively small 'once you've eliminated the bad, mad,
drunk and over the hill', as former whip Tristan Garel-
Jones memorably put it. Over time, as longstanding PMs
find, the problem becomes worse. The proportion of
unappointable backbenchers naturally grows as ex-
ministers join the ranks of the discontented.

The process itself is usually messy and often politically damaging. As reshuffle season approaches, there are often weeks of speculation in the media (with interested parties in and out of government suggesting their own candidates for the sack, demotion or promotion). Often more people are tipped for promotion than for sacking. This does little for the confidence of ministers. It also has little to do with performance. From the perspective of a lifetime banker, and short-term minister, Mervyn Davies (Lord Davies of Abersoch) noted (MR, in office 2009–10) that ministers had

> to stop worrying about their next job – because politicians just worry about their standing, what the Prime Minister thinks of them. If you are in a company, you don't spend all day thinking about what the CEO thinks of you. But they do in politics. I just was shocked at how much influence the Prime Minister has, because at the end of the day, there is no board of directors. The Prime Minister decides on the reshuffle.

There is no formal system of appraisals which applies in any other organisation, either in the public or the private sector. The late Sir Jeremy Heywood (PCRC, question 252) was sceptical about whether an appraisal system would ever be introduced, because it is unclear who would do the appraising. The 360-degree ministerial appraisals organised by Zoe Gruhn of the Institute for Government are quite normal elsewhere. They invariably contained a number of interesting insights into the performance and personalities of those involved. By definition, they are only seen by those appraised. I remember a quite damning one was finished on the day of a reshuffle but confidentiality rightly prevailed – and the minister survived for a year or two longer. But such exercises are hard to organise, because they involve civil servants and outsiders, and politicians are very nervous about leaks. Francis Maude, who enthusiastically supported appraisals and development for ministers as Cabinet Office minister, noted (MR, in office 1985–92 and 2010–16) that he would not be too optimistic that it is suddenly going to change. He is the only minister publicly to have acknowledged that he went through a 360 appraisal. 'But it was all a bit artificial. It was useful, I got some useful insights out of it, but in terms of managing my career, it didn't make any difference. So it made me a better minister.' From the perspective of a former Cabinet Secretary and Head of the Civil Service, Gus O'Donnell (PCRC, p19) acknowledged the difficulties: 'I had a fairly elaborate appraisal system for myself to get 360-degree feedback. That is very normal, but in a political world people would find it very hard. They would be very nervous about having appraisals out there in public.'

Downing Street advisers often pull together views from the Chief Whip, trusted senior ministers (though, as in the case of Gordon Brown, they can also be defending their own supporters) and, informally, with feedback from Permanent Secretaries (who invariably have their own views on which ministers should be dropped). Jonathan Powell noted (2010, pp148–9) that the advice of the Chief Whip was taken into account, but 'Dennis Skinner was an even better source on who was doing well in the chamber as the most regular attender amongst MPs'. And he sometimes thought it would be better to ask ministers' drivers who 'usually had a far better assessment of them than their Permanent Secretaries'.

Sir Jeremy Heywood, who saw more reshuffles than most from his long periods in 10 Downing Street (PCRC, question 227), commented that reshuffles are primarily political rather than Civil Service events, though officials did get involved in advising on the pressures facing particular departments at any time, over legislation or implementation of policy.

Sir George Young, who was in and out of government five times over nearly four decades, regretted (MR, in office 1979–86, 1990–7, 2010–12, 2012–14 and 2016–) that, as a former Leader of the Commons and former Chief Whip, he could not have done more career development. 'We didn't do nearly enough HR, career development, managing people who are going through a difficult period.' He talked to some private sector companies who were prepared to help, but they then realised it would have to go in the register of interests, and they would have to declare it as a donation, and, at that point, they backed off. The more traditional role of the whips is as talent spotters, as well as spotters of those not doing so well. 'You would see that some junior ministers were struggling, and so when you had a reshuffle conversation with the Prime Minister, you'd say, I really think so and so needs a break, they are not coping; they are in trouble at Question Time; and they are a liability and they ought to be moved on. And one of the things that David [Cameron] has done is to bring people back, which makes it easier to get rid of people' – of which more later.

Lord Turnbull, a former Cabinet Secretary as well as Permanent Secretary in two departments, told the PCRC inquiry that ministerial competence did get judged –

But what are the criteria of it? Is it whether you are a

good manager? Do you think strategically? Do you have a consistent pattern of delegation? Or are you good on television or, what used to be the case, because he is very good in the House? I think that counts a lot less, but clearly if you are not good in the House it counts against you. Running your department really effectively comes quite low down because I don't think there is any systematic way in which it gets reported.

The clash of Civil Service and political cultures is highlighted by Patricia Hewitt in talking (MR, in office 1998–2007) about her move from the Treasury to the Department for Trade and Industry in 1999. She had no idea that a move to become E-commerce minister was coming. Sir Andrew Turnbull, as he was then as the Treasury Permanent Secretary, 'was absolutely furious. Basically he said, "We've just got you up to speed, just got you nicely trained, you're a really good Treasury minister, and what happens? This is typical, this is so frivolous!" That was the flavour of it. You know, you're being whisked away to something else.'

Moreover, as Sir Bob Kerslake, when Head of the Civil Service, told the PCRC inquiry, it is hard to classify ministers in managerial terms. 'All ministers are a minister in a hurry. All ministers are going to be demanding. They will all want to achieve big things and achieve them as quickly as possible, and they all will expect and have the right to challenge if we are not moving things forward in the way they want to see happen.'

Whether the reshuffle is forced by a sudden ministerial resignation or is less hurried and intended to refresh a government, the changes invariably appear rushed in execution, with cameras in Downing Street and endless television – and now social media – coverage about people of whom most voters have never heard. Heywood (PCRC, question 235) said the unique thing about the British system was that

> we have these rather abrupt dismissals and changeovers. It feels a bit chaotic on reshuffle day, particularly if suddenly a minister has to appear before Parliament to answer questions on a brief of which he or she has no real awareness. There are obvious awkwardnesses on the day itself and the day afterwards, but I don't think that spreading pain over a number of days would greatly enhance the situation, if at all.

The absence of appraisal, or even forewarning, means that the sack or demotion usually comes as a shock – facing the chop after silence for a year. Some ministers seek to disappear, usually abroad, for a day or two in the hope that they cannot be found on reshuffle day and the Prime Minister will give up on sacking them. That worked both in the Thatcher and Blair years and ensured that ministers survived at least until the next reshuffle. Powerful patrons (notably Gordon Brown, in the Blair era) can intervene to protect their supporters. Some try to negotiate their way out of the sack, some are tearful and some are startled, having expected to be promoted. In recent years the sacking has usually been done on the night before the appointments, and away from the media glare in the Prime Minister's room in the House of Commons rather than in the view of television cameras in Downing Street.

Even at the top level, moves can be unexpected. Neither

Jack Straw nor Margaret Beckett expected to become Foreign Secretary when they were appointed in 2001 and 2006. Jack Straw recalls in his memoirs (p325) how several months before the 2001 general election he had told Tony Blair that he would like a move from the Home Office 'because I was running out of road'. His preference, which he thought the Prime Minister had agreed, was to take over John Prescott's huge department covering transport, planning, local government and the regions. 'JP was keen on the idea and called me on election day to agree the choreography for a friendly handover.' Number 10 had instructed senior ministers to be back in London by 11 a.m. on the morning after the election. The hours went past without a word. Straw checked: 'don't call us, we'll call you'. He guessed there was some other drama going on – there was, over the future of Anji Hunter, Blair's long-term adviser. Finally, at 5 p.m., he had enough of sitting around and decided to go to Downing Street and wait there. At around 6 p.m., he was called into the PM's room: '"I'm not giving you JP's job," he said. "I'm making you Foreign Secretary."' Straw uttered an expletive and almost fell off his chair. '"Don't you want the job, Jack?" "I do want it, thank you very much. I simply was never expecting it. I thought Robin [Cook] was staying."' Straw's surprise at becoming Foreign Secretary was matched by Cook's surprise at being moved – and was repeated five years later when Straw was replaced by Margaret Beckett.

In that case, the original plan had been to appoint Charles Clarke as Foreign Secretary, but Blair no longer thought this was possible in view of a series of well-publicised problems at the Home Office over the release of foreign prisoners. Instead, Clarke was offered Defence or Trade and Industry but declined and decided he would rather go to the back-benches – ending what had been a promising Cabinet career. According to Jonathan Powell's account (2010, p146),

> Our hopes of him as a counterweight to Gordon Brown were finished. We looked desperately for a replacement for the Foreign Office. We nearly opted for David Miliband, but we decided in the end he was still too inexperienced. Putting him into that position at that moment would have made him a target for the Gordon Brown death machine. So instead we chose Margaret Beckett.

Her reaction was as blunt as Straw's.

Expectations build up not only in the media but also among ministers, thinking that it is now their time to move up. David Waddington recalls (pp163–4) that, at the time of the 1987 general election, having been a Minister of State for over four years, 'I was bound to be moved. It seemed to me that there were only two possibilities. I was going to be either Chief Whip or Solicitor-General.' On the day after the election, he got a call at 10 p.m. from the Prime Minister inviting him to be Chief Whip.

> I later learned from Nigel Lawson that I was second choice for Chief Whip. The Prime Minister wanted John Major, but Nigel wanted him in his Treasury team as Chief Secretary and Nigel won the day. When I went in No 12 (the Chief Whip's Office) on the Saturday morning someone had forgotten to put away John Wakeham's notes, and in those my name appeared as a possible Solicitor-General. Whether John Major would have become

Prime Minister had he spent a sizeable part of the 1987
Parliament as Chief Whip is extremely doubtful. If I had
been made Solicitor-General I certainly would not have
become Home Secretary.

Promotions to the Cabinet can also be a complete surprise. Nicky Morgan (MR, in office 2012–16) had only been
in the Commons for four years when she moved from being
Financial Secretary to the Treasury to being Education
Secretary.

> It was a complete surprise. You literally just get a call.
> There was talk about a reshuffle, but I had been led to
> believe that George [Osborne] was happy with the Trea-
> sury team and he wasn't anticipating a move before the
> general election. Then the phone goes on a Tuesday
> morning: 'Can you come to Downing Street in about ten
> minutes?' And I said 'Yes' and they said, 'Exactly ten
> minutes and that's it.' You don't know anything until you
> sit down in front of the Prime Minister. I think I went
> back to the Treasury, picked up my stuff and said 'I'm
> off' and literally within about half an hour I was arriving
> at the Department for Education.

The main focus, particularly of senior civil servants, is on
the top jobs, at Cabinet level. In Charles Clarke's words
(PCRC, question 185), junior ministers are seen as 'rather
marginal figures ... So the junior ministers become, relatively speaking, adornments to the body politic rather than
decision-takers in that area. That is a very bad thing, because,
particularly with large departments, you need ministers of

immigration, policing, or whatever it may, secondary education or higher education, who are big figures.' Jonathan
Powell has talked (2010, p147) about how the appointment of
junior ministers is

> a mass production exercise. Switch [the 10 Downing
> Street telephone operators] gets five or six about-to-be
> ministers stacked up on the phone, and then they are put
> through to the Prime Minister one after another. The
> private secretary's job is to stick the right bit of paper in
> front of the Prime Minister to make sure that he appoints
> the right person to the right job. There were frequent
> shouts from the den asking what on earth the job was that
> the next caller was supposed to be doing; and, if they
> asked questions, the stock reply from Tony was that we
> would get back to them with the details.

One result is that there is little sense of building a ministerial team. Secretaries of State may or may not be consulted on
changes to their junior ministers, but often the choice is very
limited – and in some cases a junior minister may be appointed
specifically to balance out a more senior one – 'to mark, in the
football sense, the Secretary of State', which can 'institution-
alise conflict' (Clarke again). The contrary view is that giving
Secretaries of State more say would produce factions in
charge of particular areas of policy.

Insofar as they make any wider impact at all, reshuffles
can appear evidence of prime ministerial weakness rather
than strength, most famously Harold Macmillan's 'Night of
the Long Knives' of July 1962, when a third of the Cabinet
were sacked, producing sympathy for some of those

dismissed, including Selwyn Lloyd, the Chancellor, and leading to Jeremy Thorpe's famous remark that 'Greater love hath no man than this, that he lay down his friends for his life'. In retrospect the mass sacking was not crucial in the fate of Macmillan, just as all the many reshuffles of the Wilson, Blair and Brown years were soon forgotten by the public, if not by those directly affected. That leads some advisers to argue that Prime Ministers ought to be more ruthless in getting rid of underperformers. The problem is the balance in terms of ministerial effectiveness in cutting short the tenure of good ministers by promoting or shifting them to fill the gaps.

Sir Jeremy Heywood (PCRC, question 235) noted that Prime Ministers 'always hope they are going to get a big political lift out of reshuffles. They usually don't make much difference to poll ratings or the strength or credibility of the government. You just have to get through them and get back to normal business.' Reshuffles seldom in themselves have a big impact on policy, in terms of the major priorities of a government, because that is settled. A policy is decided at the top level, and the appointment of a new Secretary of State, let alone a new Minister of State or under-secretary, will not affect it. There are exceptions, when a new Secretary of State is intended to shift the direction of policy or, at least, its public perception. The need to improve presentation is often cited as a reason to undertake a reshuffle.

Rarer, and more memorable, are reshuffles which are intended to shift the direction of a government. That was, for example, true of Margaret Thatcher's September 1981 reshuffle, when she sacked or sidelined several of her 'wet' critics – notably replacing Jim Prior with Norman Tebbit at

Employment, with the aim of accelerating the pace of legislation limiting trade union powers, and bringing Nigel Lawson and Cecil Parkinson into the Cabinet. Later, in May 1986, the replacement of Keith Joseph by Kenneth Baker was intended to give fresh momentum to education reform, and led to the creation of the national curriculum, a stronger inspection regime and a new generation of more independent state-financed schools. In the Blair years, the appointment of Alan Milburn as Health Secretary was similarly meant to accelerate NHS reform. In many other cases, it is often more a case of seeking greater competence rather than a fresh direction.

As earlier chapters have indicated, so much of government is about detail and implementation, and frequent changes of ministers do disrupt the flow of administration – preparing how a policy will work and seeing the changes through. Nick Raynsford, himself a long-serving minister responsible for London and housing, argued (PCRC, written evidence) that the scope and frequency of reshuffles had 'increased to the point where they have serious adverse impacts on the effectiveness and efficiency of government'. The three main impacts are: 'One, creating perverse incentives in favour of short-termism in policy development; two, conversely making implementation of longer-term projects in policy initiatives more difficult; and three, undermining the development of effective and coherent ministerial teams in individual departments.'

John Penrose, who had a business background and held two parliamentary secretary posts with a period as a senior whip in between, praised (MR, in office 2010–16 and 2018–) David Cameron for being better than most Prime Ministers in not reshuffling people very often, but even getting the average length of time in a particular position to over two years was still too short.

> From a ministerial point of view, if you're going to carry something through, if you're quick and you're effective, you may make decisions in the first three months or maybe in the first six if it's a really complicated problem. If you're not quick and not decisive, then it will take you twice as long. And then if it's a big project it will take at least a year and possibly three or four years to complete. If you get reshuffled, the chances for a change of direction, which will not necessarily be helpful, are very high. There are plenty of stakeholders, both within the government and outside it, in whose interest it is not to present a new minister with the thing they don't want to carry on. So there is always the danger that difficult projects won't get picked up by your successor unless they've got the wit to come and ask you what it was that you think needs to be done.

There is seldom time for organised handover discussions – because a minister is moving on to to a new job, and is understandably preoccupied with that, or has been sacked, and does not have the inclination for such a meeting with his or her successor. Limiting such handovers is seen by some former ministers as giving opportunities to civil servants. Ben Bradshaw (PCRC, p17) believes that the aftermath of reshuffles is when 'the Civil Service often sees an opportunity to try to delay or even thwart policies they don't like or try to persuade an incoming minister to reach a different conclusion from their predecessor'.

Reshuffled ministers are at an inherent disadvantage compared with those appointed when a party comes to power after an election, when they may have been shadowing an area for several years. John Reid, who held nine different posts over a decade, said (PCRC, p11) that for his first post as Armed Forces minister, he had spent seven years reading military history, meeting the troops, discussing with people.

> In other cases, such as Transport, I had no particular knowledge, no particular interest. The first day I was at Transport, they were doing the roads review in Parliament, which consisted of me at the despatch box and Glenda Jackson, the under-secretary, tearing pages out of a large briefing book to put in front of me when somebody asked me what were the latest plans for the A373 going through somewhere or other.

Similarly, Nicky Morgan notes,

> you don't have the luxury of having been in opposition and then being elected to government to think, 'OK I've had time to prepare my policy programmes and what I want to do.' You've got to hit the ground running. You're inheriting other people's policies and then potentially making changes, because normally the PM will say, 'I'd like you to do more or less of that' or whatever it is.

She thought it 'quite extraordinary that we put people in these positions with absolutely no training whatsoever – no transitional period, no handover period. It's mind-boggling. People outside government, outside Whitehall, cannot believe that is what happens.'

A contrasting view is taken by Theresa Villiers, who found (MR, in office 2010–16) the transition from number two at Transport to being Northern Ireland Secretary

> not that difficult. It was far easier than the transition from opposition to government. When I arrived they gave me the whole transition set of papers, including a history of the island of Ireland from 1171, which says a lot! Some people think that is when the trouble started, and others say it is much earlier than that. I was certainly relatively cautious at first in terms of saying anything in public, but right from the start I enjoyed the role.

David Jones found (MR, in office 2010–14 and 2016–17) the move from Minister of State to Secretary of State easy. 'Of course, I'd been working in the Wales Office for over two years, so when I did become Secretary of State it was pretty seamless. I had the same staff. I was dealing with precisely the same issues. My diary was virtually unchanged. So it was extremely easy.'

Equally challenging can be a promotion from junior to middle-ranking minister with greater responsibilities and prominence. Looking back to the 1980s, Sir George Young reflected (MR, in office 1979–86, 1990–97, 2010–12, 2012–14, 2016–) that the big jump for him was going from parliamentary under-secretary to Minister of State under Michael Heseltine, 'partly because there was a lot of delegation to ministers of state, that was quite a big jump, from doing the adjournment debates, getting the bills through, signing the letters to actually driving policy. That was quite a big step, perhaps almost a bigger step than backbenchers to under-secretary. Minister of State to Secretary of State, again a big jump.'

The downside of reshuffles is that those sacked are still around. Jonathan Powell, Tony Blair's former chief of staff, pointed out (in evidence to the Public Administration Com-mittee, Eighth Report, 2009–10, question 32) that Prime Ministers faced a tricky equation when they had been there a long time:

> the balance between the appointed and the disappointed, and the problem with ministers who are MPs is that they do not go away when you sack them; they sit around on the backbenches and make your life miserable. So it may be an advantage to have ministers who come from outside because at least they will go away when you sack them rather than still being there.

But Powell himself has discussed (2010, p145) demotion as an alternative to sacking, citing the thoughts of Machiavelli: 'Venice even makes the mistake of thinking that a citizen who has held office, should be ashamed to accept a lower ... for a republic rightly places more hope and confidence in a citizen who from a high command moves to a lower than in one who from a lower command rises to a higher because of their experience'. Easier said than done.

There is a distinction between those demoted from the Cabinet to a post outside in the same reshuffle and those who go onto the backbenches for a period and then return at a lower level a year or two later. This is part of a welcome tendency noted below to bring back former ministers for a second, or even third or further period in office.

Among the first group, Geoff Hoon was demoted in 2006 from being Leader of the Commons to being Europe minister outside the full Cabinet, before rising again to become Chief Whip and then Transport Secretary in the Brown years. Stephen Timms and Tessa Jowell both moved from full Cabinet status to serving outside, as did Greg Hands after the formation of the May administration, before he resigned in 2016 ahead of the Commons vote on the extension of Heathrow airport.

The broken service group includes Harriet Harman, who had a year in the Cabinet from 1997 to 1998 before spending three years on the backbenches, returning to government as a minister outside the Cabinet from 2001 until 2007, when she was restored to full Cabinet status by Gordon Brown. Margaret Beckett served in four Cabinet positions, including an unexpected year as Foreign Secretary, before leaving government in 2007, only to return for a final year as Minister of State for Housing. Ann Taylor served as Leader of the Commons and Chief Whip for the first Blair government, and served on the backbenches before returning to government as a Minister of State in the Lords from November 2007 until the 2010 election. David Jones was dropped as Wales Secretary in 2014 only to return two years later as Minister of State in the new Department for Exiting the European Union for eleven months. Having resigned as Home Secretary at the end of April 2018, Amber Rudd returned to the Cabinet five and a half months later as Work and Pensions Secretary. The upheavals associated with Brexit have meant that a number of junior ministers, such as Stephen Hammond and John Penrose, have also returned to government some years after they were first dropped (in both cases having given interviews in the Ministers Reflect series).

As noted earlier, Sir George Young is in a class of his own for movements up and down the greasy pole. Even leaving aside his movements in and out of government in the Thatcher and Major years, he was Leader of the Commons and Chief Whip in the Cameron government and then, after a period on the backbenches and retiring from the Commons, returned as a middle-ranking Lords whip in the May administration.

What can be done? Fewer, more limited, and better planned reshuffles, is the obvious answer, but that is, of course, subject to events and can be wishful thinking in view of the sudden resignations which are part of the pattern of politics and which have ripple effects across government. Even with that important proviso, there is plenty of scope for improvement.

First, despite widespread scepticism, more can be done on appraisals and mentoring, so that ministers are not just left to flounder, and then suffer an often brutal dismissal. Ministers can be advised, and helped.

Second, while occasional changes are needed and desirable, to weed out the underperforming and to promote the promising, they can be phased. Moving a minister in post for less than two years should be the exception. Having eight Housing ministers in just over eight years, and four in two years, may have been the by-product of unusual political turmoil, but it stands strangely alongside the aim of making housing a government priority. The turnover is not itself responsible for successive governments' problems in developing a sustainable housing policy, but it clearly does not help.

Third, the recent practice of bringing back ministers who have been dropped is not only desirable in itself but also provides flexibility in reshuffles. The in and out movements have been accelerated by the political upheavals of 2015–17, with the general election, the Brexit referendum, the change of Prime Minister and then the further general election. Leaving aside the moves out and in at Cabinet level, of Michael Gove, Liam Fox, Damian Green and Amber Rudd, since 2010 there have been recalls, in some cases short-lived, for Alistair Burt and Oliver Heald (twice), Nick Gibb in the same role at Education, John Penrose, Stephen Hammond, David Jones, Alan Duncan, Chris Skidmore, Robert Goodwill and the recidivist of them all, Sir George Young (who has served five separate times in government from 1979 until the time of writing, in nine different roles and in both Houses). These repeat ministers are significant not only for the experience they bring to government but also by the mere fact that recall encourages others who have been dropped to see that there is always the possibility of a return to office.

# CHAPTER ELEVEN

# Crises and the Media

'Richard Wilson [Home Office Permanent Secretary] took me to the window and it was a bright May day. It was May the 3rd, 1997. And he said, "What can you see in the sky, Jack?" And I said "A clear blue sky." He said, "Yes, it's a very dangerous moment! At any moment in this department, an Exocet will come out of a clear blue sky and" – pointing at my feet – "explode right there. You have to deal with it because this is the Home Office."'

– Jack Straw, Cabinet minister 1997–2010,
Ministers Reflect interview, 2016

'Once you find yourself in a real crisis set clear objectives, devise strategy from the centre and pursue it with real aggression. And remember at all times that however bad it is, it will end.'

– Alastair Campbell, Downing Street head of communications
1997–2003, in reflections 2014

Crises can seldom make a minister, but they can, and do, break them. It is a mark of a successful minister that they can survive them. They are an important part of defining what makes a long-lasting minister. By definition, crises are totally unexpected, like the Exocet missile which Sir Richard Wilson described in his conversation with Jack Straw on taking office. The Home Office has faced more such difficult surprises than any other department, as the memoirs and reminiscences of successive Home Secretaries show – from prison breakouts when the department ran prisons before 2007, via the opposite of a break-in at Buckingham Palace to, now, more regularly, terrorist attacks and disclosures about immigration problems. Willie Whitelaw vividly recounts in his memoirs how within a few weeks in the summer of 1981 he had to cope with two Royal security incidents as well as Provisional IRA attacks in London and riots in different parts of the country. While Whitelaw's short temper could lead him to make snap offers to resign, these moods did not last long. The inner resilience created by his wartime experiences, the loyalty of advisers and colleagues, and a sense of public duty ensured that he stayed the course and survived.

Kenneth Baker, Home Secretary for less than eighteen months at the start of the Major government, told Jack Straw (p201): 'Just remember, Jack, as Home Secretary, there'll be fifty sets of officials working on schemes to undermine your government and destroy your political career; and the worst is, not only will you not know who they are, but neither will they.' No wonder, Straw noted, that the Home Office was correctly regarded as a graveyard for ambitious politicians – 'in politics, the first rule is to survive'.

The unexpected crises of the Home Office can be personally draining. After a series of high-profile prison breakouts in 1966, including the Soviet spy and traitor George Blake and a number of convicted murderers, even the unflappable Roy Jenkins (in Campbell, 2014, p280) admitted, 'My nerve was a bit shaken, I ought to have been steadier under fire but it is easier to say this in retrospect than it was to sustain during the barrage of daily bombardments'. The key to his survival lay in a formidable Commons performance against a Conservative censure motion. As Jenkins recalled thirty years later (Campbell, p279),

> That half hour was the nearest I have ever got to experiencing the thrill which I imagine big game hunters felt when they stalked a tiger, or matadors when they inserted the blade into the right side of the bull. It was all slightly farcical, for it neither helped to recapture Blake nor to make me a better (or worse) Home Secretary. Nevertheless it was by far the greatest parliamentary triumph I ever achieved.

It also made him a leadership contender, as Harold Wilson nervously noted. This far-off episode is a reminder that a necessary, though not sufficient, condition for handling, and surviving, crises is to have command of the Commons. Now, the media reaction would be a greater influence than half a century ago.

In many cases, the Home Secretary cannot be blamed personally, but, in others, he or she is held responsible. In all cases, however, the Home Secretary is expected to be accountable, to Parliament and the media, to explain what has happened. The success of some Home Secretaries, like Jenkins, Whitelaw and Straw, in surviving such episodes and the failure of others to do so, like Charles Clarke and Amber Rudd, who were offered a move, or had to resign (often unfairly when it became clear that failings were mainly on the official side), reflects some clear lessons in handling crises.

These include demonstrating you are clearly on top of, rather than at the mercy of, events; have been fully open with the public, the media and particularly with MPs in the House of Commons; and that you are taking action to deal with the cause of the crisis.

Jack Straw faced a diverse range of challenges, particularly in his four years as Home Secretary and nearly three years as Justice Secretary – English football fans rioting in Belgium and needing to be repatriated; the discovery of fifty-eight dead bodies in the back of a lorry at Dover; a one-day unannounced strike by prison officers. Straw's view (MR, in office 1997–2010) is that

> what you have to know about these situations is to understand that you've got to get on top of the issue straight away and not mess around. Crises will always get worse if you are not seen to be taking control immediately. So I had a sort of crisis mode, which I think sometimes used to take people by surprise, because, normally, I think I'm fairly relaxed. I did my best to be well-mannered with people all the time, but I was absolutely clear about things, about what had to happen and what you had to do and you had to get on top of it.

Alastair Campbell, Tony Blair's communications adviser in opposition and in government for nearly a decade, has drawn a distinction between a media frenzy, of which there are many, and a genuine crisis, of which there are few. This is partly a matter of timing – is it a twenty-four- or forty-eight-hour essentially ephemeral event, or does it last longer and have wider implications? He has argued that governments should not accept they are in a crisis simply because everyone says they are. In his ten years with Tony Blair, Campbell reckons there were six genuine crises but hundreds of situations that were described as such. Campbell has highlighted the lorry drivers' strike in late summer 2000 over the level of petrol duties, which struck a chord with the public. For a time, the government appeared to have lost control as the blockades – aided by mobile phone communication between the pickets – threatened everyday supplies. Indeed, it was the risk of the NHS running out of fuel and supplies that brought the crisis to a head and led the protagonists to end their action. But it was a very nervous time for ministers and senior civil servants as they discovered the fragility of supply chains and of the way the big oil companies worked.

The second big crisis was the foot-and-mouth outbreak of spring 2001, which led to the postponement of the planned general election by a month. The burning of cattle on a large scale and the initial difficulties isolating the outbreak both created an impression that the government was not in control and damaged tourism and the image of the UK. These incidents led to big changes in central government's contingency planning, which proved important later after the 9/11 attacks and particularly after the July 2005 terrorist attacks in London. There was a time during both the fuel supply and the foot-and-mouth episodes when the government appeared to be at the mercy of events which were rapidly getting out of control. Voters were worried at what might happen and at the apparent failure of the government, and of ministers, to be in charge. There is usually a way out, but it is not always immediately apparent, as the full facts are not available.

Accounts of the handling of crises not only highlight

plenty of dos and don'ts but are also a learning process for the ministers concerned. That applied particularly during the banking crisis of 2007–9. Alistair Darling (MR, in office 1997–2010) was hit, first, by the collapse of Northern Rock in the late summer of 2007, shortly after he became Chancellor. He says his legal training was useful in 'learning to focus on the things that matter and then let the other things look after themselves'. He stresses that the key thing is that 'media does matter. How you project yourself, the fact you've got to exude confidence. We got into real trouble over Northern Rock because it looked like we'd lost control, the "runaway bank" and so on, whereas we didn't have that problem a year later.' That was also a lesson in the power of twenty-four-hour television, where you get the same picture being shown over and over again, which gives the impression things are getting worse. There happened to be few Northern Rock branches, and one of them was near west London, where the BBC and Sky were. People were

> good-natured – 'Oh, I'm just queuing up because I saw them [the queues] on the television.' There was another run on a Northern Rock bank in November [2007], but two things were different. One is the instructions were, 'If people want their money out, don't argue, pay it', and secondly, 'Get them off the street', even if they're all standing in the staff room at the back. So it can't be seen. It was pouring with rain as well, which meant nobody was inclined to come out and join in!

Darling says the Northern Rock episode taught him lots of things:

one is media management; if you let things get out of
control, you're ruined. I mean the Royal Bank of Scotland was the biggest bank in the world at the time. If it
had shut it would have brought the entire banking system
with it. And you think about it: no money, no food, no
petrol, not just here, across Europe, America – so the
stakes were pretty high! And that's why both Gordon
and I were absolutely convinced that we would do whatever it took, and we had to throw absolutely everything
at it, because that's the only way you'd get a firewall and
stop it going on.

The dramas of October 2008 have been widely discussed, but
they underlined the importance of the Treasury building up
its crisis management capability, both internally and recruiting externally from the City, to handle the unprecedented
challenge to the stability of the financial system.

Media deadlines and appearances mattered here. Darling
stresses that part of being a minister is

how you project yourself – what impression do you
give? Do you sound calm and measured, even if inside
you may think, 'Goodness, I'm flying by the seat of my
pants here'? But how you come across is terribly important. And no doubt you can think of umpteen examples
of ministers who have done a really bad *Today* programme and the grim reaper is at the door within hours.

The *Today* programme deadlines proved to be very important during the height of the financial crisis, adding to the
pressure on the bankers to agree. During the talks with the

banks, he would say in the evening that 'I'm going to bed at eleven o'clock and I've got to be up to do the *Today* programme at seven and I'm not doing it half asleep'. He left it to his officials and to Paul Myners, who had been drafted in as a Treasury minister in the Lords because his background was in finance and could talk to bankers in the language they understood (see Chapter Nine).

Long-serving ministers often remark on the increased prominence of media issues. One illustration is that one of the two special advisers allocated to a Secretary of State is now designated as the media adviser as opposed to the policy adviser. David Howell (Lord Howell of Guildford) had been a Cabinet minister in the first Thatcher administration, and then returned twenty-seven years later as a Minister of State in the Cabinet Office. He describes (MR, in office 1970–4, 1979–83, and 2010–12) a change in the priority given to press and media matters. In the 1980s, he would

> begin with a morning meeting with ministers, and later on we'd call in the press people and the PR people and say, 'This is where we're going. This is how we're going to handle A, B and C. This is our defensive position here. This is a new initiative we're taking ... Now my impression of the Foreign Office, twenty-five or thirty years later, was the other way round. The first call, the first people into the Secretary of State, are the PR people and the press officers to work out where the hell we're going. What are they saying, what are the media saying. Then later on in the morning, the ministers are brought in to work it out and knock around the great policy issues and problems and events. So there you have a very, very

symbolic change. Because the government is at this side of the Internet revolution in the 2010s, they are looking over their shoulder and very much more governed by the bombardment of public opinion and media opinion and the vast range of media links. Government in the 1980s was able to proceed on a certain line and deal with the media afterwards.

Lord Howell overstates his point, since politicians have always been concerned with the media. Go back to the 1850s and Palmerston used to ride with Delane, the great mid-nineteenth-century editor of *The Times*, to discuss and, in modern language, to leak, state secrets. In the last century, Lloyd George and Neville Chamberlain actively courted the press leaders of their day, as, of course, did Harold Wilson in his prime in the 1960s. What has changed, and where Lord Howell has a strong point, is the immediacy and urgency of the media pressures – the need to respond now and the limitations that imposes on ministers' time to consider responses to events. The media was never really an afterthought, but it has become an urgent priority in decision-making.

There is a tendency to stress the increased role of the media, as opposed to, say, Parliament. That is true on a fifty- or sixty-year time span, looking back to when broadcasters, in particular, were more deferential towards politicians in the 1950s, and the tone was set by the main newspapers. But that changed in the 1970s and 1980s, when the balance moved to the broadcasters, particularly with the arrival of twenty-four-hour news, and then again from the late 1990s onwards with the spread of the Internet and social media. The real change in the influence of the media on how government works, and

the priority given by ministers and civil servants to responding to the media, occurred earlier. It was the 1980s and early
1990s, when ministers lost the time and space to reflect before
reacting to some news announcement. It was then that the
permanent campaign became dominant. Journalists became
more assertive in relation to politicians.

Tom Baldwin, a buccaneering journalist turned media
adviser to Ed Miliband, has produced a lively and candid
book charting these changes. Writing of the period from the
1990s onwards (2018, pp 25–6), 'even as sections of the press
seemed intent on undermining respect for politics, there was
a tumescent self-regard among political journalists at the time
that was generally not justified by the quality of our product'.
Reporters, and particularly some columnists, saw themselves
as more important than the politicians. That attitude was
reinforced by the long periods of one-party dominance when
the opposition was weak, first under Margaret Thatcher and
then under Tony Blair. Of course, there have always been
aggressive interviewers – though Sir Robin Day was unusual
in his time in his persistent questioning of politicians like Sir
John Nott. But Day was a strong believer in the parliamentary system, and did not give the impression of world-weary
scepticism, even cynicism, towards ministers of the likes of
John Humphrys and Jeremy Paxman. Whatever the motive,
the result has been an increasingly negative slant of stories
and greater hostility towards the politicians and the political
class.

What has changed more recently, and has reinforced these
trends, is the nature of the media – from a relatively small
number of established organisations, both broadcasters and
newspapers, to more of a free-for-all in which any blogger or

independent group with followers can have enormous influence on the political debate. Politics by Twitter creates an instant marketplace for political news in which each development is shared instantly. Social media has had a huge impact on politics, fuelling the rise of populism and putting constraints on the role of politicians. These developments are even more pronounced in Washington, as Sean Spicer, the beleaguered White House press secretary for seven months at the start of the Trump administration, reflected in his defensive, but revealing, memoir (2018, p242): 'Twitter is not glue. It is a solvent. It is breaking us down and breaking us apart. With Twitter at the centre, substantive issues that require more than 280 characters get short shrift.' Spicer quoted a former journalist, Peter Hamby, on the change in balance in media attitudes and ethics:

> With Instagram and Twitter-primed iPhones, an ever more youthful press corps, and a journalistic reward structure in Washington that often prizes speed and scoops over context, campaigns are increasingly fearful of the reporters who cover them. Any perceived gaffe or stumble can become a full-blown narrative in a matter of hours, if not minutes, thanks to the velocity of the Twitter conversation that now informs national reporters, editors and television producers. Twitter is the central news source for the Washington-based political news establishment.

Apart from an increased awareness of media deadlines – and now of the immediacy of social media – the other key lesson drawn by Darling and other ministers from crises in various departments was that they exposed weaknesses in Whitehall and the Civil Service. You have to have the right governing back-up. In particular, he stresses 'the loss of institutional knowledge is quite a big thing. One of the points which is worth reflecting on is that obviously you don't need more civil servants than you need, but if you start losing people who know about things, you lose that sort of knowledge.' The financial and subsequent crises have highlighted problems from an undesirably high turnover of civil servants, in large part a product of government cutbacks in staff numbers.

The run-up to the Olympics in London in 2012 provided a number of acute challenges of governing, since this was a major project with a fixed timetable which could not be allowed to slip, unlike many public sector infrastructure schemes. National prestige was involved. From the many crises he faced during his four years at the Home Office, Damian Green says (MR, in office 2010–14 and 2016–17) the queues at Heathrow in the run-up to the Olympics

> were probably the most serious, where there were a constant series of meetings, visits to Heathrow, negotiations with the authorities there. That was an interesting example, because there was no high politics involved at all; what we had to do and what proved extremely difficult was to get competent people running minute-by-minute operations on the ground. It shows how what feels like 'Surely that's just a bit of admin', in the end it is down to ministerial effort – the Prime Minister was getting involved as well, all the way up the line.

The solution was a very practical, straightforward one:

The rule of any airport is that once a queue is built up, you take hours to get it back, so you just have to stop them building up again first. What they used to do was send a tannoy message into the back room, where they were all having coffee, saying, 'Please will someone come out, we need to fill up a few more benches', and everyone just ignored it. If the manager went in and said, 'You, you and you, go sit on benches 10 to 15', then you've solved it – it was as simple as that. This should not have to entail ministerial intervention, but you discover it's actually that kind of thing of sending a senior official who comes up and says, 'This is what you need to do' and you say, 'Right, this is now what we're going to do.'

Sir Hugh Robertson, then Olympics minister, observed the handling of the G4S security contract. He describes (MR, in office 2010–14) the Prime Minister's performance at the meeting in the Cabinet Room the day the G4S contract finally collapsed as

the best example of clear, incisive leadership that I saw in four and half years in government. The way he got everybody round the table, summed up what had gone wrong, got to the bottom of what we needed to do and the issues that were involved, translated that into what needed to be done to put it right and then got everybody geared up. The sting in the tail was, 'I want everybody back in two days, so if you have any problems we need to know about [them] beforehand. I don't want anybody sitting round this table in two days' time telling me that they've not done what they're supposed to do. Is that clear? Thank you very much.' You could have heard a pin drop. He's a clever guy, but it was a perfect example of how to sum up a difficult, complex issue and then do what was required to save an Olympics at a time when the press was banging at the door and saying you can't keep the event safe.

There is a distinction between these types of immediate crises, where the government has to take action to tackle an immediate and potentially deteriorating problem, and others, often as, if not more, damaging politically, where the problem is the disclosure of serious mismanagement or maladministration. Both require a demonstration that ministers are in charge: that the problem has been addressed. Candour and openness are essential. You must not be seen to be hiding anything. But the type of response is slightly different.

Alistair Darling experienced one of these crises in his packed three years as Chancellor – notably in the autumn of 2007, shortly after the Northern Rock crisis, when the HMRC lost computer discs with the data of millions of recipients of child benefit. The first question was one of accountability. The HMRC is structured with its own board to keep ministers away from collectiing people's taxes.

However, if what you might call the despatch box risk doesn't go away from you, there's no way you can manage to lose the personal details of half the population. You could say, 'Well, actually, it's this organisation down here that's done it, it's nothing to do with us …

The fact that they didn't tell ministers for three weeks that this had gone missing tells you an awful lot – their instinct was to try and sort things out and then they had very little comprehension of how the public were going to take this. And the time I was told I had to announce to the House of Commons was about four to five days, because you had to tell the banks to start flagging up these accounts. You had to speak to the Information Commissioner, all sorts of people. It was one of these things that HMRC is one of these non-departmental bodies, but it's still ministers who have to answer for it.

As I discussed in Chapter Eight, Darling was always very aware of the need to take the House of Commons seriously, and this stood him in good stead.

I remember somebody said, 'Do you need to tell them everything that's happened?' and I said, 'Well, look, you know, the old cover-up cry, you just need to say everything.' I said, 'This is so horrific, frankly, that if you chuck in another two things for good measure it won't make any difference.' So it was interesting that, although there was the ritual anger, if you like, from the back-benchers, people I think understood what had happened – although there was universal amazement that anyone would be allowed to post all this information in an unregistered packet and on two CDs that you could have bought in the supermarket. Incidentally, I don't think they ever left that building. I think they would have surfaced long before now.

Ed Balls had a few external crises of this type in his three years as Secretary of State for Children, Schools and Families (MP, in office 2006–10). His first was the failure to mark SATs tests,

> which was, within the world of education and children and parents, a massive big deal. And we made a mistake on that – I made a mistake on that personally – which was that there are three things that you need to do. You have to be clear about what's happening and know it. You have to be clear about how you are going to manage accountability and responsibility, but you also have to show grip. The three things can contradict each other, or there are tensions between them. In the case of SATs testing, we didn't fully know what was happening, and we thought this was a failure to manage the process from the regulatory agency. I should have gone out, on the very first day, and said, 'We're gripping the situation and we are discovering what's happening and we are asking these difficult questions.' And because I didn't know what was going on, and I thought these guys are screwing it up and I said to them, 'You have got to go out and explain what is going on.' And that was a big mistake on my part. If you go out and say, you know, 'I don't know what is going on, but I am going to tell you I know all about it anyway and I'm in charge', that's quite bad as well. I definitely learned from that one.

The Baby P case in Haringey in 2007 presented even more testing challenges for Ed Balls. The death of the seventeen-month-old after horrific injuries occurred in the same London borough, and involved the same child welfare authorities, that had already been seen to have failed seven years earlier in the case of Victoria Climbié. This led to a public inquiry which resulted in measures being introduced which were intended to prevent similar cases happening. Baby P's mother, her boyfriend and his brother were convicted of charges of causing or allowing the death of the child. Following the conviction, three inquiries and a nationwide review were launched, while Sharon Shoesmith, the Head of Children's Services in Haringey, was removed at the direction of Balls (and she later successfully sued for wrongful dismissal). Before the criminal case against the mother and others concluded, Balls spent a lot of time trying to work out how they were going to handle the case. As he put it, it was 'a grip thing'. Lord Laming, who conducted the Climbié review, was invited back to assess his reforms and how they were being implemented across the country. But the issue became politicised, as David Cameron raised it at Prime Minister's Questions and wrote an article in the *Standard* called 'Broken Society'. He also had

a piece of information which, stupidly, we hadn't known, which was that the Director of Children's Services had chaired her own serious case review … We didn't know why, in detail, this had happened. We were absolutely clear, we didn't run social services in Haringey anyway, but I wasn't going to be behind the curve on grip again.

So therefore we came back at 2 p.m. [after Prime Minister's questions] and said, 'We've got to understand what has happened and we have got to establish accountability, therefore we will use an emergency power to

commission an immediate cross agency review', which
Ofsted, the regulator, led. So I could say, from that
moment on, 'We are finding out what has happened, we
are not rushing to judgement. David Cameron may bay
for blood, but we are going to do this properly.' But we
went from realising we needed to do that, at 1.30 p.m., to
announcing it at 5 p.m. And we sorted everything in three
hours, so that before we got to 6 p.m., we had grip. And
we had gripped with a process which gave us the space to
learn and establish accountability. I think one of the
things I absolutely learned is that it is good to take the
time to find out what's really going on and establish the
accountability, but you can only do that if you are seen to
grip.

The emphasis is clear, and readers can count the number of
references to grip in the last two paragraphs.

Alan Johnson had a similar problem in the publication of
a damning Healthcare Commission report into what had been
happening in Stafford. He describes the challenges (MR, in
office 1999–2010):

The first bit you have to look at is how this is going to be
managed in the news, and there is always the interview
with John Humphrys on the *Today* programme the next
day. You need as much information as possible. So you're
talking about last-minute things, and this came out of the
blue. You make sure you get the press lines right; this is
where your communication spads are very important,
and those press lines are not spin, those are as factual as
you can be and as honest as you can be. Get the

department together, get all the senior people together – how do we resolve this, what do we do at Stafford now in the short term to put this right. At Health that involves people trying to persuade you that the chief executive and the chair should stay in the NHS, just be moved. This is the incredible part of the Civil Service, they don't sack anyone, either in their world or in associated worlds. They always believe in moving them on somewhere else, which is really weird. So amazingly, at Stafford, I had to argue vociferously that these people should go, not just be moved, go.

Of course, in some departments, success is heading off a public crisis. In Education, David Laws says (MR, in office 2010 and 2012–15) 'it was rare that there were things that suddenly came out of the blue and dropped on our head'. Occasionally, there might be a leaked report about a school doing terribly. But, he adds,

> usually you knew about crisis-type things, or things that could have gone wrong for a while, and you may be working to extinguish the thing before it became public. So pressures on school places and stuff like that – we were aware at one stage that there were some parts of the country that were not meeting their statutory duty to give a school place to all children, but it wasn't public, so we had time to sort it out.

Few ministers escape a crisis of some kind; that is the way of politics. Often, the difficulties originate well before they took over, or are the result of actions for which they cannot be directly blamed. But, as ministers answerable to Parliament, they will be held accountable, and be expected to explain what went wrong and what they are doing to remedy the problems. That is why they are ministers.

# CHAPTER TWELVE

# Effectiveness

'First, the most important [thing] is setting political and policy direction for your department, and you need to do that reasonably quickly, so that people can crack on with delivering for you. Second, you've got to communicate that agenda to the public. Third, you are obviously accountable to Parliament and good politicians take Parliament very seriously, not least because they learn a lot there by listening. Fourth, unfortunately, you do have to oversee the project management and delivery of your brief. Tony Blair was often, I think, guilty of the politics of wishful thinking and change through edict. The fifth big job is curiosity. It's listening and bringing insight, intelligence and information into the department. So you are kind of listener-in chief for your department. That's why visits are so important.'

– Liam Byrne, minister 2005–10, Ministers Reflect, 2016

'If civil servants thought you knew what you were doing, they would deliver for you. What they didn't like is ministers who didn't really know what they wanted to do, hadn't a clear view on policy, and just wanted to "be a minister".'

– Andrew Mitchell, minister 1992–7 and 2010–12,
Ministers Reflect, 2015

The central conundrum of this book is whether, and how,

ministers can make a difference. Some can. They are not all, or even mainly, ephemeral 'here today, gone tomorrow' figures. But it is not straightforward or easy. The earlier chapters underline the constraints that ministers face – notably not being prepared for being in charge of large organisations and being in one post for too short a time to make an impact. In one sense, the surprise is that some ministers do make a difference.

Unlike sports coaches, who each have their individual theories about how to get their team or athlete to the top, there is widespread agreement among ministers – and civil servants – about what it takes to make an impact. This is, of course, not just a list of the varying roles which ministers perform as discussed in Chapter One. It is about how they are performed. There is a danger of confusing activity for achievement. Ministers can comfort themselves with busy diaries even though it is harder to identify where they have made a real difference. Meeting lots of lobbyists and responding to countless adjournment debates to a virtually empty House of Commons apart from an attendant bored whip is nobody's idea of real effectiveness.

In the Gordon Brown era two former colleagues from the Institute for Government, Simon Parker and Michael Hallsworth, did a review of the subject. Looking at evidence from business, schools and local government, they showed that leadership does matter, but that it only explains a relatively small proportion of the success of an organisation. In business, chief executive personality traits such as agreeableness, conscientiousness, emotional stability and openness all predict leadership success by influencing top team dynamics and corporate culture. They were writing about the period from 2005 onwards of Cabinet Office capability reviews which looked at the performance management of departments. This was focused on Civil Service leadership rather than the more contentious subject of political leadership. The authors showed that there was no relationship between average ministerial tenure and improvement in capability reviews, underlining the division between the management of a department by senior civil servants and its political leadership by ministers.

Attempts to draw parallels between chairs of public companies and Secretaries of State only get you so far – yes, successful chairs and Secretaries of State both have to be decisive, engaging, authoritative, have strategic awareness and be good communicators, but the objectives and pressures on a PLC chair and a minister are very different. It is the very political nature of their roles – such as taking Parliament seriously – where ministers' assessments of effectiveness differ not only from business executives but also from civil servants. For ministers, a good performance in the Commons is a mark of success, even if nobody outside Westminster notices. This is one reason, as discussed earlier, why so few politicians or businessmen make the transition from one sector to the other, and also why it is so hard to pin down clear-cut definitions of effectiveness for ministers.

The classic model sees ministers providing strategic policy leadership, direction and goal-setting – a clear vision and objectives. That emerged clearly in the views of both politicians and civil servants in the 2011 study *The Challenge of Being a Minister* and in the Ministers Reflect interviews. Andrew Mitchell is typical in stressing (MR, in office 1992–7 and 2010–12) the need 'to be very clear about what you want to achieve. If you want to be an effective minister, know how you define effective. You need to have a small number of clear objectives and pursue them.' Similarly, Jacqui Smith says (MR, in office 1999–2009), 'Decide the things that are really important to you early on and communicate them to the department.' The 2011 study and other inquiries have shown that civil servants like working for ministers who have a clear strategic vision and who are committed to transformation. They want to become associated with a high-profile, and successful, minister.

Moreover, as Nicola Hughes pointed out in her review *How to be an effective minister* (2017, p21), it is not just about being able to define priorities, it is also a matter of being able to make tough decisions quickly. As Alan Johnson stresses (MR, in office 1999–2010), 'It's no good waiting for a week's time because you'll have another whole set of problems come up that you have to make a decision on. And the Civil Service want you to be decisive. They want to give you the arguments for and against, but once you've decided, they will follow.' Ministers with legal or business backgrounds, or who were used to distilling information, found this an advantage when making decisions, and most ministers trusted their instincts.

At the opposite end of the spectrum, Civil Service leaders are seen as primarily concerned with administering departments – appointments, pay, promotion, discipline and audit functions, and, now more disputed, responsibility for policy advice. There are also areas of overlap where, depending on personality or experience, ministers may, or may not, choose to exercise a leadership role in conjunction, or sometimes in competition, with Permanent Secretaries, such as long-term organisational leadership, management of projects, people management and organisational values. The balance has shifted since the 1950s and 1960s, towards a more activist generation of ministers being more committed to organisational change and project management, with widely varying degrees of success.

There is also broad agreement on the need for effective ministers to build constructive relationships with their officials, and then to get the best out of people. This involves not only being decisive in choosing a policy and sticking to it but also making decisions on the basis of the best information. This means listening to officials and valuing their contributions. Civil servants have largely similar lists of ministers who exclude much of their departments and prefer to work with a small group of special advisers or trusted officials. Every business school or leadership guru would agree. Yet not many ministers have worked in large organisations comparable in size to a government department, and even those who have been special advisers mainly have political skills developed from operating in Westminster and Whitehall rather than necessarily understanding how big projects can be implemented. Alan Johnson, who had worked his way up as a full-time union official in the Union of Communication Workers, was rated highly by his civil servants for understanding them and how a big organisation worked. He says (MR, 1999–2010) that his main advice to an incoming minister 'would be to ensure that their private office is functioning properly and they take some time to talk to their private office and understand what everyone's responsibilities are and what they need to do'. Similarly, he treated his fellow ministers as a team. 'The traditional weekly meetings are important.

You've got to give ministers and junior ministers the time to listen to their views on things and to make them feel [what] very important people they are in the machine.'

Ministers need to be clear about how they want to work. Jacqui Smith, again: 'Communicate to your private office how you want to live your life, but be realistic about the fact that being a minister is damn hard work and, frankly, if you say, "I don't want to do any work at the weekend", you are probably being unrealistic about what being a minister is about.' She also stresses the need to develop 'relationships with the key civil servants that will deliver the policy priorities that are most important to you and get a sort of feeling of trust and understanding between you about what you want to do'.

Effective ministers have to show that they can operate with other departments, and particularly with 10 Downing Street and the Treasury. Mitchell also underlines the importance for a Secretary of State of demonstrating clout in Whitehall. 'In order to command the support of civil servants in your department, they need to know that you can get things done, that you can work the Whitehall machine and deliver results. That's extremely important.' In the Ministers Reflect interviews, several ministers appreciated the multifaceted nature of their roles. Liberal Democrat Paul Burstow (MR, in office 2010–12) saw his task as being 'to set policy direction, to hold officials to account for the execution of policy, to act as an advocate and representative of government to stakeholders and to help with the overall communication of the department's position as formed by ministers'.

Ministers are the main public contacts with outside organisations, both listening to them and trying to persuade them to support the government (indeed, their diaries can be too full of such stakeholder meetings). John Penrose says (MR, in office 2010–16 and 2018–) that 'sometimes lobby groups can be really helpful. The art of being a minister is to spot where they've really got a point, alongside the other stuff where they're being utterly self-serving. Being able to pick your way through that particular minefield is a crucial skill.' He gives the example of maintaining the balance between the competing religious, medical and business organisations concerned with gambling:

> not only from the point of view of your own personal morality, but also from the point of view of being seen to be above reproach and equally accessible. The simple question to ask yourself is, 'Who is going to benefit from this piece of seemingly reasonable advice that someone is suggesting to me?' And if it is not the person who is offering this piece of advice, it might actually be worth listening to. If it is the person who is in front of me, there's a possibility that it's still worth listening to nonetheless, but tread with caution.

The definition of effectiveness in practice differs substantially between Secretaries of State and more junior ministers. The former can hope to hold the same office for longer, enough time to introduce, and implement, policies which will really make a difference. The ambitions of the latter are bound to be more limited in both time and scope. Damian Green says (MR, in office 2010–14 and 2016–17) that

> effective ministers have a clear idea of what they want to

achieve over a realistic timescale, which can be one year or two years; much more than that and you're gone. Maybe as a Secretary of State you can have more time. Know what you want to do, transmit that as soon as you can after you arrive and then worry away at it so at the end you can say, 'We did that.' And be realistic in what you can achieve.

There are, however, common factors between junior and senior ministers. In particular, as discussed in the opening chapters of this book, there is a bias towards activity and newness as opposed to being custodians, managing and looking after existing programmes – even though most of government consists of the latter. That feeds an interest in legislating. Ministers believe they are more likely to be remembered for acts they have sponsored – or rather taking through a bill since the impact for better or worse will generally not be clear until well after they have moved on to a new role.

Ministers see themselves as providing policy direction – as implementers of their party manifestos, with a commitment to reform and change. That was epitomised by Steve Hilton, David Cameron's iconoclastic policy adviser, in the first half of the coalition years. One of his party tricks, usually delivered in a T-shirt, no shoes and socks, was to show the amount of paper that went from ministerial office to ministerial office in Whitehall in what are known as write-rounds. This is a collective process of clearing decisions outside meetings, now done by e-mails rather than by sending paper messages from department to department. Hilton argued that only a minority of these exchanges – around 30 per cent – related to the main commitments in the then coalition agreement, with 40 per cent about implementing EU regulations and 30 per cent to 'random things'. But that ignores the fact that most of government is not about launching new initiatives but about making sure existing programmes work – that pensions are paid on time, that NHS operations are carried out, etc. While most of the administration of existing programmes falls on civil servants, ministers are accountable when failings occur on programmes which voters often care about much more than shiny new initiatives. That underlines the complexity of ministers' roles.

Jacqui Smith, who served in five roles over ten years, including Chief Whip and Home Secretary, noted the dilemma (MR, in office 1999–2009) that 'you either had to decide if you wanted to deliver your predecessor's initiative, which I sometimes did, or you had to decide whether you were going to dump that and move to the thing you wanted to do, which you almost certainly wouldn't get the chance to see through to the end'. It is not just the influence of the inherited agenda. Many ministers would also admit that they have little choice in practice in the decisions they do take – and that a minister of a different party would have done precisely the same as them.

The scope for original input – either on a party or a personal basis – is limited, though this does not alter the incentives for ministers eager to make a mark by launching new initiatives. That is reinforced by the rise in the number of career politicians who are keen to be active – or rather to make themselves more visible. That raises the question: does a proliferation of ministers clog up the decision-making process, hamper decision-making and absorb resources which

could be better spent elsewhere? Is the impact largely negative, as critics of the rising number of junior ministers
suggested in the first chapter? On this view, the more ministers there are, the more work has to be found for them. What
may be described as the Chris Mullin view feeds the stereo-
type of the unnecessary and irrelevant Under-Secretary of
State for Paperclips and Statues, appointed to keep up the
numbers of the payroll vote obliged to support the government in the House of Commons. Yet there is an alternative,
more positive view – supported by Institute for Government
research – that junior ministers are not only learning how to
serve at a higher, Minister of State or even Cabinet level but,
in particular, they can also make an impact in their own right
in their current posts. Of course, there is a distinction between
the number of ministers and whether they have a positive or
negative impact.

In general, junior ministers who do make an impact have
help and support from more senior ministers. The late Tessa
Jowell launched the cross-departmental Sure Start programme as Public Health minister. She stressed (MR, in office
1997–2010):

> You need a sponsor and a patron in order to do some-
> thing difficult and innovate like that. My sponsor was
> Gordon Brown and my patron was David Blunkett [then
> Education and Employment Secretary]. The idea of Sure
> Start is something that I conceived on the strength of my
> own experience of the invaluable influence of health vis-
> iting. David and I had talked about it a lot in the context
> of a large and very successful national voluntary organ-
> isation called Home-Start, which essentially provided

support for new parents. So that was how it all started, but in a way, government at that time found it very difficult to deal with a description of policy which was about relationships – building good and nurturing relationships between mothers and their new babies.

Junior ministers have always done much of the essential behind-the-scenes work in carrying through legislation in committees, in responding to adjournment debates, in dealing with casework (often onerous in some departments) and in meeting delegations. Moreover, they can be crucial in implementing policies decided higher up in departments. The Institute for Government study (Emma Norris and others, 2014) examined the implementation of policies in four social policy areas: the London and City Challenges school improvement programme from 2003 to 2011, starting in London, and later in Greater Manchester and the west Midlands; the 2001 fuel poverty strategy; the expansion of the Sure Start children's centres; and auto-enrolment in the workplace pensions programme, introduced in stages from 2012. Their conclusion (p19) was that 'policy areas where junior ministers were closely involved had the best prospects for delivering. Junior ministers were generally better placed to guide the process of translating broad policy goals into policy that can be implemented, and staying close to – but not on top of – departmental officials'. They were also involved in keeping up the momentum of policy and in working across government. 'As a consequence of their role, continuity of junior ministers appeared to be as significant as that of senior officials. Turnover required vital relationships to be rebuilt and introduced the risk of new ministers trying to make their

mark on policy that had already been agreed with stakeholders'. This underlines the fine balance between a positive and
constructive role for junior ministers, at the same time as
fears that short tenures will encourage activity for the sake of
it. There is no contradiction. Ministerial activity is likely to be
more constructive if a minister is given a reasonable length
of time to get to grips with a brief, and to implement changes.

The Ministers Reflect interviews also have several examples of junior ministers clearly making a difference: Steve
Webb, the Liberal Democrat Pensions minister for the whole
of the coalition, introduced a number of lasting reforms,
notably the successful auto-enrolment programme; David
Freud in the Lords on welfare reform; Sir Hugh Robertson, as
mentioned above, on the Olympics; and Lynne Featherstone
in pressing for legal changes to permit equal marriage. A
common pattern is the focus on achievable goals, support from
more senior ministers (including in the coalition those from
another party) and time to take through the policy. Revealingly, female ministers are more explicit on these points,
perhaps because they have thought more about the pressures.
Time is crucial, since moving a minister around too often is
bound to be disruptive, as a successor takes time to learn a new
brief. At the time of writing, there had been four Housing
ministers in a little over two years, and eight since 2010.

The impact of ministers can be seen more broadly in
studies of policy successes and failure. Jill Rutter, my former
Institute for Government colleague and a former senior civil
servant, organised a fascinating series of seminars in 2010–
11, entitled 'Reunions' on the format of the BBC Radio series
– in part to counter the fashionable view that most government policies were failures. The list was obviously not

comprehensive, and was in part picked from a survey of members of the Political Studies Association (political academics) in 2010, asking them to identify the most successful policies of the last thirty years. The top three were privatisation, the introduction of the national minimum wage and Scottish devolution. Three more recent cases were added – the ban on smoking in public places, pensions reform in 2002–6 and the 2008 Climate Change Act. A subsequent report, 'The "S" Factors', picked out the main lessons: understanding the past and learning from failure; opening up the policy process; being rigorous in analysis and the use of evidence; taking time and building in scope for adaptation; recognising the importance of individual leadership and strong personal relationships; creating new institutions to overcome policy inertia; and building wider constituencies of support. Rutter and her fellow authors concluded that:

> People matter and individuals can make a significant difference to policy outcomes. This is not to say that many of the policies would not have happened without the particular individuals involved – nor that strong leadership is a guarantee of success – that there was a distinctive contribution made by individuals in each of these cases. Moreover, most of the case studies were characterised by open, honest and trusting relationships between ministers and civil servants.

In particular, John Hutton played a key role in brokering the pensions changes produced by the Pensions Commission chaired by Adair Turner and with the support of Tony Blair in manoeuvring with Gordon Brown at the Treasury. Ian

McCartney played a major role in preparing the minimum wage proposals following the report by George Bain and the Low Pay Commission. On devolution, Donald Dewar, first as Secretary of State for Scotland and then as First Minister, and Lord (Derry) Irvine, as Lord Chancellor and chair of the Cabinet committee on constitutional reform, ensured that the detailed proposals were rigorously tested before being brought forward and enacted. On privatisation in the 1980s, the driving force was a small group of ministers, notably Nigel Lawson (as both Energy Secretary and then Chancellor), Kenneth Baker and John Wakeham. A key factor noted by participants in the policy reunions was the high quality of the working relationships between ministers (and members of independent commissions) and civil servants. Many of the officials stayed with their subjects much longer than has become normal. (The later study on implementation on four social policy areas mentioned above followed on the 'S' Factors reunions and report.)

This emphasis on the successful, positive impact of ministers is contrary to the dominant public impression of policy failures, as summed up in *The Blunders of our Governments* by Ivor Crewe and the late Anthony King. They offer a long list – the mis-selling of private pensions, sterling's exit from the ERM in 1992, the poll tax, tax credits, farm support, the recovery of assets from criminals, a series of IT failures and cost overruns, identity cards, amongst others – which includes both mistaken policies in inception and those which went wrong in implementation. Of course, policymaking and implementation cannot be divided, but there are cases where the basic policy decision was justifiable but the execution was flawed. King and Crewe distinguish between human errors and system failures, making a number of strong points along the way about groupthink and operational disconnect. In particular, they highlight the problems produced by musical chairs, the high rate of turnover of ministers – as exampled by the four different Secretaries of State involved in devising and introducing the poll tax (though students of this episode are split about how significant this was, given that the key decision to introduce the tax all at once was taken by an experienced minister, Nicholas Ridley). The authors argue (p330) fairly that: 'The notion that ministerial turnover promotes collective Cabinet discussion – and therefore, presumably, blunder avoidance – suffers from further defects. Ministers are reluctant to interfere, and seldom do interfere, in the affairs of departments other than their own; if they stray onto others' turf, others may stray onto theirs.'

An updated version of King and Crewe would no doubt devote much space to the travails of Universal Credit and of the handling of the Windrush generation of immigrants. Both reflect flaws in the interaction between ministers and officials. Iain Duncan Smith came to office in 2010 committed to a radical overhaul of the benefits system, but faced problems from the start over the inherent complexity of the project as well as IT difficulties, Treasury scepticism and (as discussed in Chapter Five) the rate of turnover of officials involved in implementing the project. The controversy over Windrush and the handling of immigration revealed shortcomings at both ministerial and Civil Service levels, and a rare public admission that officials had let down former Home Secretary Amber Rudd in not providing the right support for her over immigration targets.

King and Crewe do acknowledge government successes

– the creation of green belts, the Clean Air Act, the introduction of the breathalyser and compulsory seat belts, privatisation, the national minimum wage and the ban on smoking in public places – all with long gestation periods. But their overall emphasis on failure in the title and balance of the book means that many of the positive aspects are downplayed.

The authors also highlight a theme of this book – ministers as activists and in a hurry, keen to act with haste. Rapid turnover in post, and the associated phenomenon of excessive activism, are rightly deplored. They also subscribe to the view that officials are more reluctant to 'speak truth to power', in the overused phrase, when the real position, as discussed in Chapter Five, is more complicated. The challenge for officials is not just to raise objections but, while pointing to potential problems in policies, also to put forward possible solutions.

These issues have more recently been explored in a report from the Public Administration and Constitutional Affairs Committee (Fifth Report of Session, 2017–19, 'The Minister and the Official: the Fulcrum of Whitehall Effectiveness') based, amongst other evidence, on a wide-ranging survey by Professor Andrew Kakabadse of Henley Business School. The report noted (p10) how:

Ministers are often under pressure to act rapidly. A time frame dictated by the electoral cycle or the prospect of an even shorter ministerial tenure, and media pressure to act immediately can all contribute to the 'urgency of the political imperative'. Civil servants, on the other hand, might want more time to assess available options, running counter to this sense of urgency. Civil servants may also feel inhibited about explaining potential problems with a preferred ministerial approach.

Professor Kakabadse suggested (p10) that it could take up to a year for a newly appointed Secretary of State or Permanent Secretary to get to grips with a new post. 'Even where they have previous experience at that level, the transition to a new department can still take six months.'

All this goes back to many of the central themes of this book over inadequate preparations for office, induction when in post and excessively rapid turnover of ministerial positions.

# CHAPTER THIRTEEN

# Goodbye Minister

'I make my way back to the House of Commons. The fact that I have been asked to go to the Prime Minister's room in the Commons, rather than No 10, tells me all I need to know. When a reshuffle is underway or a new government is being formed, the appointments take place at No. 10 so that the new ministers can be photographed by the waiting press photographers as they go in: the sackings, by contrast, occur in the privacy of the PM's office in the Palace of Westminster where the press cannot penetrate. So after eighteen years on the front bench, I am being sacked.'

– Oliver Letwin, p33, *Hearts and Minds*, 2017

'When you've held a senior position, and will in all likelihood never rise that high in politics again, the end of your career is treated like a death.'

– Ed Balls, writing about his defeat in the May 2015 general election, p xiii, *Speaking Out*, 2016

All ministerial careers inevitably come to an end. Ministers resign, retire, get sacked, give up office when their party is defeated or lose their own seats in the Commons. And some, fortunately a very small number, die in office. There are many permutations, as the following pages will show – and there are limits to the length of ministerial second or third lives. At some stage, the flow of submissions stops, the red box remains empty and the ministerial driver is working for somebody else.

This is emphatically not the same as Enoch Powell's often repeated aphorism that 'all political lives, unless they are cut off in midstream at a happy juncture, end in failure, because that is the nature of politics and of human affairs'. That was said by Powell about Joseph Chamberlain in his revealing short biography in 1977, though it was really more revealing about the author than the subject. While it is a truism that 'human affairs' in terms of getting older means coming to terms with limitations, and hence failure, that does not mean all ministerial careers are inevitably failures. Or, indeed, need be, or are seen by former ministers, as failures.

Ministerial careers vary vastly in length. The short tenure in a particular post – damaging though that often is for effectiveness – does not indicate how long a minister will serve in total. While underperforming, and, in some cases, unlucky, ministers, may only serve for a couple of years, or perhaps three years in a couple of posts, anyone who reaches the Cabinet has a good chance of serving for six to eight years in total in a number of posts. Much, of course, depends on whether, and how long, your party is in power, and has not applied in the recent frantic Brexit years, where Cabinet tenures have been much shorter. Winston Churchill served as a minister for twenty-nine years, despite his long wilderness years in the 1930s, while that quintessential man-of-office R. A. Butler managed twenty-five years. Amongst more recent ministers, Kenneth Clarke served for twenty-four years as a whip and minister, from 1972 until 2014. A few other ministers (Tony Newton, Malcolm Rifkind, John Gummer and Lynda Chalker) also served as whips and ministers for the entire eighteen years of the Thatcher and Major governments. The thirteen Labour years from 1997 until 2010 ensured that a number of its leading lights also recorded long periods in office, including Gordon Brown, Alistair Darling and Jack Straw (who aptly entitled his memoirs *Last Man Standing*).

The end can come in various ways. What is striking is how relatively few departures are entirely voluntary – a minister deciding that they have done all they want, or realistically can aspire, to do and decide to leave office, and often the Commons, to pursue other interests. In the Ministers Reflect interviews, this applied to both Sir Hugh Robertson and Mark Hoban. Robertson (MR, in office 2010–14) decided to leave politics and go back into business because he took the view that

> most politicians have a life cycle and politics permanently moves on. Apart from my first year in Parliament, I've been on the Conservative Party frontbench right the way through my parliamentary career. I went on it in 2002 and got through to 2014, twelve years later, of which four and a half had been in government. I thought I'd probably had my run and I could sense there was a generation that had arrived in the big intake of 2010 coming up behind me, all of whom wanted jobs. I thought if I stayed for another five years I'd be 57, 58, it'd be much more difficult to make that change. I accepted that I'd had my moment as a minister and it wasn't going to last forever,

and once you've accepted that, it then makes sense to get out while you're still enjoying it and before people are totally fed up with you.

Such is the scepticism, even cynicism, about politicians' motives that Norman Fowler raised eyebrows in January 1990 when he stepped down from the Cabinet 'to spend more time with his family', though he returned to politics first as Conservative Party chairman from 1992 to 1994, and then as a member of the Shadow Cabinet from 1997 until 1999. He became Lord Speaker in 2016. This formula 'to spend time with the family' has been used a number of times since June 2003, when Alan Milburn resigned from the high-pressure role of Health Secretary to spend more time with his partner and two sons at their home in the north-east. He said that he did not want to miss his children growing up since you get one shot in life with kids. He added at the time that he had concluded that 'I cannot do this twenty-four hours a day, seven days a week job in a busy Cabinet post and have anything like a normal family life'. It was a question of balancing demands on his time, and, like Norman Fowler, he remained active in public life, even rejoining the Cabinet in September 2004 to oversee Labour's preparations for the 2005 general election. He then resigned for the second, and final, time before stepping down as an MP in 2010. Politicians' motives and reasons are often complicated, but there is no reason to doubt Alan Milburn's explanation – though in the background were long-standing tensions, akin to a feud, with Gordon Brown and his allies, both over NHS reforms and politically.

There are also cases of ministers stepping down in

frustration, not quite resigning in response to immediate or crisis pressures, but deciding that they had had enough and wanted to do something else. John Nott had had bruising arguments with senior Royal Navy staff over the 1981 Defence White Paper, which originally included the scrapping of the Antarctic patrol ship HMS *Endurance*. He then offered to resign as Defence Secretary following the Argentinian invasion of the Falkland Islands in March 1982, but this was refused by Margaret Thatcher. However, after the war was over he announced that autumn that he would be stepping down, as he did the following January, to resume a busy and successful business career after the 1983 election at the age of 51. He did not disguise his irritation with some colleagues and outsiders involved in the events of the previous two years, though in a private letter published thirty years later he was effusive to the Prime Minister, saying how much he admired her as a woman.

The vast majority of departures from office are less voluntary, though they are sometimes rationalised differently. Most ministers lose office when their party is defeated at a general election and they go out with their colleagues. Many long-serving ministers then decide that they will retire to the backbenches, whether through age or realising that they are unlikely to be selected for a shadow team. That applies particularly when their party has been in office for a long time and is unlikely to return to power for many years. Only three of John Major's outgoing Cabinet served as ministers again thirteen years later – Kenneth Clarke, William Hague and Sir George Young – though a further six junior ministers served at Cabinet level in either the Cameron or May administrations, and a further half dozen at junior levels.

Some ministers do not have the choice, since they have lost their Commons seats. That happened to Shirley Williams in 1979, though, after the formation of the SDP, she won a by-election in Crosby in 1981 but lost again in 1983. Seven ministers, or a third of the Major Cabinet, were defeated as MPs, as well as losing their ministerial posts after the May 1997 election. Two, Malcolm Rifkind and Michael Portillo, returned to the Commons, in 2005 and in 1999 respectively, but Rifkind never became a minister again, while Portillo retired from the Commons in 2005 to pursue an alternative career as an enthusiastic, and gaudily dressed, presenter of programmes about railways. Of the other five, all went to the Lords and did not return to the office. Of the other Conservative ministers who lost their seats, only three returned to the Commons and became ministers again – Andrew Mitchell, Alistair Burt and Greg Knight (briefly as a senior whip) – while Michael Bates became a Lords minister. Two backbench MPs who lost their seats in 1997 returned, briefly becoming ministers (Henry Bellingham and Charles Hendry), while Jonathan Evans, who had been a junior minister before 1997, and then led the Conservative MPs in the European Parliament, never served again on the frontbench.

Another group facing even greater frustrations are those ministers who lose their seats when their party wins power, or when it remains in office (even though generally with a reduced majority). Until 1926 there was the further complication that any MP admitted to the Cabinet other than at a general election was obliged to resign their seat and contest a by-election. This happened to Winston Churchill once (he found another seat), and to Charles Masterman and Arthur Griffith-Boscawen twice; on the second occasion both resigned. In the post-war era, the most well-known example of losing a seat at general election was Patrick Gordon Walker, who lost Smethwick in October 1964 when Labour narrowly won office, but was still appointed Foreign Secretary. A by-election was specially created for him in Leyton, which he lost the following January and then had to resign. He won back Leyton in the March 1966 general election and served in lower-level Cabinet posts for two years.

Defeat for sitting ministers happened to the Conservatives in 1945, 1964, 1992 and 2017, and to Labour in 1979 (Shirley Williams being the most prominent) and 2005. The best-known Conservative casualty in 1992 was party chairman Chris Patten, who never returned to the Commons but held prominent positions in public life, as the last Governor of Hong Kong and as a UK member of the European Commission. Seven other ministers also lost their seats, one of whom, Lynda Chalker, retained her post as Minister for Overseas Development but moved straight to the Lords. Of the others five returned to the Commons, replacing retiring MPs in safe seats, but only two (Michael Fallon and Francis Maude) served as ministers again. One previous backbencher, Gerald Howarth, lost in 1992 and returned five years later, before becoming a minister for two years in the 2010 coalition government.

The reduced Labour majority in 2005 saw six current or former ministers lose their Commons seats, of whom only two (Stephen Twigg and Chris Leslie) returned in 2010, and another went to the Lords. Two of the backbench losers subsequently returned to the Commons. Eleven Conservative ministers lost their seats in the 2017 general election, one of whom, Gavin Barwell, immediately became chief of staff of the Prime Minister. By contrast, in 2015, the only minister to lose her seat was Esther McVey, though she returned to the Commons two years later in place of the retiring George Osborne, and she was in the Cabinet within six months before resigning over Brexit ten months later. The Liberal Democrats, however, lost three Cabinet ministers at the 2015 general election, as well as most of their junior ministers.

There are several lessons from these trends. First, it is very tough nowadays for MPs from any party to return to the Commons, let alone resume a ministerial career. Constituency parties are reluctant to select former MPs and, by the time your party has returned to office, you will probably no longer be the rising star you once were, and can be seen as yesterday's man or woman. Second, timing is all. Not only is it best to get elected for a safe seat – subject, of course, to changes in parliamentary boundaries – but it is best to enter the Commons when your party is in opposition, so that you can gain experience in opposition and then be seen as a promising newcomer when your party wins office again. Little or none of this, such as the swings of electoral fortune or the vagaries of selection, can be planned.

The most brutal way to lose ministerial office is by getting the sack in a reshuffle. Most Prime Ministers are 'bad butchers' in the often-used phrase. No recent ones are as blunt as Attlee was reported to be in explaining to one minister in the late 1940s why he was being sacked – 'Afraid you're not up to it'. Long-running rivalries can play a part. James Callaghan and Barbara Castle had never got on, especially after he led the successful Cabinet opposition to her 'In Place of Strife' White Paper on trade union laws in 1969. When Callaghan succeeded Wilson as Prime Minister in spring 1976, Castle was one of the few Cabinet-level casualties. He used the pretext that he wanted to lower the average age of the Cabinet (she was 65 then), which she regarded as 'a phoney reason'. She later regretted not replying 'Then why not start with yourself, Jim', since Callaghan was four years older than Wilson, his predecessor.

Most Prime Ministers dislike confronting colleagues, want to be liked and don't want to make enemies. Arguing for more rigorous weeding out of the underperforming is perfectly consistent with keeping stronger performing ministers in place for longer than now.

The process is often difficult. As noted in the chapter on reshuffles, rumour, with varying degrees of being well-informed, usually circulates before the big day. Sometimes, the signals are far from subtle. David Waddington recalls (2012, p114) the story he was told in the summer of 1981 by Mark Carlisle, then Education Secretary, who felt his job was at risk in the expected September reshuffle:

> I was sad for him but it was difficult not to smile at the story he told to justify his pessimism. 'I was asked to go to Number 10 for breakfast,' he said. 'When I got there the PM told me that Keith Joseph would be joining us shortly. I did not like the sound of that because I knew Keith wanted my job. But worse was to follow. I sat at the table where there was a nice bowl of strawberries and was about to tuck in when the PM shouted: 'No, Mark! Those are for Keith. There are prunes for you on the sideboard.' 'I knew then,' said Mark, 'that the game was up.'

Parmjit Dhanda, who served as a whip and junior whip from 2005 until 2008, recalls in his candid memoirs (2015, pp281–2) that in the late summer of 2008

> colleagues were whispering in my ears that I was set for another promotion to the rung just below Cabinet, but the tingling of blades in my back told me that I'd be levered out of government ... the phone rang. 'Punjit, Punjit, it's Gordon Brown.' Of course it was. Nobody else called me 'Punjit'. I thought to myself: 'Gordon, you might as well save yourself the breath. I've already been phoned by a journalist who has been briefed by your team that you're giving my job to Sadiq Khan.' We went through a bizarre charade for a few minutes where he couldn't come to terms with the fact that he was sacking me. In fact, he even told me he was 'promoting' me. 'Gordon, just say it as it is, please.' But, no, he wanted to promote me 'in my constituency'. Ah, that kind of promotion. Unfortunately, government was becoming so dysfunctional and divided by 2008 that all manner of posts were being created to appease those who were being 'promoted' as a means of softening their sacking. People were being made 'party vice-chairs' for sunny parts of the globe or 'envoys' to whatever their personal hobby horse was. I had the opportunity to create one too but I politely declined.

He was offered a year later the specially created post of chairing a regional committee in the south-west of England, but he declined that as well, and says he would have been much happier if the Prime Minister had just said, 'Thanks, mate, but time's up and I want to clear space for someone else.'

Prime Ministers not only want to soften the blow of dismissal but also in offering either party posts or often nebulous tsar/envoy roles to ensure that the ex-minister remains loyal to the government and does not join the awkward squad, as many former ministers do. Very few former ministers can get a more substantive role, such as an ambassadorship or role as High Commissioner, as Paul Boateng did in South Africa and Valerie Amos did in Australia (in her case for a very brief period before taking up an important United Nations post) – and David Waddington served as Governor of Bermuda. But there are few such posts, and the Foreign Office always seeks to keep the number down, to protect career diplomats – unlike, for example, the highly political diplomatic appointments in the USA.

The end is quick. Oliver Letwin, always the most balanced and detached of ministers, noted (2017, p34) how

it was a startlingly quick process. One minute, you are a Cabinet minister with tasks and worries and meetings and civil servants, and a direct role in governing the country. The next minute, these things have all disappeared. Though still a legislator, you are no longer a part of the government machine; your diary is empty; your responsibilities have vanished and so have your civil servants. With great solicitude, sensitivity and efficiency, they take back your passes and your keys, and arrange for your books and personal effects to be delivered over from the centre of government to your office in the Mother of Parliaments.

This is an updated version of Harold Macmillan's memory of

waking in his hospital room recovering from a prostate operation after he had resigned as Prime Minister. As his biographer notes (Thorpe, p581), 'Macmillan soon had it made clear that he was no longer Prime Minister. With almost indecent haste, Post Office engineers were disconnecting the scrambler telephone in his hospital room'.

Most former ministers appear – at least a few months after leaving office – remarkably balanced about their fate. The Ministers Reflect interviews show a recognition that political life can be arbitrary and unpredictable. Most are pleased that they had a chance to serve as ministers, knowing that it might not be for long. So, even if sometimes surprised by the end of their time in office, and unsettled at how it happened, they recognised this as an inescapable feature of politics.

Acceptance can, however, be combined with lingering resentment, particularly at what are often seen as lame excuses offered by Prime Ministers. Mark Garnier described (MR, in office 2016–18) leaving office as 'very disruptive. It's pretty brutal'. He had been the subject of newspaper allegations in 2017 over asking his secretary to purchase some sex toys as a family present. This was several years earlier, before he became a minister. He was cleared of breaching the Ministerial Code. He thought these troubles were behind him and was not expecting dismissal. He had just finished winding up a bill on the floor of the Commons and, in the car on the way home at eleven o'clock, received a call. He thought it was his wife ringing but it was the Number 10 switchboard summoning him to see the Prime Minister early the next morning at the Parliamentary Office. 'You know it's not good news when you get asked to the Parliamentary Office, but I thought given the undertakings that had been made before, this must be something else.' He was quite confused. So the next morning he wandered in:

> You have a chat with Gavin Barwell [Theresa May's chief of staff] first. I said, 'Am I being sacked?' and he said, 'Yeah you are.' So at least you're not going in to see the Prime Minister completely cold. It's very strange … So I sat down and she's obviously prepared a few words she's going to say. 'You've done a very good job and this has nothing to do with last year but we need some ministers to make way for a younger and diversified group of ministers and you've been one of the ones selected to make way.' By the way, I was replaced by a whiter, older bloke than me. Anyway, she leads with this, and I was slightly taken aback. It's quite an interesting thing because, as I was sitting there glaring quite angrily at the PM, I was conscious that it was her talking about what she saw her government doing and there was Gavin Barwell as well. But outside were three heavily armed security officers. So if you do kick off and get carried away at the wrong moment, somebody might come in and slot you with a nine millimetre. So you have got to be on your best behaviour! But I was absolutely furious about it, really, really angry, because of the whole business the previous year.

His frustration was because his role at International Trade was the best job he had in his life, playing to the skills he had developed in twenty-seven years in the private sector as an international banker. He hugely respected the civil servants with whom he worked – so 'at that level I was absolutely gutted to have lost that'.

There was both a personal and a political aspect to his loss of office – the impact on his family and children as well as rebuilding a career. He notes that new MPs start off as back-benchers, setting the target of being a minister, getting on to a Select Committee, etc. 'If you feel that your future is behind you in Parliament, then it's quite a change of life and you've got to think about this. I don't like to think that my ministerial career is now behind me. I would hope to do something else. But it's slightly frustrating.'

Garnier is frank in admitting the pain of losing office – saying he had spoken to several other ministers who lost their jobs. 'They were saying you go through this process, a Kübler-Ross model of the five stages of grief'. These are defined as denial, anger, bargaining, depression and accep-tance. The transition from one stage to the next can be long and painful. One rising Cabinet star of an earlier generation who suffered a medical breakdown talked, revealingly, of the government leaving him, rather than the other way round. It was very sad.

The unusually candid Garnier says:

You're angry, you're disappointed, you think perhaps it was a mistake, they didn't mean to sack me. It goes on and on like that and eventually you come to terms with the fact that your ministerial career is behind you and you've just got to get over it and do other stuff … It's a question of just getting on and trying to find a role to play in Parliament without getting bored, and much more importantly, without getting bitter and twisted. You've got to be positive, you've got to be upbeat.

Most of the ministers we talked to for the Ministers Reflect series had reached the acceptance stage, partly because the interviews were usually several months after they had left office.

What is striking, however, is how often former MPs and ministers talk in terms of bereavement and condolence. Apart perhaps from David Cameron and George Osborne, Ed Balls has been the best-known casualty of recent years – a high-flying minister in the Brown years and then Shadow Chancellor for most of the coalition years, but then losing his Yorkshire seat in May 2015. In his disarming memoirs (2016), he begins by reflecting that 'being present at your own funeral isn't all it's cracked up to be'. As it became evident that he had lost, he was offered condolences. No one quite knew what to say.

> If you resign, retire or are sacked from frontbench politics, it usually doesn't happen out of the blue, and there are time-worn phrases that we all know to use – 'you're a great loss to the Cabinet', 'I hope you'll continue your campaigning from the backbenches',' I'm sure you'll be back very soon'. Whereas when a high-profile figure is unexpectedly shunted out by the voters, it's more like a political death – hence some people were actually getting in touch with Yvette [Cooper, his wife], rather than me, to pass on their condolences.

Then aged 48, and before his new life in *Strictly Come Dancing*, television documentaries and as football club chairman, he protested 'I'm not dead'. He had had 'twenty-one good years in politics'. Reflecting the greater resilience of

American public figures, Larry Summers, the former Treasury Secretary and academic, as well as a longstanding friend
of Balls, advised him that defeat was not just an ending but
also a beginning, and that, in time, he would recognise also an
opportunity. 'It will take you a while, but you'll get there'.

The loss of political office has been an under-discussed
topic apart from the work of Kevin Theakston and colleagues
from Leeds University, and of Dame Jane Roberts, a former
leader of Camden Council and consultant psychiatrist.
Neither study looked specifically at former ministers though
their work covered their experience as a means of examining
defeated politicians. Professor Theakston's work has been
about the experience of former MPs – in a report for the
Association of Former Members of Parliament in 2007 and
then in a survey of MPs who left the Commons in 2010.
Dame Jane's work, entitled *Losing Political Office* (2015) and
based on extensive interviews, looked at both politicians and
former council leaders who either chose to stand down or
faced electoral defeat. This is not special pleading for former
ministers. As she argues, politicians must lose office. We must
be able to kick them out – our representative democracy
depends on us doing precisely that. And MPs, and ministers,
are going to retire at some point – few die in office. The question of how this happens has a considerable impact on the
attitudes of politicians and their potential contributions. She
argues (p18) that the loss of office matters, since politicians
'may be fearful of stepping down, seeing colleagues struggle,
or they may be uncertain about possible choices ahead'. They
have ended up staying too long as a result. Second, political
parties may lose out through 'dismissive and thoughtless
treatment of those who have been defeated', jeopardising

'the goodwill, membership and activism of committed and knowledgeable people'. Third, employers lose out 'by failing to recognise and value the skills that former parliamentarians may bring'. Lastly, wider society loses out by 'failing to harness and make use of the knowledge, skills and experience of people who have been elected representatives'.

The widely held view that former ministers, and ex-MPs generally, can parachute easily from office into well-paid private sector posts only applies to former party leaders and a handful of other very well-known names, of whom George Osborne and Boris Johnson are the most prominent examples. The picture otherwise is more mixed, especially for those who have been sacked or who lose their Commons seats. Those who manage easier, and less fraught, moves from ministerial life to outside politics are often those who have voluntarily stepped down in their fifties, such as Mark Hoban and Hugh Robertson.

Otherwise, the Theakston study in 2007 (p20) found that the widely held perception that MPs make a smooth transition into lucrative private sector employment is mistaken. In actual fact, many former MPs encounter great difficulties in resuming a career outside of politics or finding new work, with a significant number citing the problems caused by being out of the loop for an extended period in relation to their previous careers as a major factor. It can take several months to find a new job, with around two-fifths (according to the 2010 study) earning less than when they were MPs. The labour market can look upon former MPs as lacking any valuable skills or experience. In 2010 there was the additional, powerful legacy of the MPs' expenses scandal, which tarnished the reputation of politicians generally, regardless of whether an individual had been at fault. There is also the particular paradox for the career/professional politicians, which many ministers are, or were. Once they lose office, especially if they leave the Commons, they lose their career and profession – and therefore their adjustment is even greater.

# CHAPTER FOURTEEN

# Conclusions

'Be very clear what you're there for. If you're a Secretary of State that's very important, but it doesn't matter where you are as a minister – why are you there? It's not just to sign the letters or to do adjournment debates when five people and a dog are sitting in the House of Commons. You're there as a politician, you're not there as an administrator.'

– Alistair Darling, Cabinet minister, 1997–2010,
in Ministers Reflect interview, 2016

'Eighty per cent of the decisions he took as Chancellor were decisions that would be made by any minister, Labour or Conservative. A further 10 per cent were decisions that any Conservative minister would make. It was the last 10 per cent of decisions that were his own and in which he hoped to leave his mark.'

– George Osborne, former Chancellor of the Exchequer, to King's College, London, economic history seminar, as reported in the *Independent*, December 2016

Ministers can make a difference – though not as much as they would like and claim. They face constraints all around – of programmes inherited from predecessors, of fragile parliamentary majorities, at times of divided parties, the whims of party leaders, of unrealistic expectations and, above all, of time. And those are just the factors outside their control, before taking account of their varying approaches to office. Some have the personalities to mobilise support within departments, in Parliament and outside to be effective, and others do not.

This book has explored the uncertain life of ministers, largely in their own words, and it is hard not to have sympathy for most, who work hard, largely unappreciated and are soon forgotten. Yet most leave office, or, rather, look back on their time as ministers, with at least small satisfaction that they achieved something.

It could, and should, be better. The lessons are not hard to find.

First, we have far too many ministers. The flagrant evasion by Prime Ministers of all parties of the legislation limiting the number of paid ministers is both revealing and damning. The creation of unpaid ministers on top of the statutory limit is entirely for reasons of patronage and bolstering a Commons majority and nothing to do with good government. (This is leaving aside parliamentary private secretaries, paid party posts, trade envoys and policy tsars.) Privatisation of previous state industries and devolution within the UK has been followed by an increase in the number of ministers, not a decline. Indeed, the proliferation of ministers contributes to bad government by encouraging activism by ministers to make a mark and be noticed.

Second, ministers have inadequate preparation for serving in office. The parliamentary and political skills they learn as MPs are important but insufficient for understanding how large organisations like government departments work and how major, multi-year projects should be run.

Third, the appointment of ministers to particular roles is too casual and ill thought out. Appointments are often made mainly for party and factional balance rather than matching skills and experience to roles. And new ministers are often given no clear guide as to what is expected of them.

Fourth, ministers are in post for far too short a time. The Brexit-related changes may be exceptional, but the average tenure in post of two years or less for 55 per cent of ministers in 1979–97 and of 78 per cent of those in 1997–2010 is too short for most to master their briefs let alone make an impact. It is even worse for good and effective government that the churn in the Civil Service is also far too high. The result is that ministers, with rare exceptions, are not in office long enough to take through projects.

Fifth, there is no serious system of appraisal to assist ministers, to tell them how they are doing and how they could improve, as is normal for the leaders of most other public and private sector organisations. So when the axe comes in a reshuffle, it is often an unpleasant surprise.

Sixth, broadening the range of potential ministers by recruiting from outside Westminster has had only a limited, and mixed, impact. Some Lords ministers with party backgrounds and outside experience have proved to be successful in office but too many of the Goats recruited from outside politics have not adjusted and have left within a couple of years. In general, only those few given specific specialist tasks have made an impact.

A common reply to these criticisms is a shrug of the shoulders and the grudging admission that it is all politics

— whether in the way ministers are appointed or in their short tenures in office. Reshuffles are seen as an unavoidable part of politics. Damian Green, who has experienced the ups and downs of political life, reflected after his first departure from office (MR, in office 2010–14 and 2016–17):

> We all know that ministers are hired and fired for a number of reasons, and we sort of all accept that as 'That's the way things are'. Well, they needn't be. The real revolution for politicians would be to say, 'We're now going to treat you like a sort of manager in a company, and we're to have development programmes and you're going to have training and you're going to be assessed regularly and in an objective way and your future progress will depend on that.' And you get to that stage and everyone says, 'Oh, it is impossible because in the end, Prime Ministers will want more women and more northerners or they'll just dislike people and want to get rid of them.' Well a strong-minded Prime Minister will say, 'No, actually, what I want is to run an effective government, and I'm going to do it that way.' So that will be one way to incentivise ministers, and the other thing is all about knowledge, that all politicians should know how Whitehall works and Whitehall should know how Parliament works and why Parliament is important. And both sides of that equation seem to me to be surprisingly deficient.

The real fault lies with successive Prime Ministers who have not taken the development of their ministers seriously enough. It is now twenty-two years since we had a Prime

Minister who served as junior minister and therefore understood the challenges and frustrations of their position. No recent Prime Minister has taken the development of their shadow team, and hence potential Cabinet and other ministers, sufficiently seriously, as both Patricia Hewitt and Francis Maude have complained. Party leaders have not involved themselves, nor indicated that ministerial development is, and should be, an important priority. The prevailing attitude is that future ministers already have a lot of the skills from their time in the House of Commons or will pick them up in office. And, as I discovered as Director of the Institute for Government, there is a limited amount that well-intentioned external organisations can do. The initiative has to come from party leaders.

So any change manifesto is inevitably presented with a degree of scepticism, of hope over experience, but, at least, setting aspirations for better government may expose some of the current inadequacies.

First, reduce the maximum number of ministers and close the loophole allowing unpaid ministers. This could start with a review of the 1975 legislation setting a statutory upper limit on the number of paid ministers. The Public Administration Select Committee proposed just before the 2010 election that the number of ministers should be cut by around a third, halving the number of parliamentary private secretaries by restricting them to one for each department or Cabinet minister, and limiting the total size of the payroll vote in the Commons to 15 per cent of its total membership. The government did not engage with the committee's arguments in its response.

Second, opposition parties should set up proper training

and development for their teams in opposition to learn about how government and the management of programmes work – separate from the access talks with the Civil Service about opposition plans ahead of general elections. This should be supplemented by development and appraisal when ministers are in office organised by a senior minister.

Third, new ministers should be given specific roles and, where possible, objectives, either from the Prime Minister for Secretaries of State, or agreed with the latter for junior ministers, which are regularly monitored as part of regular appraisal and support for ministers.

Fourth, Prime Ministers should seek to exercise restraint on the frequency and scale of reshuffles, as David Cameron did in the first half of the coalition. Of course, changes are necessary either when ministers are forced to resign for some reason, or to weed out those who don't measure up. But the aim should be to ensure that other ministers, at all levels, are given at least two years in any post, and three or four years for a Secretary of State. Prime Ministers should extend the recent practice of bringing back experienced ministers who have been dropped in earlier years. This is to help avoid wider changes – in the process reducing the wider ripple effect of reshuffles.

Will any of this happen? As Brexit unfolds, there are, of course, many more pressing issues. And the political tensions and conflicts at Westminster, and within the main parties, that the Brexit arguments have exposed go much deeper to questions of national identity than my examination of the life of ministers. But if we want both more effective ministers and more effective government, these ideas should be reconsidered.

# Bibliography

Allen, Peter, and Cowley, Philip, 'The Rise of the Professional Politician?', Chapter 21 in Leston-Bandeira, Cristina and Thompson, Louise, *Exploring Parliament*, Oxford University Press, 2018.

Baker, Kenneth, *The Turbulent Years: My Life in Politics*, Faber and Faber, 1997.

Baldwin, Tom, *Ctrl Alt Delete: How Politics and the Media Crashed Our Democracy*, C. Hurst and Co. Publishers, 2018.

Ball, James, and Greenway, Andrew, *Bluffocracy*, Biteback Publishing, 2018.

Balls, Ed, *Speaking Out: Lessons in Life and Politics*, Hutchinson, 2016.

Blair, Tony, *A Journey*, Hutchinson, 2010.

Brown, Gordon, *My Life, Our Times*, Bodley Head, 2017.

Bruce-Gardyne, Jock, *Ministers and Mandarins: Inside the Whitehall Village*, Sidgwick and Jackson, 1986.

Byrne, Christopher, and Theakston, Kevin, *Leaving the House: the challenge for MPs after leaving Parliament*, London School of Economics blog, 2015.

Byrne, Christopher, and Theakston, Kevin, 'Leaving the House: The Experience of Former Members of Parliament Who Left the House of Commons in 2010', *Parliamentary Affairs*, volume 69, issue 3, 2016.

Campbell, John, *Roy Jenkins: A Well-Rounded Life*, Jonathan Cape, 2014.

Clark, Alan, *A Life in His Own Words: The Edited Diaries, 1972–99*, edited by Ion Trewin, Weidenfeld and Nicolson, 2010.

Cowley, Philip and Kavanagh, Dennis, *The British General Election of 2010*, Palgrave Macmillan, 2010.

——*The British General Election of 2015*, Palgrave Macmillan, 2015.

——*The British General Election of 2017*, Palgrave Macmillan, 2018.

Crossman, Richard, *The Charm of Politics*, Hamish Hamilton, 1958.

Crossman, Richard, *Insights (the godkin lectures)*, Jonathan Cape, 1972.

Davison, Nehal, *Supporting Politicians to lead in government, Insights from the Institute for Government, 2008–15*, Institute for Government, 2015.

Dhanda, Parmjit, *My Political Race: An Outsider's Journey to the Heart of British Politics*, Biteback Publishing, 2015.

Diamond, Patrick, *The End of Whitehall?: Government by Permanent Campaign*, Palgrave Macmillan, 2019.

Donoughue, Bernard, *Westminster Diary: A Reluctant Minister under Tony Blair*, I. B. Taurus, 2016.

Freeguard, Gavin, *Whitehall Monitor 2019*, Institute for Government, 2019.

Goodwin, Matthew, Milazzo, Caitlin, *UKIP*, Oxford University Press, 2015.

Guerin, Benoit, McCrae, Julian and Shepheard, Marcus, *Accountability in Modern Government: Recommendations for Change*, Institute for Government, 2018.

Hazell, Robert, and Yong, Ben, *Putting Goats Amongst the Wolves: Appointing Ministers from Outside Parliament*, Constitution Unit, 2011.

Heclo, Hugh, and Wildavsky, Aaron, *The Private Government of Public Money*, Macmillan, 1974.

Hennessy, Peter, and Shepherd, Robert, *Reflections: Conversations with Politicians*, Haus Publishing, 2017.

Heppell, Timothy, Atkins, Judi, and Theakston, Kevin, 'The Rise of the Novice Cabinet Minister: The Career Trajectories of Cabinet Ministers in British Governments from Attlee to Cameron', *Political Quarterly*, 84 (3), 2017.

Honeyman, Matthew, *Former Special Advisers in Cabinet*, briefing note and blog, Constitution Unit, 2013.

Hoskyns, John, *Just in Time: Inside the Thatcher Revolution*, Aurum Press, 2000.

HC, Public Administration Committee, Skills for Government, Ninth Report, Session 2006–07, HC 93.

HC, Public Administration Committee, Good Government, Eighth Report of Session 2008–09, HC 297.

HC, Public Administration Committee, Goats and Tsars: Ministerial and other appointments from outside Parliament, Eighth Report of Session 2009–10, March 2010, HC 330.

HC, Public Administration Committee, Too Many Ministers?, Ninth Report of Session 2009–10, March 2010, HC 457.

HC, Public Administration Committee, Government Responses to the Committee's Eighth and Ninth Reports of Session 2009–10: Goats and Tsars: Ministerial and other appointments from outside Parliament, and Too Many Ministers?, Second Report of Session 2010–11, HC 150.

HC, Public Administration Committee, Smaller Government: What do Ministers do?, Seventh Report of Session 2010–11, HC 530.

HC, Political and Constitutional Reform Committee, The Impact and Effectiveness of Ministerial Reshuffles, Second Report of Session 2013–14, June 2013, HC255.

HC, Public Administration and Constitutional Affairs Committee, The Ministers and the Official: The fulcrum of Whitehall Effectiveness, Fifth Report of Session 2017–19, June 2018, HC 497.

Howe, Geoffrey, *Conflict of Loyalty*, Macmillan, 1994.

Hughes, Nicola, *How to be an effective minister: What ministers do and how to do it well*, Institute for Government, March 2017.

Hutton, John, and Lewis, Leigh, *How to be a Minister: A 21st Century Guide*, Biteback Publishing, 2014.

Ipsos MORI Veracity Index, Ipsos MORI, November 2018.

Kakabadse, Andrew, written evidence to Public Adminstration and Constitutional Affairs committee inquiry into Civil Service Effectiveness, CSE 14.

Kaufman, Gerald, *How to be a Minister*, Faber and Faber, 1980.

Kavanagh, Dennis and Butler, David, *The British General Election of 2005*, Palgrave Macmillan, 2005.

King, Anthony, and Crewe, Ivor, *The Blunders of our Governments*, Oneworld, 2013 and 2014.

Lang, Ian, *Blue Remembered Years: A Political Memoir*, Politico's Publishing, 2002.

Letwin, Oliver, *Hearts and Minds*, Biteback Publishing, 2017.

Maude, Francis, Speaker's Lecture, The Future of the Civil Service, September, 2017.

Moore, Charles, *Margaret Thatcher: the Authorized Biography*, Volume One: Not for Turning, Allen Lane, 2013.

Mullin, Chris, *A View from the Foothills: The Diaries of Chris Mullin*, Profile Books, 2009.

Norris, Emma, Kidson, Marc, Bouchal, Petr and Rutter, Jill, *Doing them Justice: Lessons from four cases of policy implementation*, Joseph Rowntree Foundation and Institute for Government, 2014.

Osborne, George, contribution to King's College, London, seminar on post-war economic history, as reported by John Rentoul in the *Independent*, 7 December 2016.

Palmer, Alasdair, *The Return of Political Patronage: How Special Advisers are taking over from civil servants and why we need to worry about it*, Civitas, 2015.

Parker, Simon, and Hallsworth, Michael, *Ministerial Effectiveness, Review of evidence*, Institute for Government, 2010–11.

Paun, Akash, *Shuffling the Pack, A brief guide to government reshuffles*, Institute for Government, 2012

Powell, Jonathan, *The New Machiavelli: How to Wield Power in the Modern World*, Bodley Head, 2010.

Renton, Tim, *Chief Whip: The role, History and Black Arts of Parliamentary Whipping*, Politico's Publishing, 2004.

Richards, David, *New Labour and the Civil Service: Reconstituting the Westminster Model*, Palgrave Macmillan, 2008.

Riddell, Peter, *Honest Opportunism: How We Get the Politicians We Deserve*, Hamish Hamilton, 1993.

Riddell, Peter, and Haddon, Catherine, *Transitions: preparation for changes of government*, Institute for Government, 2009.

Riddell, Peter, Gruhn, Zoe, and Carolan, Liz, *The Challenge of Being a Minister, Defining and developing ministerial effectiveness*, Institute for Government, 2011.

Riddell, Peter, and Haddon, Catherine, *Transitions: Lessons Learned, Reflections on the 2010 UK General Election – and looking ahead to 2015*, Institute for Government, 2011.

Riddell, Peter, *In Defence of Politicians – In Spite of Themselves*, Biteback Publishing, 2011.

Roberts, Jane, *Losing Political Office*, The Open University Business School, 2015.

Roberts, Jane, *Losing Political Office*, Palgrave Macmillan, 2017.

Rutter, Jill, Marshall, Edward and Sims, Sam, *The 'S' Factors: Lessons from IfG's policy success reunions*, Institute for Government, 2012.

Sasse, Tom and Norris, Emma, *Moving On: The costs of high staff turnover in the Civil Service*, Institute for Government, 2019.

Silva, Rohan, 'I'm so proud to have worked with irreverent indispensable Sir Jeremy', *Evening Standard*, 25 October 2018.

Spicer, Sean, *Politics, The Press and the President*, Biteback, 2018.

Straw, Jack, *Last Man Standing: Memoirs of a Political Survivor*, Macmillan, 2012.

Tebbit, Norman, *Upwardly Mobile: An Autobiography*, Weidenfeld and Nicolson, 1988.

Thatcher, Margaret, *The Downing Street Years*, HarperCollins, 1993.

Theakston, Kevin, *Junior Ministers in British Government*, Basil Blackwell, 1987.

Theakston, Kevin, Gouge, Ed and Honeyman, Victoria, 'Life After Losing or Leaving: The experience of Former Members of Parliament', A Report for the Association of Former Members of Parliament, 2007.

Theakston, Kevin, Gill, Mark and Atkins, Judi, *Ministerial Foothills: Labour Government Junior Ministers 1997–2010*, Parliamentary Affairs, volume 67, issue 3, July 2014.

Thorpe, D. R., *Supermac: the Life of Harold Macmillan*, Chatto & Windus, 2010.

Tiernan, Anne, and Weller, Patrick, *Learning to be a Minister: Heroic Expectations, Practical Realities*, Melbourne University Press, 2010.

Unwin, Brian, *With Respect, Minister: A View from Inside Whitehall*, I. B. Tauris, 2016.

Waddington, David, *Memoirs: Dispatches from Margaret Thatcher's Last Home Secretary*, Biteback Publications, 2012.

Weller, Patrick, *The Prime Minister's Craft: Why Some Succeed and Others Fail in Westminster Systems*, Oxford University Press, 2018.

Whitelaw, William, *The Whitelaw Memoirs*, Aurum Press, 1989.

Wicks, Malcolm, 'What Ministers Do', *Political Quarterly*, volume 83, issue 3, 2012.

# Ministers Reflect Interviews

Baroness Anelay, Conservative, minister 2010–17, interviewed 26 June 2018.

Ed Balls, Labour, minister 2006–10, interviewed 7 July 2016.

Greg Barker (now Lord), Conservative, minister 2010–14, interviewed 13 November 2015.

Dame Margaret Beckett, Labour, minister 1975–9, 1997–2007 and 2008–9, interviewed 12 July 2016.

Nick Boles, Conservative, minister 2012–16, interviewed 28 November 2017.

Ben Bradshaw, Labour, minister 2001–10, interviewed 13 September 2016.

Jeremy Browne, Liberal Democrat, minister 2010–13, interviewed 15 October 2015.

Paul Burstow, Liberal Democrat, minister 2010–12, interviewed 26 October 2015.

Alistair Burt, Conservative, minister 1992–7, 2010–13, 2015–16 and 2017–19, interviewed 1 November 2016.

Liam Byrne, Labour, minister 2005–10, interviewed 7 September 2016.

Sir Vince Cable, Liberal Democrat, minister 2010–15, interviewed 7 July 2015.

Kenneth Clarke, Conservative, minister 1972–4, 1979–97 and 2010–14, interviewed 8 February 2016.

Sir Nick Clegg, Liberal Democrat, minister 2010–15, interviewed 19 April 2018.

Stephen Crabb, Conservative, minister 2012–16, interviewed 24
October 2016.

Alistair Darling (now Lord), Labour, minister 1997–2010,
interviewed 20 July 2016.

Lord (Mervyn) Davies of Abersoch, Labour, minister 2009–10,
interviewed 6 June 2016.

Jonathan Djanogly, Conservative, minister 2010–12, interviewed
27 October 2015

Sir Alan Duncan, Conservative, minister 2010–14 and 2016–,
interviewed 30 June 2015.

Iain Duncan Smith, Conservative, minister 2010–16, interviewed
11 July 2016.

Lord (Andrew) Dunlop, Conservative, minister 2016–17,
interviewed 10 October 2017.

Sir Michael Fallon, Conservative, minister 1988–92 and 2012–17,
interviewed 3 July 2008.

Lord (Edward) Faulks, Conservative, minister 2014–16,
interviewed 9 November 2016.

Lynne (now Baroness) Featherstone, Liberal Democrat, minister
2010–15, interviewed 7 July 2015.

Liam Fox, Conservative, minister 1994–7, 2010–11 and 2016–,
interviewed 27 October 2015.

Mark Francois, Conservative, minister 2010–16, interviewed 1
November 2016.

George Freeman, Conservative, minister 2014–16, interviewed 30
November 2016.

Lord Freud, Conservative, minister 2010–16, interviewed 26
January 2017.

Sir Edward (now Lord) Garnier, Conservative, minister 2010–12,
interviewed 20 October 2015.

Mark Garnier, Conservative, minister 2016–18, interviewed 13
March 2018.

Damian Green, Conservative, minister 2010–14 and 2016–17,
interviewed 9 July 2015.

Lord (Stephen) Green of Hurstpierpoint, Conservative, minister
2010–13, interviewed 10 September 2015.

Justine Greening, Conservative, minister 2010–18, interviewed 1
May 2018.

Dominic Grieve, Conservative, minister 2010–14, interviewed 20
July 2015.

Stephen Hammond, Conservative, minister 2012–14 and 2018–,
interviewed 16 July 2015.

David Hanson, Labour, minister 1998–2001 and 2005–10,
interviewed 25 May 2016.

Harriet Harman, Labour, minister 1997–8 and 2001–10,
interviewed 19 May 2017.

Sir Nick Harvey, Liberal Democrat, minister 2010–12, interviewed
24 June 2015.

Sir Oliver Heald, Conservative, minister 1995–7, 2012–14 and
2016–17, interviewed 8 September 2015.

John Healey, Labour, minister 2001–10, interviewed 24 May 2016.

Lord Heseltine, Conservative, minister 1970–74, 1979–86, and
1990–7, interviewed 3 May 2017.

Patricia Hewitt, Labour, minister 1998–2007, interviewed 11 July
2016.

Mark Hoban, Conservative, minister 2010–13, interviewed 14 July
2015.

Lord (David) Howell, Conservative, minister 1970–74, 1979–83
and 2010–12, interviewed 22 September 2015.

Sir Simon Hughes, Liberal Democrat, minister 2013–15,
interviewed 24 September 2015.

Chris Huhne, Liberal Democrat, minister 2010–12, interviewed 7
July 2015.

Lord (Philip) Hunt of Kings Heath, Labour, minister, 1998–2003
and 2005–10 interviewed 13 May 2016.

Alan Johnson, Labour, minister 1999–2010, interviewed 11
October 2016.

David Jones, Conservative, minister 2010–14 and 2016–17,
interviewed 8 September 2015 and 18 January 2018.

Tessa Jowell (Baroness, now deceased), Labour, minister 1997–2010, interviewed 12 July 2016.

Jim (now Lord of Weymouth) Knight, Labour, minister 2005–10, interviewed 28 April 2016.

Baroness Kramer, Liberal Democrat, minister 2013–15, interviewed 18 January 2016.

David Laws, Liberal Democrat, minister 2010 and 2012–15, interviewed 4 February 2016.

Oliver Letwin, Conservative, minister 2010–16, interviewed 15 December 2016.

Lord (Ian) Livingston, Conservative, minister 2013–15, interviewed 7 July 2015.

Tim Loughton, Conservative, minister 2010–12, interviewed 16 July 2015.

Lord Mandelson, Labour, minister 1997–8, 1999–2001 and 2008–10, interviewed 18 April 2018.

Lord Marland, Conservative, minister 2010–13, interviewed 19 August 2015.

Lord (Francis) Maude, Conservative, minister 1985–92 and 2010–16, interviewed 1 June 2016.

Patrick McLoughlin, Conservative, minister 1989–97 and 2010–18, interviewed 6 March 2018.

Lord McNally, Liberal Democrat, minister 2010–13, interviewed 21 July 2015.

Andrew Mitchell, Conservative, minister 1992–7 and 2010–12, interviewed 9 June 2015.

Michael Moore, Liberal Democrat, minister 2010–13, interviewed 27 January 2016.

Nicky Morgan, Conservative, minister 2012–16, interviewed 19 December 2016.

Lord Myners, Labour, minister 2008–10, interviewed 7 June 2016.

Robert Neill, Conservative, minister 2010–12, interviewed 22 October 2015.

Lord (Jim) O'Neill, Conservative, minister 2015–16, interviewed 17 January 2017.

John Penrose, Conservative, minister 2010–12, 2015–16 and 2018–, interviewed 18 October 2016.

Mark Prisk, Conservative, minister 2010–13, interviewed 14 July 2015.

Sir Hugh Robertson, Conservative, minister 2010–14, interviewed 6 July 2015.

Jacqui Smith, Labour, minister 1999–2009, interviewed 2 June 2010.

Caroline Spelman, Conservative, minister 2010–12, interviewed 19 November 2015.

Baroness Stowell, Conservative, minister 2011–16, interviewed 14 September 2017.

Jack Straw, Labour, minister 1997–2010, interviewed 3 May 2016.

Desmond Swayne, Conservative, minister 2014–16, interviewed 25 October 2016.

Jo Swinson, Liberal Democrat, minister 2012–15, interviewed 17 June 2015.

Hugo Swire, Conservative, minister 2010–16, interviewed 13 December 2016.

Stephen Timms, Labour, minister 1998–2010, interviewed 28 September 2016.

Kitty Ussher, Labour, minister 2007–9, interviewed 16 June 2016.

Ed Vaizey, Conservative, minister 2010–16, interviewed 8 December 2016.

Theresa Villiers, Conservative, minister 2010–16, interviewed 15 November 2016.

Lord (Jim) Wallace, Liberal Democrat, minister 2010–15, interviewed 17 July 2015.

Baroness Warsi, Conservative, minister 2010–14, interviewed 24 April 2017.

Steve Webb, Liberal Democrat, minister 2010–15, interviewed 9 June 2015.

John Whittingdale, Conservative, minister 2015–16, interviewed 26 October 2016.

David Willetts, Conservative, minister 1994–6 and 2010–14, interviewed 20 July 2015.

Sir George (now Lord) Young, Conservative, minister, 1979–86, 1990–97, 2010–12, 2012–14 and 2016–, interviewed 21 July 2015.

The main interviewers in the Ministers Reflect project for the Institute for Government, each doing more than ten interviews, were Nicola Hughes, Jen Gold, Peter Riddell, Daniel Thornton and Catherine Haddon. Fifteen other members of the IfG staff conducted interviews.

# Index